Authors

This GCSE guide was co-written with Kerry Lewis, author of Mr Bruff's guides to [the] Tempest' and Amazon best sellers 'Mr Bruff's Guide to Grammar' and 'Mr Bruff[Guide to] English Literature'. Kerry has been a member of the mrbruff.com team since May 2014. You can follow her on Twitter @Mrs_SPaG.

Dedication

Kerry Lewis would like to thank Andrew Simmons for his support with the final draft of this guide. He has spent a considerable amount of his time reviewing chapters and offering his expertise, which includes alternative interpretations. As always, this is greatly appreciated.

She would also like to thank history expert Julie Boden for her thoughts on the 'Political Backdrop of Ancient Rome' chapter.

Finally, she would like to thank Mark Forsyth for clarifying via Twitter (@inkyfool) the terminology *paralipsis*. Any keen student of rhetoric should consider reading his book 'Elements of Eloquence', which is highly recommended.

Introduction

William Shakespeare's 'Julius Caesar' contains the drama of conspiracies, supernatural omens, betrayal, assassination, revenge, ghosts, and battles. These themes are just as electrifying today as they were when the play was written. The play is hugely rewarding both for those who see it performed and those who read it on the page. However, some of Shakespeare's language can be a little challenging in places for students.

In this exciting collaboration, Andrew Bruff has translated the complete text of the play into modern English while Kerry Lewis has written the analysis, considering key elements of language, structure and form and context, which are the areas for assessment in all GCSE English literature courses.

It is worth mentioning that, in addition to his wide range of revision guides, Mr Bruff has a flourishing YouTube channel with hundreds of videos focusing on GCSE English language and English literature as well as the A' levels in English literature and language. His videos have been viewed over 2 million times across 198 nations—sample them on https://www.youtube.com/user/mrbruff. Mr Bruff can be contacted at info@mrbruff.com
We hope that you find this revision guide useful!

Contents

Part 1: The Origins of the Play

By the time that Shakespeare had written 'Julius Caesar', he was a highly accomplished and financially successful playwright. He had a list of historical plays under his belt, which included Henry VI parts I, II and II and Richard III; he had also written the revenge tragedy 'Titus Andronicus' that was set in ancient Rome.

The first recorded performance of Shakespeare's 'Julius Caesar' is in September 1599 when Swiss tourist Thomas Platter the Younger watched an afternoon performance at The Globe Theatre and enthusiastically recorded his impressions in his diary. Although we will never definitively know when the play was written, the 1599 performance suggests that it was written after the comedies 'Much Ado about Nothing', 'Twelfth Night' and 'As You Like It. 'Julius Caesar' is unique because this is the first time that Shakespeare had written a political play set in ancient Rome about real historical characters. With its fast pace, incredible oratory, conspiracy, assassination, civil war, supernatural omens and ghost, it was truly exciting to watch.

'Julius Caesar' can be defined as a tragedy, as the main character's downfall is the result of a tragic flaw in his character. However, the central figure of Caesar dies in Act 3. Hence, it is often argued that the tragic hero is Brutus, a leading conspirator and assassin, whose sincere but mistaken belief that he was acting for the public good led to his downfall.

'Julius Caesar' is based on historical events, and Shakespeare probably used Thomas North's translation of 'Plutarch's Lives of the Noble Greeks and Romans' as his main source of information. Caesar, an important politician and military leader in ancient Rome, was born about 100 BC. You might remember from your history lessons that he invaded Britain in 55 BC. More details of his life in relation to the politics of the time are provided in the next chapter.

Published in the 1623 First Folio, 'Julius Caesar' reveals some interesting anachronisms (elements from the wrong period in time). For example, there are references to clocks, which were not used in ancient Rome because they had not been invented. Shakespeare bent facts to suit his dramatic ends and, as we shall later see, he played loose with all sorts of conventions to do with time, place and action. Nevertheless, his themes are timeless, as we shall see when we review the political backdrop of the play in the next chapter.

Part 2: The Political Backdrop of Ancient Rome

The Roman Republic, founded in 509 BC, was a powerful military state which elected its leaders; its rule extended over North Africa, Italy, France, Spain, Greece, most of the Iberian Peninsula and the eastern Mediterranean. In 44 BC, the Roman Senate (the central political institution in ancient Rome) granted Julius Caesar the title of *dictator perpetuo* (Dictator for Life). This was the end of five hundred years of almost uninterrupted senatorial government of the Roman Republic and its territories.

The Republican Government

In ancient Rome, two classes of people had their voice in government: the patricians (aristocrats) and the ordinary people (plebeians). When the Republic was first established, only patricians ruled, but this changed over time. The republican government developed to include three institutions:

- **The Senate:** this consisted of 300 patricians (i.e. aristocrats), who were elected as members of the Senate and held posts for life. The Senate was the equivalent of a parliament—in English terms, the House of Lords. Patricians, however, had overall control of the government. Plebeians could not be elected as members of the Senate.
- **Tribunes of the people:** these were two officials who represented the plebeians. They had their own assembly and could propose laws.
- **The consuls:** A consul was the equivalent of a head of state and, from the 4th century BC, one was a patrician and one was a plebeian. The two Consuls were approved by the plebeians and elected by the Senate. They were elected to rule together for a year—this was a safeguarding mechanism to stop one man from having too much power.

Dictators

In times of war, consuls had the right to command armies. If the Republic had an emergency, one consul could be elected as dictator (or supreme commander) for six months only. In a break from tradition, Julius Caesar was granted the title of Dictator for Life—hence the concern felt by many that he would become a tyrant.

Backdrop of Civil Unrest

In Rome, there was a long history of struggle between the plebeians and the patricians for political control of the Republic. The plebeians, who greatly outnumbered the patricians, were very unhappy with patrician control of the Senate. Furthermore, there was much ill-feeling and jealousy aroused by the luxurious lifestyles of the patricians who often neglected public service in pursuit of pleasure.

In due course, wealthy men with private armies began to emerge; they used their influence to eliminate their enemies and control the powers of the Senate. Three of these men were Julius Caesar, Pompey the Great and Marcus Licinius Crassus, who formed a political alliance known as the First Triumvirate. They had a private agreement to support each other and did not baulk at achieving their aims through violence. Over time, however, their relationship began to crumble. Eventually, Crassus died at the Battle of Carrhae in 53 BC and Julia, who was Pompey's wife and Caesar's daughter, died in childbirth; thus, the last link in Caesar and Pompey's alliance disappeared.

Meanwhile, in Rome, a city steeped in political corruption, chaos and assassinations, the atmosphere worsened. Events began to move rapidly. Pompey aligned himself with the patricians, who regarded Caesar as a threat to Rome. From Gaul (France), Caesar set off with his army and illegally crossed the River Rubicon into northern Italy, an act of clear aggression. In response to this threat, Pompey was elected dictator by the Senate in 49 BC and tasked with the challenge of fighting

Caesar, now his enemy. Within months, Pompey had to abandon Rome and was forced to go to Greece to raise an army. He was followed there by Caesar and beaten at the battle of Pharsalus in 48BC. Pompey fled to Egypt where a few months later, he was assassinated by Cleopatra's brother, who was anxious to remain on friendly terms with the growing power of Caesar.

Caesar followed the trail to Egypt and became the lover of Cleopatra; with Roman support, she was re-installed as queen of Egypt. She claimed that Caesar was the father of her son Caesarion, but he refused to acknowledge paternity.

Caesar the Ruler

Caesar initiated many reforms in the months before he was assassinated. For example, he restructured the Senate to better represent the people; he reorganised local government; created the Julian calendar; relieved debt; introduced a fairer tax system; and rebuilt Carthage and Corinth, which had been destroyed by war. These actions made him popular with the plebeians.

Although he was careful to fill the Senate with his allies, some members of the Senate worried that Caesar aspired to become king—Rome had not been ruled by a king for nearly five hundred years. Two of Caesar's highest profile opponents were Cassius and Brutus, who plotted against him because they were anxious about his ambitions for kingship. Ironically, Brutus's ancestors had helped to drive King Tarquin out of Rome centuries before. History repeated itself, and Brutus would play a similar role in the downfall of Caesar.
However, such is the unpredictability of politics that, two years after he was assassinated, Caesar 'The Divine Julius' was deified (turned into a god).

Political Consequences of his Assassination

Caesar's adopted heir and grand-nephew Octavian formed a Second Triumvirate with Mark Antony and Marcus Lepidus to bring to justice Caesar's assassins. Brutus and Cassius were duly defeated at the battle of Philippi in 42 BC. Later, the Second Triumvirate fractured like the first, and the young but ruthless Octavian first side-lined and then banished Marcus Lepidus.

After this, he defeated Mark Antony and Cleopatra's combined forces at the battle of Actium. Mark Antony and Cleopatra committed suicide, leaving Caesarion, soon murdered on the orders of Octavian, to succeed his mother as ruler of Egypt. Cleopatra's three remaining children, fathered by Mark Antony, were taken to Rome and paraded in gold chains behind a statue of their mother. Octavian then gave the children to his sister Octavia (Mark Antony's divorced fourth wife, whom he had abandoned in favour of Cleopatra) to raise as her own.

In 27 BC, seventeen years after the assassination of Julius Caesar because of his presumed ambition to become king, Octavian became the first Roman emperor and took the name Caesar Augustus. Ironically enough, the Roman Republic did not become a monarchy: it became an empire ruled by one man, an emperor. With this event, the hopes of Cassius, Brutus and the whole republican movement were completely destroyed.

Significance of the Play to the Elizabethans

A play about Julius Caesar had historical resonance for the English since they would have been aware of his 55 BC invasion of Britain and the subsequent Roman occupation.

The play was first performed in the reign of Queen Elizabeth I (1558-1603). Elizabethan audiences would have instinctively contrasted their situation to that of the Romans: they would have considered that they had more freedom than the citizens of the Republic of Rome because Queen Elizabeth I needed the consent of parliament to pass laws and levy taxes. The English were aware that they owed their loyalty to the queen, but they regarded the rule of 'Good Queen Bess' or 'Gloriana' as fair and just: she was not, in their eyes, a tyrant.

Another point of comparison was social stability: the political turmoil in ancient Rome had in some ways been paralleled by that of the recent past. In 1536, Queen Elizabeth's father, King Henry VIII, had declared himself the head of the Church of England, rejecting the authority of the Roman Catholic Church. Consequently, Catholic conspirators attempted numerous plots to seize the crown. There was a short period of Catholic rule under the reign of Queen Mary I, also known as Bloody Mary because of the number of Protestants she burnt at the stake. Political and religious turmoil bubbled away intermittently under the reign of her successor, the Protestant Queen Elizabeth I. However, she survived numerous attempts on her life by conspirators who wanted to place the Catholic Mary Queen of Scots on the throne, and Elizabeth established a stable, prosperous Protestant state. Nevertheless, the threats of political and religious conflict were never far away. The fate of Rome was an object lesson for Shakespearean playgoers, reminding them what could easily happen, even in an apparently well-regulated society.

Perhaps the most significant reason for the popularity of the play was that it embodied a particular anxiety of many Elizabethans of the time. When 'Julius Caesar' was first performed in 1599, anxiety was high because the unmarried and childless queen refused to name an heir to the throne of England. This created insecurity about the succession and concern about the possibilities of a civil war. Shakespeare therefore explored contemporary concerns about leadership and violence through 'Julius Caesar' in its setting of ancient Rome.

Timeless Themes
Themes of leadership, succession and civil war continue to recur in every society in every age, making the play just as relevant today as it was in Elizabethan times.

Shakespeare's Adaptations of Time Frames
According to Plutarch the historian, Caesar defeated the remaining supporters of Pompey in March 45 BC and returned to Rome in October of the same year. His assassins were defeated at the Battle of Philippi in 42 BC, so Shakespeare condensed three years of history into five days. These are summarised as follows:

Shakespeare's Timeframe	Acts & Scenes	Historical Events	Actual Timeframe
Day 1	Act 1, Scenes 1-2	Caesar returns to Rome Cassius and Brutus conspire	45 BC
Day 2	Act 1, Scene 3 Acts 2 and 3	Caesar is assassinated	44 BC
Day 3	Act 4, Scene 1	Second Triumvirate	43 BC
Day 4	Act 4, Scenes 2-3	Cassius and Brutus meet before the battle	Early 42 BC
Day 5	Act 5	Final battle	October 42 BC

Changing the timeframe of historical events leads to greater tension, excitement and a faster-pace.

The play begins when the citizens are waiting for Caesar to enter Rome after he has defeated Pompey's remaining supporters.

Part 3: Translating Act 1 Scene 1

ORIGINAL TEXT	MODERN TRANSLATION
ROME. A STREET.	**ROME. A STREET.**
Enter FLAVIUS, MARULLUS, and certain Commoners	*Enter FLAVIUS, MARULLUS, and certain Commoners*
FLAVIUS Hence! Home, you idle creatures get you home!	**FLAVIUS** Get away from here! Go home, you lazy men, go home!
Is this a holiday? What, know you not, Being mechanical, you ought not walk	Is today a holiday? Don't you realise, Belonging to the artisan class, you're not supposed to walk around
Upon a labouring day without the sign Of your profession? Speak, what trade art thou?	On a work day without wearing Your work clothes? Tell me, what's your trade?
FIRST COMMONER Why, sir, a carpenter.	**FIRST COMMONER** I am a carpenter, sir.
MARULLUS Where is thy leather apron and thy rule? What dost thou with thy best apparel on? You, sir, what trade are you?	**MARULLUS** Where is your leather apron and your ruler? Why are you wearing your best clothes? You, sir, what's your trade?
SECOND COMMONER Truly, sir, in respect of a fine workman, I am but, as you would say, a cobbler.	**SECOND COMMONER** Truly, sir, compared to a fine workman, I am, as you would say, a mere cobbler.
MARULLUS But what trade art thou? Answer me directly.	**MARULLUS** But what's your trade? Give me a straight answer.
SECOND COMMONER A trade, sir, that I hope I may use with a safe conscience, which is, indeed, sir, a mender of bad soles.	**SECOND COMMONER** It is a trade, sir, which I hope I practice with a clear conscience. My trade is, indeed sir, a repairer of bad soles.
MARULLUS What trade, thou knave? Thou naughty knave, what trade?	**MARULLUS** What trade, boy? You worthless boy, what's your trade?
SECOND COMMONER Nay, I beseech you, sir, be not out with me. Yet, if you be out, sir, I can mend you.	**SECOND COMMONER** No, sir, I beg you, don't be put out with me. However, if your sole's worn out, sir, I can mend you.
MARULLUS What meanest thou by that? 'Mend' me, thou saucy fellow!	**MARULLUS** What do you mean by that? 'Mend' me, you cheeky fellow!
SECOND COMMONER Why, sir, cobble you.	**SECOND COMMONER** I mean I can cobble you, sir – mend your shoes.
FLAVIUS Thou art a cobbler, art thou?	**FLAVIUS** You are a cobbler, are you?

SECOND COMMONER

Truly, sir, all that I live by is with the awl. I meddle with no tradesman's matters, nor women's matters, but with awl I am, indeed, sir, a surgeon to old shoes. When they are in great danger, I recover them. As proper men as ever trod upon neat's leather have gone upon my handiwork.

FLAVIUS

But wherefore art not in thy shop today?
Why dost thou lead these men about the streets?

SECOND COMMONER

Truly, sir, to wear out their shoes, to get myself into more work. But, indeed, sir, we make holiday to see Caesar and to rejoice in his triumph.

MARULLUS

Wherefore rejoice? What conquest brings he home?

What tributaries follow him to Rome
To grace in captive bonds his chariot-wheels?
You blocks, you stones, you worse than senseless things,
O you hard hearts, you cruel men of Rome,
Knew you not Pompey? Many a time and oft
Have you climb'd up to walls and battlements,
To towers and windows, yea, to chimney-tops,

Your infants in your arms, and there have sat
The livelong day, with patient expectation,
To see great Pompey pass the streets of Rome.

And when you saw his chariot but appear,
Have you not made an universal shout
That Tiber trembled underneath her banks
To hear the replication of your sounds
Made in her concave shores?
And do you now put on your best attire?
And do you now cull out a holiday?
And do you now strew flowers in his way

That comes in triumph over Pompey's blood?
Be gone!
Run to your houses, fall upon your knees,
Pray to the gods to intermit the plague
That needs must light on this ingratitude.

FLAVIUS

Go, go, good countrymen, and for this fault,

Assemble all the poor men of your sort,
Draw them to Tiber banks, and weep your tears

SECOND COMMONER

Truly, sir, I make my living using the awl. I don't meddle in other tradesmen's business, nor in the business of women, but when it comes to the awl, I am, indeed, sir, a surgeon to old shoes. When they are in great danger, I re-sole them. The most handsome men who ever walked upon leather have walked upon my handiwork.

FLAVIUS

But why aren't you in your shop today?
Why are you leading these men through the streets?

SECOND COMMONER

Truly, sir, to wear out their shoes and so to get myself some more work. But really, sir, we took some holiday to see Caesar and to celebrate his victory.

MARULLUS

Why celebrate? What victory is he bringing home with him?
What captives are following him to Rome
To pay honour, in fetters, to his chariot wheels?
You blockheads, you stone- hearted, unfeeling people,
Oh, you hard- hearted, cruel men of Rome,
Didn't you know Pompey? Many times, very often
You've climbed up the walls and battlements,
To the towers and windows, and even to the chimney tops,
With your babies in your arms and sat there
The whole day long, patiently waiting
To see great Pompey pass through the streets of Rome.
And as soon as you saw his chariot appear,
Didn't you make a universal shout, so loud
That the river Tiber shook her banks
On hearing the echo of your shouts
Resounding against her shoreline?
And now are you putting on your best clothes?
And now are you taking a holiday?
And now are you strewing flowers in the path of Caesar
Who comes celebrating victory over Pompey's sons?
Away with you!
Run to your houses, fall on your knees,
Pray to the gods to withhold the disaster
That you deserve for such ingratitude.

FLAVIUS

Go, go, good countrymen, and to make up for doing this wrong,
Gather together all the poor men like yourselves,
Lead them to the banks of the river Tiber and all of you weep your tears

— disgusted by Caesar's supporters

Into the channel till the lowest stream	Into the river until even at the lowest ebb the river level
Do kiss the most exalted shores of all.	Swells enough to reach the highest banks of all.
Exeunt all the Commoners	*Exeunt all the Commoners*
See whether their basest metal be not moved.	Let's see if that doesn't cut them to the quick.
They vanish tongue-tied in their guiltiness.	They're leaving tongue- tied, they're so guilty.
Go you down that way towards the Capitol.	You go down that way towards the Capitol.
This way will I. Disrobe the images	I'll go this way. Undress the statues
If you do find them deck'd with ceremonies.	If you find them decorated in honour of Caesar.
MARULLUS	**MARULLUS**
May we do so?	Are we allowed to do that?
You know it is the feast of Lupercal.	You know it's the feast of Lupercal.
FLAVIUS	**FLAVIUS**
It is no matter. Let no images	That doesn't matter. Make sure that no statues
Be hung with Caesar's trophies. I'll about	Are decorated with Caesar's trophies. I'll walk around
And drive away the vulgar from the streets.	And drive away the common people from the streets.
So do you too, where you perceive them thick.	You do the same wherever you see a crowd of them.
These growing feathers pluck'd from Caesar's wing	If we pluck these growing feathers from Caesar's wings
Will make him fly an ordinary pitch,	We will prevent him from flying too high,
Who else would soar above the view of men	Otherwise he will soar so high that he'll be out of sight of ordinary men
And keep us all in servile fearfulness.	And he will keep us all in a state of fear and servility.
Exeunt	*Exeunt*

Part 4: Analysing Act 1 Scene 1

Shakespeare employs contrasts to introduce the themes of language, class and politics; the contrasting views in this scene will set the tone for future discord, thereby foreshadowing events. At the beginning of the scene, it is clear that the tribunes (or government officials) Flavius and Marullus, hold different views from the 'Commoners': the 'carpenter' and 'cobbler' are excited about Caesar's victory; the tribunes are suspicious. The difference in rank is immediately apparent because the higher-status tribunes speak in **blank verse** while the lower-status characters employ **prose**.

Blank verse is easy to identify because each line begins with a capital letter and the line might not finish at the end of the page (it looks like a poem). It consists of unrhymed lines of ten syllables of alternating stress (if the lines are rhymed, this is called **iambic pentameter**). In the following example, the stressed syllables are underlined:

> You _blocks_, you _stones_, you _worse_ than _senseless_ _things_!

The regular rhythm of blank verse is like a beating heart. In this example, it suggests a heart pounding in anger when Marullus berates the plebeians.

Shakespeare does not always stick to the rules for creating blank verse, however. Sometimes, he adds or drops syllables. He also varies the rhythm. For example, in the first line of the play, Flavius states:

> Hence! Home, you idle creatures, get you home!

The double stress (which is called a spondee if you want to impress the examiner) and alliteration of '[h]ence! Home' intensify the impact of Flavius's anger, heightening feelings of class divisions and conflict. The plebeians are 'idle creatures'; the adjective 'idle' is unnecessary and insulting while the noun 'creatures' dehumanises the manual workers, who have no individual names in the play. Moreover, Flavius defines them by their work status, indicating that they represent the large number of plebeians of the time who, if they were valued at all, were valued for their labour. The assonance of 'hence' and 'get', coupled with the open vowel sound of 'home', emphasises Flavius's view of the vacant nature of the plebeians, and (except for 'idle creatures'), the use of single syllable words puts greater emphasis on those feelings. The repetition of 'home' at the end rounds off the alliterative impact. We therefore see that Shakespeare matches the rhythm of his blank verse to the topic and mood of his speeches, and the whole line is a punchy start to a violent play.

A close study of the characters' language reveals a lot about their contrasting social status and attitudes. Flavius first addresses the manual workers with the plural 'you'; then, when he speaks to them individually, he switches to the singular 'thou', typically used when addressing someone of a lower social class. The tribunes also employ lots of interrogatives, which indicate their higher status because they control and guide the conversation. They quiz the plebeians about their class: 'Speak, what trade art thou?'. The tribunes are not interested in names but where the plebeians stand in the social hierarchy. The latter are easily identified because they are wearing their 'best apparel' (clothes). This demonstrates their political allegiance: the Elizabethan audience would have interpreted both clothing and bearing to communicate resistance. By viewing Roman class relationships through Elizabethan cultural assumptions, we therefore see an example of the anachronisms mentioned in parts 1 and 2 of this guide. The fact that the tribunes expect the manual workers to be wearing their work clothes emphasises their status as subordinates whose function is to serve.

We see more contrasts between the two classes when Marullus employs insulting adjectives to establish his authority, calling the second commoner a 'naughty' [worthless] knave' and a 'saucy [cheeky] fellow'. The parallel sets of adjective and noun illustrate his dismissive attitude and sense of entitlement to speak so freely. To a modern audience, his verbal abuse is surprising, as he risks retaliation. This illustrates that the divisions between the classes in Elizabethan eyes were more defined than today—although, as we know, there were changing.

In contrast to blank verse, the plebeians speak in **prose**, which is easy to identify because it looks like paragraphs in a novel. Prose, often used by low-status characters, is also the language of comedy. Thus, we see humour with the cobbler's pun when he says that he is 'a mender of bad soles'. This is a pun on *souls*, suggesting that corruption is rife in Rome. Shakespeare uses this moment of the play to show that the cobbler is quicker witted than his supposed better. He is a typical cheeky, sharp-witted character (a little like the many apprentices in early 17th century literature), and perhaps Shakespeare is stating that we should not take ordinary people for granted. All this feeds into the play's discussion about upsetting the *natural order* of things where everyone is expected to behave in a way appropriate to their rank. In this part of the scene, we certainly see that the tribunes may be in authority but they do not necessarily have authority. Moreover, Marullus does not understand the cobbler's answers to his questions, symbolising his inability on a wider level to understand why the plebeians are supporting Caesar.

Marullus's speech, in blank verse, is the more formal, educated rhetoric of the upper-classes, which contrasts with the sarcastic impertinence of the quick-witted cobbler. Which, implies Shakespeare, is the more authentic and effective way of speaking? The answer is that each has its place.

The power of words—or oration—to change the opinions of others is dominant in the play. Marullus's speech emphasises his authority and contains a range of rhetorical devices to challenge the crowd's beliefs:

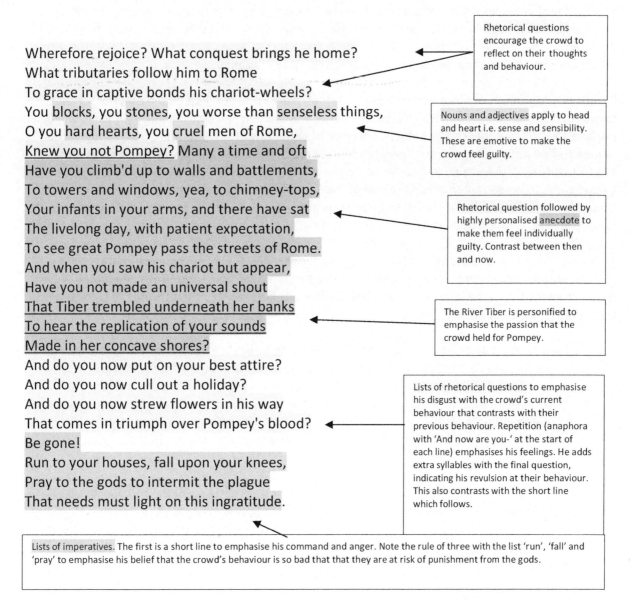

Wherefore rejoice? What conquest brings he home?
What tributaries follow him to Rome
To grace in captive bonds his chariot-wheels?
You blocks, you stones, you worse than senseless things,
O you hard hearts, you cruel men of Rome,
Knew you not Pompey? Many a time and oft
Have you climb'd up to walls and battlements,
To towers and windows, yea, to chimney-tops,
Your infants in your arms, and there have sat
The livelong day, with patient expectation,
To see great Pompey pass the streets of Rome.
And when you saw his chariot but appear,
Have you not made an universal shout
That Tiber trembled underneath her banks
To hear the replication of your sounds
Made in her concave shores?
And do you now put on your best attire?
And do you now cull out a holiday?
And do you now strew flowers in his way
That comes in triumph over Pompey's blood?
Be gone!
Run to your houses, fall upon your knees,
Pray to the gods to intermit the plague
That needs must light on this ingratitude.

Rhetorical questions encourage the crowd to reflect on their thoughts and behaviour.

Nouns and adjectives apply to head and heart i.e. sense and sensibility. These are emotive to make the crowd feel guilty.

Rhetorical question followed by highly personalised anecdote to make them feel individually guilty. Contrast between then and now.

The River Tiber is personified to emphasise the passion that the crowd held for Pompey.

Lists of rhetorical questions to emphasise his disgust with the crowd's current behaviour that contrasts with their previous behaviour. Repetition (anaphora with 'And now are you-' at the start of each line) emphasises his feelings. He adds extra syllables with the final question, indicating his revulsion at their behaviour. This also contrasts with the short line which follows.

Lists of imperatives. The first is a short line to emphasise his command and anger. Note the rule of three with the list 'run', 'fall' and 'pray' to emphasise his belief that the crowd's behaviour is so bad that that they are at risk of punishment from the gods.

One of the major themes of the play is oration: the power of speech to change people's minds with the weapons of rhetoric—or military power when all else fails. It is worth emphasising that rhetoric was deemed as important a skill in Elizabethan England as it was in Ancient Rome. Marullus's speech is a paler foreshadowing of Antony's oration to change the minds of the crowd at Caesar's funeral. Antony will manipulate the plebeians through a range of emotions, some of which we now see with the tribunes. You might be familiar with the *good cop, bad cop* technique in which a suspect is subjected to harsh interrogation by a bad cop, and then a gentler line of questioning from the good cop, who wins the co-operation of the grateful suspect. In this scene, after Marullus's threats of 'disaster' from the gods because of the crowd's 'ingratitude', Flavius follows with a softer approach, addressing the crowd as 'good countrymen', telling them to 'weep' on the banks of the Tiber. This has the desired effect, as seen in the embedded stage direction when 'they vanish tongue-tied in their guiltiness'.

Flavius and Marullus's speeches are interesting on other levels. Firstly, the fickleness of the crowd had contemporary relevance in Elizabethan England, as it reflected concerns that, if Elizabeth did not name an heir, there might be another civil war (the previous one had been the Wars of the Roses between the houses of York and Lancaster, 1455-1485). Secondly, some members of the audience might recall the disturbances that took place under Elizabeth's rule and that of her predecessors.

Thirdly, the rhetoric illustrates how a crowd can be swayed, preparing the audience for Brutus's and Antony's speeches to influence public opinion after Caesar is later assassinated. A modern audience might additionally reflect on the role of rhetoric in more recent times. Churchill and Hitler, for very different purposes, used powerful rhetoric to mobilise public opinion.

Flavius and Marullus's concern about Caesar's sudden rise to power might be a metaphor for the Elizabethans' apprehensions about the potential for very sudden and catastrophic political change in England (possibly engineered by Catholic Europe). In sixteenth century Europe, French and Spanish monarchs had absolute power; this threatened the English political system, in which nobles and elected representatives could to a certain extent work with Elizabeth I. As we are aware, when Caesar came to power, this marked the end of the Roman Republic. By deciding to include the thoughts of Flavius and Marullus, Shakespeare is drawing the audience's attention to the dangers of European centralisation of power.

There is irony in that one aspect of Flavius's and Marullus's behaviour reflects that of the mob. At the end of the scene, they plan to '[d]isrobe the images' (take the decorations off the statues). Just as the crowd will take the law into its own hands after Caesar's funeral, the tribunes now consider breaking the law themselves.

The function of the statues is similar to political advertising campaigns today: they aim to persuade. Caesar's supporters have erected the statues because Romans associated statues with important politicians and Gods. They were therefore establishing Caesar's position in society, planting the subconscious thought that he is associated with the gods. Caesar's politically astute campaigners are also preparing the masses for his coronation, thus enabling a smoother transition to power. The symbolic purpose of the statues is therefore similar to the persuasive rhetoric of the tribunes in the scene.

The 'disrobing' of the statues is not only an attack on the ancient customs of the religious feast of Lupercalia, a Roman public holiday, but also an attack on symbols which celebrate Caesar's imminent arrival. Taking away the decorations represents a breakdown both of traditional cultural identity and the current political order. This anticipates the breakdown of social and political relationships to come.

ORIGINAL TEXT	MODERN TRANSLATION
A PUBLIC PLACE.	**A PUBLIC PLACE.**
Flourish. Enter CAESAR; ANTONY, *for the course;* CALPURNIA, PORTIA, DECIUS BRUTUS, CICERO, BRUTUS, CASSIUS, and CASCA; *a great crowd following, among them a Soothsayer.*	*Flourish. Enter* CAESAR; ANTONY, stripped *for the course;* CALPURNIA, PORTIA, DECIUS BRUTUS, CICERO, BRUTUS, CASSIUS, and CASCA; *a great crowd following, among them a Soothsayer.*
CAESAR Calpurnia!	**CAESAR** Calpurnia!
CASCA Peace, ho! Caesar speaks.	**CASCA** Everyone, be quiet! Caesar is speaking.
CAESAR Calpurnia!	**CAESA** Calpurnia!
CALPURNIA Here, my lord.	**CALPURNIA** I am here, my lord.
CAESAR Stand you directly in Antonius' way When he doth run his course. Antonius.	**CAESAR** Stand directly in Antonius' path When he runs his holy course. Antonius.
ANTONY Caesar, my lord?	**ANTONY** Yes, Caesar, my lord?
CAESAR Forget not, in your speed, Antonius, To touch Calpurnia; for our elders say, The barren, touched in this holy chase, Shake off their sterile curse.	**CAESAR** Antonius, in your haste, don't forget To touch Calpurnia; because our elders say, The infertile woman, who is touched in this holy race, Will be freed from the curse of sterility.
ANTONY I shall remember: When Caesar says, 'Do this,' it is perform'd.	**ANTONY** I shall remember: When Caesar says, 'Do this,' it is done.
CAESAR Set on, and leave no ceremony out.	**CAESAR** Proceed, and don't forget to perform any of the rituals.
Flourish	*Flourish*
SOOTHSAYER Caesar!	**SOOTHSAYER** Caesar!
CAESAR Ha! Who calls?	**CAESAR** Who is calling me?

CASCA
Bid every noise be still; peace yet again!

CAESAR
Who is it in the press that calls on me?
I hear a tongue shriller than all the music
Cry 'Caesar!' Speak. Caesar is turn'd to hear.

SOOTHSAYER
Beware the ides of March.

CAESAR
What man is that?

BRUTUS
A soothsayer bids you beware the ides of March.

CAESAR
Set him before me; let me see his face.

CASSIUS
Fellow, come from the throng; look upon Caesar.

CAESAR
What say'st thou to me now? Speak once again.

SOOTHSAYER
Beware the ides of March.

CAESAR
He is a dreamer. Let us leave him. Pass.

Sennet. Exeunt all except BRUTUS and CASSIUS

CASSIUS
Will you go see the order of the course?

BRUTUS
Not I.

CASSIUS
I pray you, do.

BRUTUS
I am not gamesome: I do lack some part
Of that quick spirit that is in Antony.

Let me not hinder, Cassius, your desires;
I'll leave you.

CASSIUS
Brutus, I do observe you now of late:
I have not from your eyes that gentleness

CASCA
Please be quiet everyone; let silence resume!

CAESAR
Who is it in the crowd who's calling me?
I can hear a voice and it's shriller than all the music
Calling out 'Caesar!' Speak. Caesar is listening.

SOOTHSAYER
Beware of March 15th.

CAESAR
Who is that man?

BRUTUS
A soothsayer is telling you to beware of March 15th.

CAESAR
Bring him to me; let me see his face.

CASSIUS
You, fellow, come away from the crowd; come before Caesar.

CAESAR
What do you have to say to me now? Say it again.

SOOTHSAYER
Beware of March 15th.

CAESAR
He is a fantasist. Let us leave him. Advance.

Sennet. Exeunt all except BRUTUS and CASSIUS

CASSIUS
Are you going to watch the progress of the race?

BRUTUS
Not me.

CASSIUS
Please come.

BRUTUS
I am not a frivolous sport- lover: I lack something
Of that lively and prompt disposition that Antony has.
Don't let me keep you from going, Cassius;
I'll be on my way.

CASSIUS
Brutus, I have been studying you recently:
I have not observed in your eyes that well-bred courtesy
And manifestation of love that I was accustomed to.
You have too stubborn and too hostile a disposition

And show of love as I was wont to have.
You bear too stubborn and too strange a hand
Over your friend that loves you.

BRUTUS
Cassius,
Be not deceived: if I have veil'd my look,
I turn the trouble of my countenance
Merely upon myself. Vexed I am
Of late with passions of some difference,
Conceptions only proper to myself,
Which give some soil, perhaps, to my behaviors;

But let not therefore my good friends be grieve -

Among which number, Cassius, be you one-
Nor construe any further my neglect,

Than that poor Brutus, with himself at war,
Forgets the shows of love to other men.

CASSIUS
Then, Brutus, I have much mistook your passion,
By means whereof this breast of mine hath buried
Thoughts of great value, worthy cogitations.
Tell me, good Brutus, can you see your face?

BRUTUS
No, Cassius; for the eye sees not itself
But by reflection, by some other things.

CASSIUS
'Tis just;
And it is very much lamented, Brutus,
That you have no such mirrors as will turn
Your hidden worthiness into your eye,
That you might see your shadow. I have heard,
Where many of the best respect in Rome,

Except immortal Caesar, speaking of Brutus,
And groaning underneath this age's yoke,
Have wish'd that noble Brutus had his eyes.

BRUTUS
Into what dangers would you lead me, Cassius,

That you would have me seek into myself
For that which is not in me?

CASSIUS
Therefore, good Brutus, be prepared to hear;

And since you know you cannot see yourself
So well as by reflection, I, your glass,

Towards your friend who loves you.

BRUTUS
Cassius,
Don't be misled: if my expression is concealed,
The troubled look is directed
Entirely towards myself. I am worried
Recently by conflicting emotions,
Thoughts pertaining only to me,
Which are, perhaps, adversely affecting my
behaviour;
So therefore, my good friends must not be
troubled—
And, Cassius, I number you among my friends—
Nor must you make anything more of my neglect of
you,
Than that poor Brutus, who is at war with himself,
Is forgetting to demonstrate love to others.

CASSIUS
Then, Brutus, I have misunderstood your feelings,
And it's caused me to keep to myself
Important thoughts and contemplations.
Tell me, good Brutus, can you see your face?

BRUTUS
No, Cassius; because an eye cannot see itself
Unless it's reflected in something else.

CASSIUS
That's true;
And it is very much regretted, Brutus,
That you don't have any mirrors which can reflect
Your hidden worthiness back to yourself,
So that you could see your image. I have heard,
Many people in Rome who're held in the highest
estimation,
Next to immortal Caesar, speaking of you, Brutus,
And groaning under the weight of this government,
Wishing that noble Brutus' eyes were seeing clearly.

BRUTUS
What sort of dangers are you trying to lead me into
Cassius,
That you want me to look inside myself
For something that isn't there?

CASSIUS
So far as that is concerned, good Brutus, get ready
to listen;
And since you know that you can't see yourself
Any more clearly than by looking at your reflection, I
shall be your mirror,

Will modestly discover to yourself
That of yourself which you yet know not of.
And be not jealous on me, gentle Brutus:
Were I a common laugher, or did use
To stale with ordinary oaths my love

To every new protester; if you know
That I do fawn on men and hug them hard,
And after scandal them; or if you know
That I profess myself in banqueting
To all the rout, then hold me dangerous.

Flourish, and shout

BRUTUS
What means this shouting? I do fear the people
Choose Caesar for their king.

CASSIUS
Ay, do you fear it?
Then must I think you would not have it so.

BRUTUS
I would not, Cassius; yet I love him well.
But wherefore do you hold me here so long?
What is it that you would impart to me?
If it be aught toward the general good,
Set honour in one eye and death i' the other,
And I will look on both indifferently;
For let the gods so speed me as I love
The name of honour more than I fear death.

CASSIUS
I know that virtue to be in you, Brutus,
As well as I do know your outward favour.
Well, honour is the subject of my story.
I cannot tell what you and other men
Think of this life; but, for my single self,
I had as lief not be as live to be
In awe of such a thing as I myself.
I was born free as Caesar, so were you;
We both have fed as well, and we can both
Endure the winter's cold as well as he.
For once, upon a raw and gusty day,
The troubled Tiber chafing with her shores,

Caesar said to me, 'Darest thou, Cassius, now
Leap in with me into this angry flood,
And swim to yonder point?' Upon the word,
Accoutred as I was, I plunged in
And bade him follow; so indeed he did.
The torrent roar'd, and we did buffet it
With lusty sinews, throwing it aside
And stemming it with hearts of controversy.

And will show you without exaggeration
Things about yourself which you don't know yet.
And don't be suspicious of me, noble Brutus:
If I were a common jester, or was inclined
To cheapen my affection by using commonplace oaths
To every new acquaintance; if you saw
That I flatter men and hug them tightly,
And later libel them; or if I were inclined to
Declare friendship at banquets
To the whole common rabble, then go ahead and call me dangerous.

Flourish, and shout

BRUTUS
Why are they shouting? I'm afraid the people
Have chosen Caesar for their king.

CASSIUS
Is that what you're afraid of?
Then I assume that you don't want him to be king.

BRUTUS
I don't, Cassius; even though I love him very much.
But why are you keeping me here so long?
What is it that you want to say to me?
If it is anything at all to help the well-being of Rome,
Put honour in one eye and death in the other,
And I will look on both indifferently;
For let the gods make me prosper only when I love
Acting with honour more than I fear death.

CASSIUS
I recognise that integrity within you, Brutus,
As well as I recognise your face.
Well, honour is the subject of my story.
I don't know what you and other men
Think of this life; but as for me,
I would just as soon be dead rather than live
To worship a man as ordinary as myself.
I was born as free as Caesar, so were you;
We both have eaten as well, and we can both
Endure the winter's cold weather as well as him.
Once, on a cold and blustery day,
The restless river Tiber was crashing against its banks,
Caesar said to me, 'Cassius do you dare, right now
To jump with me into this wild river,
And swim to that point over there?' Straight away,
Smartly dressed as I was, I plunged in
And invited him to follow; and so, he did.
The torrent roared, and we fought against it
With brawny muscles, overcoming it
And thwarting its strength with hearts eager for competition.

But ere we could arrive the point proposed,	But before we could reach the place we were heading to,
Caesar cried, 'Help me, Cassius, or I sink!'	Caesar cried, 'Help me, Cassius, or I will sink!'
I, as Aeneas, our great ancestor,	And just as Aeneas, our great founder of the Roman nation,
Did from the flames of Troy upon his shoulder	Emerged from the flames of Troy, bearing on his shoulders
The old Anchises bear, so from the waves of Tiber	His elderly father Anchises, so I emerged from the waves of the Tiber
Did I the tired Caesar. And this man	Carrying the tired Caesar. And this man
Is now become a god, and Cassius is	Has now become a god, and I, Cassius am
A wretched creature and must bend his body	A wretched creature who must bow low
If Caesar carelessly but nod on him.	If Caesar so much as carelessly nods my way.
He had a fever when he was in Spain,	He had a fever when he was in Spain,
And when the fit was on him, I did mark	And when the fever was at its height, I noticed
How he did shake; 'tis true, this god did shake;	How much he was shaking; it's true, this god was shaking;
His coward lips did from their colour fly,	The colour drained from his cowardly lips,
And that same eye whose bend doth awe the world	And that same eye whose gaze fills the world with wonder
Did lose his lustre; I did hear him groan;	Lost its radiance; I heard him groan;
Ay, and that tongue of his, that bade the Romans	Yes, and that tongue of his, that ordered the Romans
Mark him and write his speeches in their books,	To obey him and write his speeches on their writing tablets,
'Alas!', it cried, 'Give me some drink, Titinius,'	Cried, 'Fetch me a drink of water, Titinius,'
As a sick girl. Ye gods, it doth amaze me	Just like a sick girl. Ye gods, it does stupefy me
A man of such a feeble temper should	That a man with such a feeble constitution should
So get the start of the majestic world,	Outstrip the whole world,
And bear the palm alone.	And carry off the prize alone.
Shout. Flourish	*Shout. Flourish*
BRUTUS	**BRUTUS**
Another general shout?	More loud shouting?
I do believe that these applauses are	I can't help but think that this applause is
For some new honours that are heap'd on Caesar.	For some new honours that are being bestowed on Caesar.
CASSIUS	**CASSIUS**
Why, man, he doth bestride the narrow world	Why, Caesar straddles the narrow world
Like a Colossus, and we petty men	Like a giant, and we petty men
Walk under his huge legs and peep about	Walk under his huge legs and peep out
To find ourselves dishonourable graves.	To find slaves' graves for ourselves.
Men at some time are masters of their fates;	Men can be masters of their fate;
The fault, dear Brutus, is not in our stars,	The fault, dear Brutus, is not due to our star signs,
But in ourselves, that we are underlings.	But it is due to ourselves, that we are slaves.
Brutus and Caesar. What should be in that 'Caesar'?	Brutus and Caesar. What is so important about the name Caesar?
Why should that name be sounded more than yours?	Why should that name resound more famously than yours?
Write them together, yours is as fair a name;	Write them together, yours is just as good a name;
Sound them, it doth become the mouth as well;	Pronounce them, yours sounds just as good;
Weigh them, it is as heavy; conjure with 'em,	Weigh them, yours is just as heavy; conjure up spirits with them,
'Brutus' will start a spirit as soon as 'Caesar'.	'Brutus' will call forth a ghost just as well as 'Caesar'.
Now in the names of all the gods at once,	Now in the name of all the gods at once,

Upon what meat doth this our Caesar feed,
That he is grown so great? Age, thou art shamed!

Rome, thou hast lost the breed of noble bloods!
When went there by an age, since the great flood,
But it was famed with more than with one man?

When could they say, till now, that talk'd of Rome,

That her wide walls encompass'd but one man?
Now is it Rome indeed and room enough,
When there is in it but one only man.
O, you and I have heard our fathers say,
There was a Brutus once that would have brook'd

The eternal devil to keep his state in Rome

As easily as a king.

BRUTUS
That you do love me, I am nothing jealous;
What you would work me to, I have some aim:
How I have thought of this and of these times,

I shall recount hereafter. For this present,
I would not - so with love I might entreat you -
Be any further moved. What you have said
I will consider; what you have to say
I will with patience hear, and find a time
Both meet to hear and answer such high things.

Till then, my noble friend, chew upon this:
Brutus had rather be a villager
Than to repute himself a son of Rome
Under these hard conditions as this time
Is like to lay upon us.

CASSIUS
I am glad
That my weak words have struck but thus much show
Of fire from Brutus.

BRUTUS
The games are done and Caesar is returning.

CASSIUS
As they pass by, pluck Casca by the sleeve,
And he will, after his sour fashion, tell you
What hath proceeded worthy note to-day.

Re-enter CAESAR and his Train

BRUTUS
I will do so. But, look you, Cassius,
The angry spot doth glow on Caesar's brow,

Tell me what meat does this Caesar eat,
That has made him grow so great? This era should be ashamed!
Rome, you have lost the art of breeding noble stock!
When was there ever an age, since the great flood,
When Rome wasn't celebrated for more than one great man?
Until now, when could anyone who was talking about Rome say,
That her extensive walls embraced only one man?
Now all of Rome has room enough,
For only one man.
You and I have heard our fathers talk,
Of a different Brutus, your ancestor, who would have tolerated
The eternally damned devil maintaining his court in Rome
Rather than let a King reign.

BRUTUS
I have no doubt that you love me;
I can guess what you want to persuade me to do:
My opinion about this and what's happening here in Rome now,
I shall tell you later. For this moment,
I don't want – if I may ask you as a friend –
To be persuaded any more. What you have said
I will mull over; what you are going to say
I will listen to patiently and find a time
Suitable to listen to and answer such important affairs.
Until then, my noble friend, consider this:
I, Brutus, would rather be a villager
Than call myself a citizen of Rome
Under such hard conditions as this time
Is likely to put us through.

CASSIUS
I am glad
That my weak little speech has provoked even this much declaration
Of protest from Brutus.

BRUTUS
The games are over and Caesar is returning.

CASSIUS
As they pass by, take hold of Casca by the sleeve,
And he will, in his usual sour way, tell you
What has happened that's worthy of note today.

Re-enter CAESAR and his Train

BRUTUS
I will do so. But look Cassius,
Caesar's expression is clearly angry,

And all the rest look like a chidden train:	And all the rest look as if they've been severely told off:
Calpurnia's cheek is pale, and Cicero Looks with such ferret and such fiery eyes As we have seen him in the Capitol Being cross'd in conference by some senators.	Calpurnia's face is pale and Cicero's eyes Look as fiery and blood shot As they do when we see him in the Capitol Debating and arguing with the senators.
CASSIUS Casca will tell us what the matter is.	**CASSIUS** Casca will tell us what's the matter.
CAESAR Antonius.	**CAESAR** Antonio.
ANTONY Caesar?	**ANTONY** Caesar?
CAESAR Let me have men about me that are fat, Sleek-headed men and such as sleep a- nights. Yond Cassius has a lean and hungry look; He thinks too much: such men are dangerous.	**CAESAR** Let me be surrounded by men who are fat, Smooth-combed men and the sort who sleep at night. Cassius, over there, has a lean and hungry look; He thinks too much: that sort of man is dangerous.
ANTONY Fear him not, Caesar; he's not dangerous; He is a noble Roman and well given.	**ANTONY** Don't be afraid of him, Caesar; he's not dangerous; He is a noble Roman and is well disposed.
CAESAR Would he were fatter! But I fear him not; Yet if my name were liable to fear, I do not know the man I should avoid So soon as that spare Cassius. He reads much, He is a great observer and he looks Quite through the deeds of men. He loves no plays, As thou dost, Antony; he hears no music; Seldom he smiles, and smiles in such a sort As if he mock'd himself and scorn'd his spirit That could be moved to smile at any thing. Such men as he be never at heart's ease Whiles they behold a greater than themselves, And therefore are they very dangerous. I rather tell thee what is to be fear'd Than what I fear; for always I am Caesar. Come on my right hand, for this ear is deaf, And tell me truly what thou think'st of him.	**CAESAR** I wish he were fatter! But I am not afraid of him; Yet if I were prone to fear, I don't know a man I would more readily avoid Than that thin Cassius. He reads a lot, He is keenly observant and he looks Behind men's actions to determine their motives. He has no love for plays, In the way you do, Antony; he doesn't listen to any music; He very rarely smiles and when he does, he smiles in such a way As if he's mocking himself and scorning his spirit For allowing anything to cause him to smile at all. Men like that are never happy When they observe someone who is greater than themselves, And therefore, they're very dangerous. I am only telling you what should be feared And not what I fear; because I alone am Caesar. Come to my right side, because this ear is deaf, And tell me truthfully what you think of Cassius.
Sennet. Exeunt CAESAR and all his Train, but CASCA	*Sennet. Exeunt CAESAR and all his Train, but CASCA*
CASCA (to Brutus) You pull'd me by the cloak; would you speak with me?	**CASCA (to Brutus)** You pulled at my cloak; do you want to speak to me?

BRUTUS Ay, Casca, tell us what hath chanced to-day That Caesar looks so sad.	**BRUTUS** Yes, Casca, tell us what has happened today That has made Caesar look so sad.
CASCA Why, you were with him, were you not?	**CASCA** But you were with him, weren't you?
BRUTUS I should not then ask Casca what had chanced.	**BRUTUS** I wouldn't be asking you what happened, Casca, if that were the case.
CASCA Why, there was a crown offered him; and being offered him, he put it by with the back of his hand, thus; and then the people fell a-shouting.	**CASCA** Well, a crown was offered to him; and when it was offered to him, he pushed it away with the back of his hand, like this; and then the people started shouting.
BRUTUS What was the second noise for?	**BRUTUS** What was the second noise for?
CASCA Why, for that too.	**CASCA** The same thing again.
CASSIUS They shouted thrice: what was the last cry for?	**CASSIUS** They shouted three times: what was the last cry for?
CASCA Why, for that too.	**CASCA** For the same thing, again.
BRUTUS Was the crown offered him thrice?	**BRUTUS** Was the crown offered to him three times?
CASCA Ay, marry, was't, and he put it by thrice, every time gentler than other; and at every putting-by mine honest neighbours shouted.	**CASCA** Yes, indeed it was and he pushed it aside three times, each time more reluctantly than the last; and each time he pushed it aside my honest countrymen shouted.
CASSIUS Who offered him the crown?	**CASSIUS** Who offered him the crown?
CASCA Why, Antony.	**CASCA** Antony.
BRUTUS Tell us the manner of it, gentle Casca.	**BRUTUS** Tell us how it happened, noble Casca.
CASCA I can as well be hanged as tell the manner of it; it was mere foolery; I did not mark it. I saw Mark Antony offer him a crown; yet 'twas not a crown neither, 'twas one of these coronets; and, as I told you, he put it by once; but, for all that, to my thinking, he would fain have had it. Then he offered it to him again; then he put it by again; but, to my thinking, he was very loath to	**CASCA** I am at a loss as how to describe it; it was just silliness; I didn't pay full attention. I saw Mark Antony offer him a crown; though it wasn't a real crown, just a small coronet; and as I told you, he pushed it aside once; but even so, in my opinion, he would have willingly had it. Then he offered it to him again; then he pushed it aside again; but in my opinion, he was very loath to take his hands off it.

lay his fingers off it. And then he offered it the third time; he put it the third time by; and still as he refused it, the rabblement hooted and clapped their chopped hands and threw up their sweaty night-caps and uttered such a deal of stinking breath because Caesar refused the crown, that it had, almost, choked Caesar; for he swooned and fell down at it. And for mine own part, I durst not laugh, for fear of opening my lips and receiving the bad air.

CASSIUS
But soft, I pray you; what, did Caesar swoon?

CASCA
He fell down in the market-place, and foamed at mouth, and was speechless.

BRUTUS
'Tis very like; he hath the falling sickness.

CASSIUS
No, Caesar hath it not; but you and I,

And honest Casca, we have the falling sickness.

CASCA
I know not what you mean by that, but I am sure Caesar fell down. If the tag-rag people did not clap him and hiss him, according as he pleased and displeased them, as they use to do the players in the theatre, I am no true man.

BRUTUS
What said he when he came unto himself?

CASCA
Marry, before he fell down, when he perceived the common herd was glad he refused the crown, he plucked me ope his doublet and offered them his throat to cut. An I had been a man of any occupation, if I would not have taken him at a word, I would I might go to hell among the rogues. And so he fell. When he came to himself again, he said, if he had done or said anything amiss, he desired their worships to think it was his infirmity. Three or four wenches, where I stood, cried, 'Alas, good soul!' and forgave him with all their hearts; but there's no heed to be taken of them; if Caesar had stabbed their mothers, they would have done no less.

BRUTUS
And after that, he came thus sad away?

Antony then offered it a third time; he pushed it aside a third time; and each time he refused it, all the people shouted and clapped their chapped hands and threw up their sweaty night-caps and exhaled such a great deal of stinking breath because Caesar refused the crown, that it almost choked Caesar; because he fainted and fell over. And as for me, I didn't dare laugh, for fear of opening my mouth and inhaling the stinking air.

CASSIUS
But slow down, please; are you saying that Caesar fainted?

CASCA
He fell down in the market-place, and foamed at the mouth and couldn't speak.

BRUTUS
That is very likely; he has epilepsy, a disease that causes you to fall.

CASSIUS
No, Caesar doesn't have the falling disease; but you and I,
And honest Casca, we have fallen under Caesar's sway.

CASCA
I don't know what you mean by that, but I am sure that Caesar fell down. If the rabble were not applauding him and hissing at him, depending on whether he pleased them or displeased them, just as they do to actors in the theatre, then I am a liar.

BRUTUS
What did he say when he came around?

CASCA
Indeed, before he fell, when he realised the crowd of commoners were glad that he refused the crown, he opened his jacket and offered them his throat to cut. If I had been a man of action, and hadn't taken him up on his offer, I would wish myself in hell among the villains. And so he fainted. When he regained consciousness, he said that if he had done or said anything inappropriate, he wanted them to understand that it was because of his affliction. Three or four women, where I was standing, exclaimed, 'Alas, good soul!' and forgave him with all their hearts; but we shouldn't take any notice of what they say; if Caesar had stabbed their mothers, they would have forgiven him.

BRUTUS
And after that, he came back here looking so sad?

CASCA Ay.	**CASCA** Yes.
CASSIUS Did Cicero say anything?	**CASSIUS** Did Cicero say anything?
CASCA Ay, he spoke Greek.	**CASCA** Yes, he spoke in Greek.
CASSIUS To what effect?	**CASSIUS** What did he say?
CASCA Nay, an I tell you that, I'll ne'er look you i' the face again. But those that understood him smiled at one another and shook their heads; but, for mine own part, it was Greek to me. I could tell you more news too: Marullus and Flavius, for pulling scarfs off Caesar's images, are put to silence. Fare you well. There was more foolery yet, if I could remember it.	**CASCA** No, if I tell you that, I will never look you in the face again. But those who understood him smiled at one another and shook their heads; but as for me, I couldn't understand it. I have more news to tell you too: Marullus and Flavius have been silenced, for pulling scarves off statues of Caesar. Thoroughly silenced. There was even more tomfoolery, if only I could remember it.
CASSIUS Will you sup with me to-night, Casca?	**CASSIUS** Will you eat with me tonight, Casca?
CASCA No, I am promised forth.	**CASCA** No, I have promised to dine elsewhere.
CASSIUS Will you dine with me to-morrow?	**CASSIUS** Will you dine with me tomorrow?
CASCA Ay, if I be alive and your mind hold and your dinner worth the eating.	**CASCA** Yes, if I am alive and you don't change your mind and your dinner is worth eating.
CASSIUS Good; I will expect you.	**CASSIUS** Good; I will expect you.
CASCA Do so. Farewell, both.	**CASCA** Yes, do so. Farewell to you both.
Exit CASCA	*Exit CASCA*
BRUTUS What a blunt fellow is this grown to be! He was quick mettle when he went to school.	**BRUTUS** What an abrupt man he has turned out to be! He had a lively disposition when he was at school.
CASSIUS So is he now in execution Of any bold or noble enterprise, However he puts on this tardy form. This rudeness is a sauce to his good wit, Which gives men stomach to digest his words With better appetite.	**CASSIUS** He is still courageous when he is carrying out Any bold or noble enterprise, Although he pretends to be slow witted. This rough manner is like a sauce to his genuine intelligence, Which helps people to digest what he says More willingly.

BRUTUS

And so it is. For this time I will leave you.
To-morrow, if you please to speak with me,
I will come home to you; or, if you will,
Come home to me, and I will wait for you.

CASSIUS

I will do so: till then, think of the world.

Exit BRUTUS

Well, Brutus, thou art noble; yet I see
Thy honourable mettle may be wrought
From that it is disposed: therefore it is meet
That noble minds keep ever with their likes;

For who so firm that cannot be seduced?
Caesar doth bear me hard, but he loves Brutus.
If I were Brutus now and he were Cassius,
He should not humour me. I will this night,

In several hands, in at his windows throw,

As if they came from several citizens,
Writings, all tending to the great opinion
That Rome holds of his name; wherein obscurely

Caesar's ambition shall be glanced at.
And after this, let Caesar seat him sure,
For we will shake him, or worse days endure.

Exit

BRUTUS

Yes, that is how it is. I must leave you for now.
If you would like to talk with me tomorrow,
I will come to your home; or, if you wish,
You can come to my home and I will wait for you.

CASSIUS

I will do that: until then, think about the present state of affairs in Rome.

Exit BRUTUS

Well, Brutus, you are virtuous; Yet I see
Your upstanding spirit can be twisted
Out of its natural inclination: therefore, it is fitting
That honest men should only keep company with other honest men;

Because who is so firm that he cannot be seduced?
Caesar feels ill-will towards me, but he loves Brutus.
If I were Brutus now and Brutus were me,
He would not be able to influence me, in the same way that I have just been moulding him. Tonight, I will,

Throw through his windows, several letters in different handwriting,
As if they were written by several citizens,
Letters, all concerning the great respect
That Romans have for Brutus; and all of them will indirectly
Allude to Caesar's ruthless ambition.
And after this, let Caesar make his position secure,
For we will dethrone him, or must endure even greater tranny in the future.

Exit

Part 6: Analysing Act 1 Scene 2

While Act 1, Scene 1 revealed Flavius's and Marullus's antagonism towards Caesar, Act 1, Scene 2 opens at the festival of Lupercalia with evidence of his popularity. The festival, held on February 15, was a spiritual event, which aimed to cleanse the city of evil spirits and to release health and fertility. Shakespeare's use of setting therefore introduces the theme of the supernatural.

Portents (signs or warnings that something momentous will happen) and omens (events that are predictions of the future) emerge from the beginning of this scene as a motif, a recurring idea. The soothsayer (fortune teller) warns Caesar to 'Beware the ides of March', intimating something significant will happen on that day. The line only has six syllables instead of the usual ten of blank verse to emphasise the great importance of the message. A contemporary audience would note the soothsayer's warning and associate Caesar with some sort of tragic event. Elizabethans believed that fate controlled people's lives and that their destiny was pre-determined: they had no power to change it. In their eyes, Caesar is therefore doomed.

Unlike many if not most Elizabethans, Cassius does not believe in fate. He tells Brutus: 'Men at sometime were masters of their fates. /The fault, dear Brutus, is not in our stars, /But in ourselves, that we are underlings'. In other words, we are 'underlings' (slaves) because we have chosen to be that way rather than because the gods have decided it for us. We learn in Act 5, Scene 1 that Cassius is a 'follower of Epicurus', a Greek philosopher who taught that the gods did not intervene in human lives, so we have the free will to do what we want. Cassius's Epicurean beliefs therefore motivate him to conspire against Caesar and to change the course of history himself rather than waiting for the gods to act.

By way of contrast, Brutus's attitude towards fate derives more from the philosophical school of Stoicism, which flourished in Ancient Rome and Greece. Stoics believed that the gods controlled everything in the universe and that the only way to gain wisdom and become happy was to restrain emotions. At this moment in the play, Brutus accepts Caesar's popularity despite being troubled. By hanging back from the procession, telling Cassius 'I am not gamesome', we see that Brutus is demonstrating Stoicism by refusing to join in the celebrations. He also, however, appears to be troubled, and this hints at his concerns about Caesar's rule. Brutus's Stoic approach to life explains why he later focuses on reason, ignoring his private feelings when he decides in the next act to join the conspiracy.

Another theme that dominates this scene is what we learn about a person's private self in relation to their public actions or feelings of responsibility. In Act 1, Scene 2, we see Antony briefly but, through his behaviour, we learn important facts about his private character that will be significant as the play progresses. For example, Caesar instructs Antony when 'running the course' to touch Calpurnia and Antony replies: 'When Caesar says, 'Do this,' it is perform'd'. From his response, we have evidence that, out of deep loyalty to Caesar, Antony is happy to follow orders without question. This helps the audience to understand his loyalty when he later avenges Caesar's death. It is also significant that Shakespeare has chosen to depict Antony as naked as part of the public ceremony. For Ancient Romans, male nakedness had negative connotations of slavery, as slaves were usually naked when they were auctioned to the highest bidder. This might foreshadow how, for a short time, Antony will like a slave keep his private thoughts hidden from the assassins when he appears to agree with their reasons for killing Caesar. However, for the Ancient Greeks, male nakedness had connotations of heroism—in the Olympic games, for example, the male participants competed naked. If we interpret Antony's nakedness with the more positive connotation, we see further foreshadowing of Antony as the heroic avenger.

Although Caesar is a powerful public man, there are various signs or hints of weakness in his private character in this scene. By ignoring the Soothsayer's warning, for example, we learn that Caesar sometimes lacks judgment, as he does not listen to other points of view. This lack of judgement is also symbolised by his deafness in one ear: he tells Antony 'Come on my right hand, for this ear is deaf', indicating that he hears what he chooses to hear, rather than considering a range of views. For example, Caesar ignores his private thoughts and believes Antony when the latter tells him that Cassius is 'not dangerous'. The dramatic irony produced by this statement is strong, as the audience knows that Cassius has already begun to plot.

Interestingly, Caesar's reasons for not trusting Cassius relate to how the latter neglects elements of his private life. Cassius's inability to appreciate the arts arouses Caesar's suspicions: Cassius 'loves no plays' and 'he hears no music'. Caesar sees that Cassius does not nurture his spirit: his public life and ambitions dominate his personality. Therefore, his public persona is not to be trusted and he is 'very dangerous'. Caesar is an intelligent man to understand Cassius and he is right to suspect him but, as stated above, he foolishly allows his opinion to be swayed by Antony when he says that Cassius is 'not dangerous'. Caesar is therefore fallible.

We also see that Caesar the public hero is fallible in his private life. Despite ignoring the Soothsayer's warning, he superstitiously asks Antony to touch Calpurnia as he is running in order to 'shake off' the 'sterile curse' of her being 'barren'. This illustrates that Caesar is worried that she is infertile, hinting at an ambition to found a dynasty. His apparent inability to produce an heir with Calpurnia also poses questions about his physical capability. This is his third marriage, so it is surprising that he only has one daughter (Julia) from his first marriage and an illegitimate son (Caesareon) by Cleopatra.

Shakespeare investigates the intersection between the private and public spheres through Caesar's other physical weakness: in Ancient Rome and indeed in Elizabethan England, 'the falling sickness' or epilepsy was regarded with some suspicion and ignorance. This might have made the sufferer incapable of ruling in the eyes of observers. We therefore see that Caesar is not as all-powerful as he would like to believe when we hear reports of his epileptic fit: this is a physical foreshadowing of his literal and metaphorical fall from power when he is assassinated.

In this scene, we see the influence of the Greek philosopher Aristotle through contemporary Roman beliefs about the public self in relation to manhood and honour. After Caesar's epileptic fit, Casca reports that Caesar 'offered them [the crowd] his throat to cut'. This could be because, knowing an epileptic fit was coming, he refused the crown and now feels publicly shamed. Aristotle said 'there are conditions on which life is not worth having': Caesar would rather not live with the shame of the public epileptic fit, or life without the crown, or both. We have already learnt that Casca would rather not live as a slave, and we will learn at the end of the play that Brutus would rather not live with the stain of defeat and dishonour. This foreshadows his later suicide, which is perceived as noble by Antony and Octavius, in turn heightening the contrast with Cassius's dishonourable death in Act 5.

Despite his physical weaknesses, Caesar is still regarded by the people as a great public man. When he asks forgiveness from the crowd for his epileptic fit, Casca reports they 'forgave him with all their hearts'; and, to emphasise the love the crowd has for Caesar, Casca adds 'if Caesar had stabbed their mothers, they would have done no less'. Interestingly, this comment is made only in relation to some women in the throng, which suggests that older women were not valued in Ancient Rome. The verb 'stabbed' foreshadows the means by which Caesar will die. The reference to the potential violence of the mob also foreshadows the mob rule that will take place after Caesar's funeral when Cinna the Poet is murdered. Finally, Caesar's ability to gain the goodwill of the crowd reminds us of another dominant theme in the play: oration, the power of rhetoric to influence people's hearts and minds. Although Caesar the man has physical weaknesses, his power derives from rhetoric (backed up by his army).

The ways in which the private self can accommodate the demands of the public sphere continue with Casca's cynicism about Caesar's motives for refusing the crown three times. His attitude is emphasised by his use of down-to-earth prose: 'he was very loath to lay his fingers off it'. Casca's bias is revealed through his use of the adjective 'loath' to describe Caesar's apparent reluctance to put the crown down. At this point in the play, the audience is unsure as to whether Caesar is putting on a crowd-pleasing show or being genuinely humble. The conspirators are upset primarily because hundreds of years of republican history have been overturned at a stroke. If Casca's account is accurate and Caesar is 'loath' to return the crown, this also suggests that Caesar is seduced by the temptation of absolute power—in which case the concerns of the conspirators that Caesar might misuse his power could be legitimate.

Further conflict is revealed between the private self and a public sense of responsibility when Brutus explains to Cassius that he is 'with himself at war'. The use of the third person has a distancing effect and develops the idea of Brutus rationalising his thoughts about the impact that Caesar's rule will have on Rome. At the same time, he genuinely loves his friend Caesar ('I love him very much'), and the use of the first person is more intimate, illustrating that it is not easy to rationalise feelings. The switch between the third and first person therefore enhances Brutus's internal struggles as he attempts to decide whether his private feelings of love for Caesar or his concerns about Caesar's dictatorship should dominate.

From this point until the end of the scene, Cassius takes advantage of Brutus's internal conflict by attempting to influence his thoughts through a range of rhetorical devices. We therefore see the power of words to persuade continue as a theme. He begins by flattering Brutus, calling him 'good Brutus' and 'gentle Brutus'; the positive adjectives clearly intend to appeal to Brutus as a friend. He also offers to be his mirror ('glass') to reflect his 'hidden worthiness', implying that he is so modest that he is unaware of the high esteem in which the Romans regard him. He then states that everyone 'except immortal Caesar' wishes Brutus knows how much they admire him. This veiled insult implies that Caesar is not giving his friend the recognition that he deserves. The use of the adjective 'immortal' is also sarcastic and suggests that Caesar is becoming too powerful. This phrase therefore deliberately appeals to Brutus's private self, intending to hurt his feelings by implying Caesar does not return his respect. It also reminds him of his social standing in the eyes of the public, thereby appealing to his sense of public responsibility towards the Roman citizens.

Another device that Cassius uses is to twist Brutus's words to encourage him to express his private thoughts. When Brutus says 'What means this shouting? I do fear the people/Choose Caesar for their king', Cassius throws the verb 'fear' back at Brutus and asks a leading question: 'Ay, do you fear it? /Then must I think you would not have it so'. He cleverly forces Brutus to express his point of view, which opens the conversation for Cassius to employ his rhetoric to induce Brutus to share his beliefs.

Cassius carefully selects his words to encourage Brutus to draw his own conclusions. For example, Cassius claims equality with Caesar ('I would just as soon be dead rather than live/To worship a man as ordinary as myself), but his examples illustrate that Caesar is physically inferior. Cassius builds the irony of Caesar's current position by contrasting it with his past weaknesses, recounting the times that he rescued Caesar from drowning and he nursed him through a fever. He employs sarcasm when he concludes 'this man/Has now become a god'. The blunt contrast between 'man' and 'god' heightens the differences: how can a man of such 'a feeble constitution', so lacking in essential masculinity, be considered a god?

Cassius also plays on Brutus's fears by employing simile to emphasise Caesar's ambition. He states that Caesar is 'Like a Colossus'. The Colossus of Rhodes was a huge statue of the Greek sun god Helios that stood with its feet astride the harbour entrance. The simile emphasises the awe and wonder that everyone felt at seeing one of the Seven Wonders of the World. This develops the contrast with 'petty' men who 'peep about' and are buried in 'dishonourable graves' like slaves. We have two wonderfully evocative words with 'petty' and 'peep': the *-p* and *-ee* sounds emphasise the tininess of the people scuttling about like ants between the statue's legs. They also reflect Cassius's disgust: the little people are dwarfed by the immense bulk of Caesar.

Cassius build on his ideas by employing rhetorical questions to encourage Brutus to think hard about Caesar's position:

> What should be in that 'Caesar'?
> Why should that name be sounded more than yours?
> Write them together, yours is as fair a name;   Imperatives
> Sound them, it doth become the mouth as well;
> Weigh them, it is as heavy [...]

The rhetorical questions build the pace and are followed by imperatives to ram Cassius's point home. The inverted stress with the parallel grammatical structure of 'Write them…Sound them…Weigh them…' builds momentum as he encourages Brutus to consider Caesar's reputation in relation to his own. These imperatives add urgency and passion to his message: Brutus is just as good as Caesar and therefore Caesar is no more worthy than Brutus of this godlike elevation.

Shakespeare employs soliloquy at the end of the scene so that the audience can learn more of private Cassius's thoughts. Literally meaning 'solo speech', a soliloquy is spoken by a character who assumes that he or she is alone on stage. Hence, the audience gains insight into what the character is thinking and feeling. Cassius intends to exploit Brutus's concerns about the impact of Caesar's rule on the public by plans to 'throw' forged 'writings' from 'several citizens' into his house. These letters will prove to Brutus that the citizenry also does not wish to have Caesar as king. This trick to gain Brutus's support shows that Cassius is not confident about the justice of the conspiracy. If the forged letters succeed in persuading Brutus that the citizens do not trust Caesar, Brutus will join the conspiracy and gain the support of the populace. Cassius's soliloquy confirms to the audience that he is ruthless and has no scruples about lying and manipulating others to achieve his aims.

Finally, in this scene, we see the consequences of exposing private beliefs to public judgement when we learn that 'Marullus and Flavius, for pulling scarfs off Caesar's images, are put to silence'. In other words, they have been punished, banished, removed from office or killed. This is a disturbing turn of events and one with which the audience, who has seen and listened to the pair, is likely to empathise. This is therefore a worrying hint that, behind the scenes, Caesar will allow no one to stand in his way.

ORIGINAL TEXT	MODERN TRANSLATION
The same. A street.	**The same. A street.**
Thunder and lightning. Enter from opposite sides, CASCA, with his sword drawn, and CICERO.	*Thunder and lightning. Enter from opposite sides, CASCA, with his sword drawn, and CICERO.*
CICERO Good even, Casca: brought you Caesar home? Why are you breathless? and why stare you so?	**CICERO** Good evening, Casca: did you bring Caesar home? Why are you breathless? And why are you staring like that?
CASCA Are not you moved, when all the sway of earth Shakes like a thing unfirm? O Cicero, I have seen tempests, when the scolding winds Have rived the knotty oaks, and I have seen The ambitious ocean swell and rage and foam, To be exalted with the threatening clouds; But never till to-night, never till now, Did I go through a tempest dropping fire. Either there is a civil strife in heaven, Or else the world, too saucy with the gods, Incenses them to send destruction.	**CASCA** Aren't you disturbed, when the whole earthly realm Is shaking like shifting sands? Oh Cicero, I have seen storms, in which the angry winds Have split gnarled oaks, and I have seen The forceful ocean swell, rage and foam, As if it wanted to be raised up to the storm clouds; But never until tonight, never until now, Have I experienced a storm which drops fire. Either there is a civil war in heaven, Or else the world, too insolent to the gods, Has provoked them to send destruction.
CICERO Why, saw you anything more wonderful?	**CICERO** What - have you ever seen anything that was more awe-inspiring than the things you mention?
CASCA A common slave—you know him well by sight— Held up his left hand, which did flame and burn Like twenty torches join'd; and yet his hand, Not sensible of fire, remain'd unscorch'd. Besides—I ha' not since put up my sword-- Against the Capitol I met a lion, Who glazed upon me, and went surly by, Without annoying me. And there were drawn Upon a heap a hundred ghastly women, Transformed with their fear, who swore they saw Men, all in fire, walk up and down the streets. And yesterday the bird of night did sit, Even at noon-day, upon the market-place, Hooting and shrieking. When these prodigies Do so conjointly meet, let not men say, 'These are their reasons, they are natural'; For I believe, they are portentous things Unto the climate that they point upon.	**CASCA** A common slave—you know him well by sight— Held up his left hand which flamed and burned Like twenty torches together; and yet his hand, Not feeling the pain of the fire, remained unburnt. Also—since I saw this, I have kept my sword unsheathed— Near to the Capitol I met a lion, Who gazed fixedly at me, and walked grumpily by, Without harming me. And there were Huddled together a hundred deathly white women, Clearly terrified, who swore they saw Men, totally on fire, walking up and down the streets. And yesterday the screech-owl was sitting, At midday, in the market- place, Hooting and shrieking. When these extraordinary things Happen together, we should not say, 'These things can be explained rationally'; Because I believe, they are ominous things Pointing to what's going to happen in this country.
CICERO	**CICERO**

Indeed, it is a strange-disposed time:
But men may construe things after their fashion,
Clean from the purpose of the things themselves.
Come Caesar to the Capitol to-morrow?

CASCA
He doth; for he did bid Antonius
Send word to you he would be there to-morrow.

CICERO
Good night then, Casca: this disturbed sky
Is not to walk in.

CASCA
Farewell, Cicero.

Exit CICERO. Enter CASSIUS.

CASSIUS
Who's there?

CASCA
A Roman.

CASSIUS
Casca, by your voice.

CASCA
Your ear is good. Cassius, what night is this!

CASSIUS
A very pleasing night to honest men.

CASCA
Who ever knew the heavens menace so?

CASSIUS
Those that have known the earth so full of faults.

For my part, I have walk'd about the streets,
Submitting me unto the perilous night,
And, thus unbraced, Casca, as you see,

Have bared my bosom to the thunder-stone;
And when the cross blue lightning seem'd to open
The breast of heaven, I did present myself
Even in the aim and very flash of it.

CASCA
But wherefore did you so much tempt the heavens?

It is the part of men to fear and tremble
When the most mighty gods by tokens send
Such dreadful heralds to astonish us.

CASSIUS

Indeed, it is an abnormally upset time:
But men tend to interpret things in their own way,
Quite differently from their true meaning.
Is Caesar coming to the Capitol tomorrow?

CASCA
He is; because he asked Antonius
To pass on a message to you that he would be there
tomorrow.

CICERO
Good night then, Casca: this unsettled weather
Is not good for walking in.

CASCA
Farewell, Cicero.

Exit CICERO. Enter CASSIUS.

CASSIUS
Who's there?

CASCA
A Roman.

CASSIUS
I can tell it's Casca, by your voice.

CASCA
You hear correctly. Cassius, what a night this is!

CASSIUS
It is a very pleasing night to honest men.

CASCA
Who ever saw the heavens look so ominous?

CASSIUS
Those who have known how bad things are here on
earth.
As for me, I have walked around the streets,
Subjecting myself to the perilous night,
And with my jacket open like this, Casca, as you can
see,
I have bared my chest to the thunderbolt;
And when the forked blue lightning seemed to bare
The chest of heaven, I put myself
At the very spot at which it was aimed.

CASCA
But why did you so defiantly tempt the heavens like
that?
It is the role of man to fear and tremble
When the mightiest gods send signs
As dreadful warnings to dismay us.

CASSIUS

31

You are dull, Casca, and those sparks of life	You are acting as if you're stupid, Casca, and the quick wits
That should be in a Roman you do want,	That a Roman should have, are lacking in you,
Or else you use not. You look pale and gaze,	Or else you don't use them. You look pale and stare,
And put on fear and cast yourself in wonder,	And manifest fear and a state of astonishment,
To see the strange impatience of the heavens;	When you see the strange restlessness of the heavens;
But if you would consider the true cause	But if you thought about the real reason
Why all these fires, why all these gliding ghosts,	For all these fires and for all these gliding ghosts,
Why birds and beasts from quality and kind,	Why birds and animals are acting contrary to their usual natures,
Why old men, fools and children calculate,	Why old men, born idiots and children prophesy,
Why all these things change from their ordinance,	Why all these things change from their usual behaviour which was given by nature,
Their natures and preformed faculties,	From their natural characteristics,
To monstrous quality, why, you shall find	To unnatural ways, well, then you would find
That heaven hath infused them with these spirits	That heaven has imparted these spirits to them
To make them instruments of fear and warning	To make them instruments of fear and warning
Unto some monstrous state.	Of an unnatural state of affairs to come.
Now could I, Casca, name to thee a man	Now, Casca, I could name a man to you
Most like this dreadful night,	Who is just like this dreadful night,
That thunders, lightens, opens graves, and roars	Who thunders, shoots lightning, splits open graves, and roars
As doth the lion in the Capitol;	Like the lion in the Capitol;
A man no mightier than thyself, or me,	A man who is no mightier than you or me,
In personal action, yet prodigious grown,	In his personal abilities, and yet has become supernatural,
And fearful, as these strange eruptions are.	And as dreadful as these strange unnatural happenings are.

CASCA

'Tis Caesar that you mean; is it not, Cassius?	You mean Caesar; is that right Cassius?

CASSIUS

Let it be who it is: for Romans now	Let it be who it is: Romans these days
Have thews and limbs like to their ancestors;	Have muscles and limbs like their ancestors;
But, woe the while! our fathers' minds are dead,	But alas for these days! We no longer have their manly spirits,
And we are govern'd with our mothers' spirits:	And are, instead, governed by our mothers' spirits:
Our yoke and sufferance show us womanish.	Our submission to tyranny and our patient acceptance of it, reveal us to be weak like women.

CASCA

Indeed, they say the senators tomorrow	Indeed, they say that tomorrow the senators
Mean to establish Caesar as a king;	Intend to proclaim Caesar king;
And he shall wear his crown by sea and land,	And he shall wear his crown at sea and on land,
In every place, save here in Italy.	Everywhere, except here in Italy.

CASSIUS

I know where I will wear this dagger then:	I know where I will wear this dagger then:
Cassius from bondage will deliver Cassius.	Cassius will save himself from slavery.
Therein, ye gods, you make the weak most strong;	In the ability to commit suicide, you gods make the weak strong;
Therein, ye gods, you tyrants do defeat.	In the ability to commit suicide, you gods allow tyrants to be defeated.
Nor stony tower, nor walls of beaten brass,	No stony tower, no brass walls,
Nor airless dungeon, nor strong links of iron,	No airless dungeon, no strong iron chains,

Can be retentive to the strength of spirit;
But life, being weary of these worldly bars,

Never lacks power to dismiss itself.
If I know this, know all the world besides,
That part of tyranny that I do bear
I can shake off at pleasure.

Thunder still

CASCA
So can I;
So every bondman in his own hand bears
The power to cancel his captivity.

CASSIUS
And why should Caesar be a tyrant then?
Poor man! I know he would not be a wolf,
But that he sees the Romans are but sheep.
He were no lion, were not Romans hinds.

Those that with haste will make a mighty fire
Begin it with weak straws. What trash is Rome,

What rubbish and what offal, when it serves
For the base matter to illuminate
So vile a thing as Caesar! But, O grief,
Where hast thou led me? I perhaps speak this

Before a willing bondman; then I know
My answer must be made. But I am arm'd,

And dangers are to me indifferent.

CASCA
You speak to Casca, and to such a man
That is no fleering tell-tale. Hold, my hand;
Be factious for redress of all these griefs,
And I will set this foot of mine as far
As who goes farthest.

CASSIUS
There's a bargain made.
Now know you, Casca, I have moved already
Some certain of the noblest-minded Romans

To undergo with me an enterprise
Of honourable-dangerous consequence;
And I do know, by this they stay for me
In Pompey's porch: for now, this fearful night,

There is no stir or walking in the streets;

And the complexion of the element
In favour's like the work we have in hand,
Most bloody, fiery, and most terrible

Can imprison a strong mind;
But man, if he becomes weary of these worldly restraints,
Always has the power to end it all.
If I know this, then let everyone else know,
That the tyranny that I am enduring
Can be shaken off whenever I please.

Thunder still

CASCA
So can I;
So every slave carries in his own hands
The power to annul his captivity.

CASSIUS
And how can Caesar be a tyrant then?
Poor man! I know that he could not be a wolf,
If he didn't see that the Romans are like sheep.
He would be no lion, if the Romans weren't like easily preyed upon deer.
Those who want to quickly make a huge fire
Start it with little pieces of straw. What a pile of little twigs Rome becomes,
What a load of litter and wood chips, when it is used
For the vile purpose of igniting the ambitions
Of someone as worthless as Caesar! But, oh grief,
What have you caused me to say? Perhaps I am saying this
To someone who is willing to be a slave; then I know
I shall be called to account for my speech. But I am armed,
And indifferent to danger.

CASCA
You are talking to Casca and this man
Is no sneering tell-tale. Let us shake hands on it;
If you form a party to redress all these grievances,
I will walk alongside you, as far as
Whoever walks the furthest.

CASSIUS
That's a deal.
Now I have to tell you, Casca, I have already inspired
Certain individuals from amongst the noblest-minded Romans
To undertake with me a bold mission
Of honourable but dangerous consequence;
And I know, by this time, they are waiting for me
In the porch of Pompey's theatre: because now, on this fearful night,
There is no activity and no one walking in the streets;
And the appearance of the skies
Is, like the work that we must do,
Most bloody, fiery and terrible.

CASCA
Stand close awhile, for here comes one in haste.

CASSIUS
'Tis Cinna; I do know him by his gait;
He is a friend.

Enter CINNA

Cinna, where haste you so?

CINNA
To find out you. Who's that? Metellus Cimber?

CASSIUS
No, it is Casca, one incorporate
To our attempts. Am I not stay'd for, Cinna?

CINNA
I am glad on 't. What a fearful night is this!

There's two or three of us have seen strange sights.

CASSIUS
Am I not stay'd for? Tell me.

CINNA
Yes, you are.
O Cassius, if you could
But win the noble Brutus to our party—

CASSIUS
Be you content. Good Cinna, take this paper,
And look you lay it in the praetor's chair,

Where Brutus may but find it; and throw this
In at his window; set this up with wax
Upon old Brutus' statue. All this done,

Repair to Pompey's porch, where you shall find us.

Is Decius Brutus and Trebonius there?

CINNA
All but Metellus Cimber; and he's gone

To seek you at your house. Well, I will hie,
And so bestow these papers as you bade me.

CASSIUS
That done, repair to Pompey's Theatre.

Exit CINNA

CASCA
Remain hidden for a while, because someone is
approaching in a hurry.

CASSIUS
It's Cinna; I recognise him by his walk;
He is a friend.

Enter CINNA

Cinna, where are you going in such a hurry?

CINNA
To look for you. Who is that? Metellus Cimber?

CASSIUS
No, it is Casca, who is in league
With us. Are the others waiting for me, Cinna?

CINNA
I am glad that Casca is with us. What a fearful night
this is!
There are two or three of us who have seen strange
things.

CASSIUS
Are the others waiting for me? Tell me.

CINNA
Yes, they are.
Oh Cassius, if only you could
Persuade the noble Brutus to join us –

CASSIUS
Set your mind at rest. Good Cinna, take this paper,
And ensure you lay it on the chair of the chief
Roman magistrate,
Where Brutus alone will find it; and throw this one
In his window; fix this one with wax
To the statue of Brutus' ancestor, old Brutus. When
you've done all this,
Return to the porch of Pompey's Theatre, where
you will find us.
Are Decius Brutus and Trebonius there?

CINNA
Everyone is there except Metellus Cimber; and he
has gone
To look for you at your house. Well, I will go quickly,
And distribute these papers as you asked me to.

CASSIUS
When you have done that, return to Pompey's
Theatre.

Exit CINNA

Come, Casca, you and I will yet ere day See Brutus at his house: three parts of him Is ours already, and the man entire Upon the next encounter yields him ours. **CASCA** O, he sits high in all the people's hearts; And that which would appear offence in us, His countenance, like richest alchemy, Will change to virtue and to worthiness. **CASSIUS** Him and his worth and our great need of him You have right well conceited. Let us go, For it is after midnight, and ere day We will awake him and be sure of him. *Exeunt*	Come on, Casca, you and I will, before daylight, Go to see Brutus at his house: three quarters of him Is already on our side, and the entire man Will join our faction at our next encounter. **CASCA** Oh, all the people have taken him to their hearts; And the exact same things which would appear bad if we did them, Brutus' face, like richest alchemy, Will change to appear virtuous and good if he does them. **CASSIUS** Brutus and his worth and our great need of him You have fully understood. Let's go, Because it is after midnight, and before daylight We will awake him and secure him as a member of our faction. *Exeunt*

Part 8: Analysing Act 1 Scene 3

Shakespeare introduces the theme of the supernatural when Casca says 'all the sway of earth/Shakes like a thing unfirm'. Nature is upset, the earth is quaking and the atmosphere is so ominous that there appears to be 'civil strife in heaven'. In this scene, the pathetic fallacy signals the upset to the natural order caused by the threats that are amassing against Caesar. The noises of the thunderstorm would have been created by using fireworks, thunder sheets, or by rolling a cannon ball along a wooden trough; these sound effects emphasise a world turned upside down in an apocalyptic night of terror.

The portents of Caesar's death are on a huge scale and impossible to stage, so Shakespeare compensates for this by painting vivid pictures through dialogue to create horror in the minds of the audience. He commands the attention of the audience through eye-witness accounts of the five prodigies (amazing events), and Casca employs strong visual imagery when he reports what he has seen to Cicero. The scale of the omens can be seen with his use of lists:

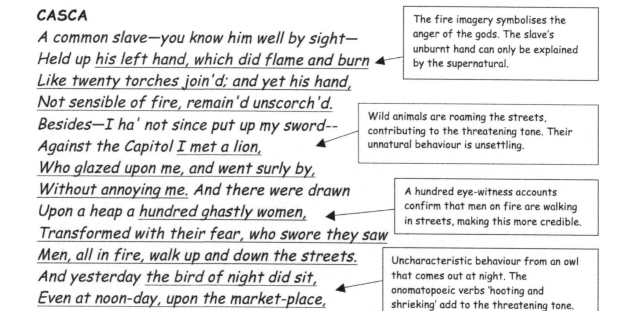

CASCA
A common slave—you know him well by sight—
Held up <u>his left hand, which did flame and burn</u>
<u>Like twenty torches join'd; and yet his hand,</u>
<u>Not sensible of fire, remain'd unscorch'd.</u>
Besides—I ha' not since put up my sword--
Against the Capitol <u>I met a lion,</u>
<u>Who glazed upon me, and went surly by,</u>
<u>Without annoying me.</u> And there were drawn
Upon a heap a <u>hundred ghastly women,</u>
<u>Transformed with their fear, who swore they saw</u>
<u>Men, all in fire, walk up and down the streets.</u>
And yesterday <u>the bird of night did sit,</u>
<u>Even at noon-day, upon the market-place,</u>
<u>Hooting and shrieking.</u>

> The fire imagery symbolises the anger of the gods. The slave's unburnt hand can only be explained by the supernatural.

> Wild animals are roaming the streets, contributing to the threatening tone. Their unnatural behaviour is unsettling.

> A hundred eye-witness accounts confirm that men on fire are walking in streets, making this more credible.

> Uncharacteristic behaviour from an owl that comes out at night. The onomatopoeic verbs 'hooting and shrieking' add to the threatening tone.

With the extended imagery of fire connoting hell, and birds and animals behaving out of character, these events appear to herald the end of the world: the prodigies are impossibilities, making it unthinkable to ignore the omens. The question is: what do they mean? While Casca believes they are bad omens, Cicero comments 'men may construe things after their fashion'. In other words, people interpret things in their own way, so interpretations might be very different from the real meaning. This comment is interesting, as it reveals Cicero to be a Sceptic, one who believes that to know things as a certainty is impossible. This comment foreshadows Cassius's incorrect interpretation of the omen of carrion birds in Act 5, Scene 2 before he dies.

Shakespeare's decision to link supernatural events to Caesar is significant because firstly, it reflects his huge importance as an historical figure and secondly, it poses the question of the inevitability of fate. As we have seen, Elizabethans generally believed that fate controlled an individual's life and destiny, and that no-one had the power to change what fate had in store. This was depicted by the symbolic wheel of fortune, on which a person's luck might rise or fall with the turn of the wheel. The portents therefore pose the interesting question of whether Caesar is destined to die or whether, should the omens be heeded as a warning, his fate can be averted.

Shakespeare uses the storm as a device to align the characters with good or evil. Before he exits, for example, the upstanding Cicero warns Casca 'this disturbed sky/Is not to walk in'—the night is full of supernatural terror, so citizens should avoid it. By way of contrast, Cassius enters and states 'A very pleasing night to honest men'. Cassius is exhilarated to be outside, and the horror of the omens serves as pathetic fallacy to mirror the horror of his plans to murder Caesar. Cassius believes that the conspirators are 'honest men', and the audience is reminded of his plans to employ trickery to enlist the support of honest Brutus. While Cassius is dishonest, he paradoxically believes the opposite.

It is appropriate that the conspirators meet under cover of night, as the setting helps to establish the theme of darkness concealing a secret plot. The meeting also provides Shakespeare with the opportunity to compare Cassius with Caesar. When Cassius enters, he recognises Casca's voice in the dark, and Casca comments 'Your ear is good. Cassius'. This excellent hearing contrasts with Caesar's deafness in one ear; as we have seen, this is a metaphor for his inability to discern good advice. By way of contrast, Cassius appears to be intelligent, alert and perceptive. This subtle comparison of ear imagery therefore positions Cassius as a legitimate threat to Caesar.

The storm reveals contemporary ideas about masculinity when Cassius, full of exhilaration, reports that he has deliberately put his life at risk:

> *...when the cross blue lightning seem'd to open*
> *The breast of heaven, I did present myself*
> *Even in the aim and very flash of it.*

The use of religious imagery 'heaven' and 'cross' (which also refers to the fork of lighting) would be interpreted by Elizabethans as Cassius believing that God is on his side, providing him with the confidence to tempt fate. Casca responds that 'It is the part of men to fear and tremble' when the Ancient Roman gods send these omens; however, Cassius does the opposite of 'fear and tremble', suggesting that he is not a 'man' and that he has lost all his human weakness. This reflects his lack of humanity and his arrogance.

We have dramatic irony when Cassius states that the prodigies are 'instruments of fear and warning/Unto some monstrous state'. He thinks that the omens are the result of the 'monstrous state' of Caesar's ambition to become king and that the omens are a warning about the consequences of this to Rome. Yet there is irony because it is Cassius who is in a 'monstrous state', resembling an evil being more than a human. In reality, the omens are warning about the destruction that Cassius will bring with his intention to murder Caesar. The audience will be aware of his misinterpretation because they know their history and that Caesar will be assassinated.

Cassius uses the prodigies to his own advantage when, employing a simile, he tells Casca that there is 'a man/Most like this dreadful night, /That thunders, lightens, opens graves, and roars/As doth the lion in the Capitol'. He does not directly name Caesar, as he is sounding Casca out. The simile functions to establish a problem, inviting Casca to name Caesar after which Cassius can propose the solution. The audience is therefore provided with further evidence of Cassius' skill and intelligence when developing his assassination plans.

Contemporary ideas about masculinity are invoked again when Cassius states '[b]ut, woe the while! our fathers' minds are dead' and that 'we are govern'd with our mothers' spirits:/Our yoke and sufferance show us womanish'. He regards women as second-class citizens and, in this context, 'mothers' spirits' and 'womanish' have negative connotations, implying weakness. We have already seen physical weakness with Caesar, so Cassius implies that the real reason for the portents is that Caesar is not masculine enough to rule.

Throughout Act 1, we have seen Cassius's descriptions of Caesar change. In Act 1, Scene 2, he used the adjective 'immortal' to describe Caesar. Then he claimed terms of equality, telling Brutus 'I was born free as Caesar'. He also focused on Caesar's lack of physical strength when he rescued 'tired Caesar' from the Tiber. We saw sarcasm when he said 'And this man/Is now become a god' and commented that when Caesar had a fever, 'this god did shake'. He used femininity as an insult, calling the recuperating Caesar 'a sick girl'. In this scene, his language escalates. He calls Caesar a 'tyrant' and becomes progressively more insulting, to the point that he calls Caesar 'vile a thing', thus stripping him of his humanity. By describing Caesar as weak and tyrannical, it will be easier for Cassius to kill Caesar in his 'honourable-dangerous' 'enterprise'. The juxtaposition of 'honourable' with 'dangerous' is interesting because, being aware of the risks to himself, Cassius is positioning himself as a hero. The noun 'enterprise' also has positive connotations of a bold, daring undertaking; once more, his choice of vocabulary illustrates his cleverness and ability to manipulate the thoughts of others.

In this scene, evil prevails despite the warning of the portents, which are misinterpreted. It seems inevitable that Cassius will take advantage of Brutus's credibility: he knows that Brutus will not question whether the letters, distributed under cover of night, are genuine. We learn that Cassius's conspirators need the support of 'noble Brutus' because he 'sits high in all the people's hearts'. His reputation and respectability are such that once he is completely won over to their cause, their actions will be validated in the eyes of the people. Then a new phase of their conspiracy will begin.

Freytag's Pyramid

The events so far can be analysed using Freytag's pyramid. Gustav Freytag was a nineteenth century German novelist who saw common patterns in the plots of novels and plays and developed a diagram to analyse them:

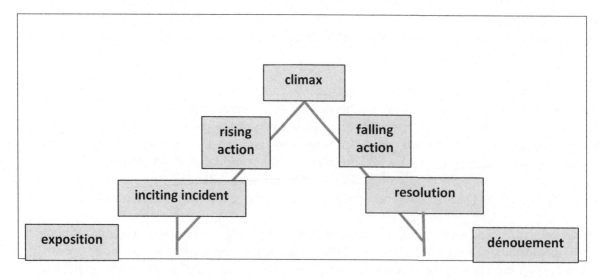

Act 1 ends the **exposition**. The audience has learnt about the setting, the characters and their concerns. In Act 1, Scene 1, we met the 'Commoners' celebrating Caesar's return, which was in direct conflict to the concerns of Marullus and Flavius. Then in Act 1, Scene 2. We met the remaining main characters, Caesar, Antony, Calpurnia, Brutus, Cassius and Casca and, in minor capacities, Portia, Decius, Cicero and the soothsayer. At the end of Act 1, Scene 2, we learnt through Cassius's soliloquy of his plan to forge letters to encourage Brutus to join the conspiracy. Finally, in Act 1,

Scene 3, amid a setting of portents and omens, Cassius has persuaded Casca to join the conspiracy. In the last part of their plans to assemble allies, Cinna will distribute the forged letters in the hope that Brutus will be persuaded to join the conspiracy.

Part 9: Translating Act 2 Scene 1

ORIGINAL TEXT	MODERN TRANSLATION
Rome. BRUTUS's orchard.	**Rome. BRUTUS's orchard.**
Enter BRUTUS	*Enter BRUTUS*
BRUTUS What, Lucius, ho! I cannot, by the progress of the stars, Give guess how near to day. Lucius, I say! I would it were my fault to sleep so soundly. When, Lucius, when? Awake, I say! What, Lucius!	**BRUTUS** Hey, Lucius, are you there? I cannot tell, by the position of the stars, How close to daybreak it is. Lucius, can you hear me? I wish that my weakness was to sleep so soundly. Come on, Lucius, come on! Wake up, I say! Come on, Lucius!
Enter LUCIUS	*Enter LUCIUS*
LUCIUS Call'd you, my lord?	**LUCIUS** Did you call, my lord?
BRUTUS Get me a taper in my study, Lucius; When it is lighted, come and call me here.	**BRUTUS** Put a candle in my study for me, Lucius; When it is lit, come and call me.
LUCIUS I will, my lord. *Exit*	**LUCIUS** I will, my lord. *Exit*
BRUTUS It must be by his death; and for my part, I know no personal cause to spurn at him, But for the general. —He would be crown'd. How that might change his nature, there's the question. It is the bright day that brings forth the adder, And that craves wary walking. Crown him! -- that! And then, I grant, we put a sting in him That at his will he may do danger with. The abuse of greatness is when it disjoins Remorse from power; and, to speak truth of Caesar,	**BRUTUS** Caesar must be put to death; and for my part, I have no self-interested reason to kick against him, But for the common political good. — He wants to be crowned. How would being king change his nature, that is the question. Favourable conditions can bring out the hidden evil in people, just as sunny days bring out poisonous adders, And that requires us to walk carefully. If we crown him, Then, I admit, we would be putting venom in him Which he could use, at will, to do harm. The abuse of power happens when it separates Compassion from power; and speaking honestly about Caesar,

I have not known when his affections sway'd	I have not known him to be swayed by his emotions
More than his reason. But 'tis a common proof,	Rather than his judgement. But it is a matter of common knowledge,
That lowliness is young ambition's ladder,	That humility is the ladder of ambition by which a young man,
Whereto the climber-upward turns his face;	Climbs upwards, towards power;
But when he once attains the upmost round,	But when he gets to the highest rung,
He then unto the ladder turns his back,	He then turns his back on his ladder of support,
Looks in the clouds, scorning the base degrees	Reaches for the skies, while scorning the lower rungs and the people
By which he did ascend: so Caesar may;	Who helped him to get there: Caesar may become like that;
Then, lest he may, prevent. And, since the quarrel	Therefore, in case he does, we must prevent him by taking anticipatory action. And since the accusation
Will bear no colour for the thing he is,	Carries no validity considering what Caesar is at this moment,
Fashion it thus: that what he is, augmented,	Let us put the case in this way: that if he is promoted,
Would run to these and these extremities;	He would resort to such tyrannical extremes;
And therefore think him as a serpent's egg	And therefore, we should think of him as a serpent's egg
Which, hatch'd, would, as his kind, grow mischievous,	Which, when it has hatched, would, like all poisonous snakes, become dangerous,
And kill him in the shell.	And so, we must kill him while he is still in the shell.
Re-enter LUCIUS	Re-enter LUCIUS
LUCIUS	**LUCIUS**
The taper burneth in your closet, sir.	The candle is burning in your study, sir.
Searching the window for a flint, I found	While I was looking on the windowsill for a flint, I found
This paper, thus seal'd up; and, I am sure	This paper, sealed up like this; and I am sure
It did not lie there when I went to bed.	It was not there when I went to bed.
Gives him the letter	*Gives him the letter*
BRUTUS	**BRUTUS**
Get you to bed again, it is not day.	Go back to bed, as it isn't daybreak yet.
Is not to-morrow, boy, the ides of March?	Is tomorrow the 15th March, boy?
LUCIUS	**LUCIUS**
I know not, sir.	I don't know, sir.
BRUTUS	**BRUTUS**
Look in the calendar, and bring me word.	Have a look at the calendar and let me know.
LUCIUS	**LUCIUS**
I will, sir.	I will, sir.

Exit Lucius	*Exit Lucius*
BRUTUS	**BRUTUS**
The exhalations, whizzing in the air,	The meteors, whizzing through the air,
Give so much light that I may read by them.	Give off so much light that I can read by them.
Opens the letter and reads	*Opens the letter and reads*
Brutus, thou sleep'st: awake, and see thyself.	Brutus, you are sleeping: wake up and look at yourself.
Shall Rome, etc. Speak, strike, redress.	Is Rome going to, etc. Speak, strike, put things right.
'Brutus, thou sleep'st: awake.'	'Brutus, you are sleeping: wake up.'
Such instigations have been often dropp'd	Such promptings to action have often been dropped
Where I have took them up.	Where I would find them.
'Shall Rome, etc.' Thus must I piece it out:	'Is Rome going to, etc.' I must try to understand what this means:
Shall Rome stand under one man's awe? What, Rome?	Is Rome going to stand in awe of one man? What, Rome?
My ancestors did from the streets of Rome	My ancestors, from the streets of Rome,
The Tarquin drive, when he was call'd a king.	Drove out Tarquin, when he was pronounced a king.
'Speak, strike, redress.' Am I entreated	'Speak, strike, put things right.' Am I being urged
To speak and strike? O Rome, I make thee promise,	To speak and strike? Oh, Rome, I promise you,
If the redress will follow, thou receivest	If things are going to be put right, you will receive
Thy full petition at the hand of Brutus.	Your full request by the hand of Brutus.
Re-enter LUCIUS	*Re-enter LUCIUS*
LUCIUS	**LUCIUS**
Sir, March is wasted fifteen days.	Sir, we're already fifteen days into March.
Knocking within	*The sound of knocking offstage*
BRUTUS	**BRUTUS**
'Tis good. Go to the gate; somebody knocks.	That's good. Go to the gate; somebody's knocking.
Exit LUCIUS	*Exit LUCIUS*
Since Cassius first did whet me against Caesar,	Ever since Cassius began to turn me against Caesar,
I have not slept.	I have not slept.
Between the acting of a dreadful thing	Between the time of carrying out a dreadful deed
And the first motion, all the interim is	After the initial impulse, the interval is
Like a phantasma or a hideous dream:	Like a nightmare or a ghastly dream:

The genius and the mortal instruments
Are then in council; and the state of man,

Like to a little kingdom, suffers then
The nature of an insurrection.

Re-enter LUCIUS

LUCIUS
Sir, 'tis your brother Cassius at the door,

Who doth desire to see you.

BRUTUS
Is he alone?

LUCIUS
No, sir, there are more with him.

BRUTUS
Do you know them?

LUCIUS
No, sir, their hats are pluck'd about their ears,

And half their faces buried in their cloaks,

That by no means I may discover them
By any mark of favour.

BRUTUS
Let 'em enter.

Exit LUCIUS

They are the faction. O conspiracy,

Shamest thou to show thy dangerous brow by night,
When evils are most free? O, then by day

Where wilt thou find a cavern dark enough
To mask thy monstrous visage? Seek none, conspiracy;
Hide it in smiles and affability:

For if thou path, thy native semblance on,

Not Erebus itself were dim enough
To hide thee from prevention.

The guiding spirit and the passions
Are then in consultation; and the condition of man,
Like a small kingdom, then suffers
A kind of violent uprising.

Re-enter LUCIUS

LUCIUS
Sir, it is your brother-in-law, Cassius, at the door,
Who wants to see you.

BRUTUS
Is he alone?

LUCIUS
No, sir. There are others with him.

BRUTUS
Do you know who they are?

LUCIUS
No, sir, their hats are pulled down over their ears,
And half of their faces are covered by their cloaks,
So, there is no way I can identify them
By their appearance.

BRUTUS
Let them come in.

Exit LUCIUS

They are the faction that wants to kill Caesar.
Oh conspiracy,
Are you ashamed to show your murderous face even at night,
When evil things most freely wander about?
Well then, by day
Where will you find a cave dark enough
To hide your monstrous face? Don't look for one, conspiracy;
Hide your monstrous face in smiles and friendliness:
For if you pursue your way, showing your true colours,
Even Hell itself would not be dark enough
To keep you from being found and stopped.

Enter the conspirators, CASSIUS, CASCA, DECIUS BRUTUS, CINNA, METELLUS CIMBER, and TREBONIUS

CASSIUS
I think we are too bold upon your rest.
Good morrow, Brutus; do we trouble you?

BRUTUS
I have been up this hour, awake all night.
Know I these men that come along with you?

CASSIUS
Yes, every man of them; and no man here

But honours you; and every one doth wish

You had but that opinion of yourself
Which every noble Roman bears of you.
This is Trebonius.

BRUTUS
He is welcome hither.

CASSIUS
This, Decius Brutus.

BRUTUS
He is welcome too.

CASSIUS
This, Casca; this, Cinna; and this, Metellus Cimber.

BRUTUS
They are all welcome.
What watchful cares do interpose themselves
Betwixt your eyes and night?

CASSIUS
Shall I entreat a word?

BRUTUS and CASSIUS whisper

DECIUS BRUTUS
Here lies the east; doth not the day break here?

CASCA
No.

Enter the conspirators, CASSIUS, CASCA, DECIUS BRUTUS, CINNA, METELLUS CIMBER, and TREBONIUS

CASSIUS
I think we are too bold, disturbing your sleep.
Good morning, Brutus; are we bothering you?

BRUTUS
I was awake already, awake all night.
Do I know these men who have come along with you?

CASSIUS
Yes, every one of them; and there's not a man here
Who doesn't highly respect you; and each one of them wishes
You had as high an opinion of yourself
As every noble Roman has of you.
This is Trebonius.

BRUTUS
He is welcome here.

CASSIUS
This is Decius Brutus.

BRUTUS
He is welcome too.

CASSIUS
This is Casca; this is Cinna; and this is Metellus Cimber.

BRUTUS
They are all welcome.
What worries have come between
You and a good night's sleep?

CASSIUS
Can I have a word with you?

BRUTUS and CASSIUS whisper

DECIUS BRUTUS
Here is the east; isn't this where daybreak occurs?

CASCA
No.

CINNA
O, pardon, sir, it doth; and yon gray lines
That fret the clouds are messengers of day.

CASCA
You shall confess that you are both deceived:

Here, as I point my sword, the sun arises,
Which is a great way growing on the south,
Weighing the youthful season of the year.
Some two months hence, up higher toward the north
He first presents his fire; and the high east
Stands, as the Capitol, directly here.

BRUTUS
Give me your hands all over, one by one. *(He shakes their hands)*

CASSIUS
And let us swear our resolution.

BRUTUS
No, not an oath. If not the face of men,

The sufferance of our souls, the time's abuse -

If these be motives weak, break off betimes,

And every man hence to his idle bed;
So let high-sighted tyranny range on

Till each man drop by lottery. But if these,

As I am sure they do, bear fire enough
To kindle cowards and to steel with valour

The melting spirits of women, then, countrymen,
What need we any spur but our own cause

To prick us to redress? What other bond

Than secret Romans that have spoke the word,

And will not palter? And what other oath

Than honesty to honesty engaged
That this shall be, or we will fall for it?

CINNA:
Oh, excuse me, sir, it is; and those grey lines
That interlace the clouds are signs of daybreak.

CASCA
You shall admit that you're both wrong:
(pointing his sword)
Here, where I point my sword, the sun rises,
Which is noticeably encroaching on the south,
Taking into consideration that it is still winter.
In about two months from now, further towards the north
The dawn will break; and due east
Stands the Capitol, right here.

BRUTUS
Give me your hands all of you, one by one. *(He shakes their hands)*

CASSIUS
And let us swear our resolution.

BRUTUS
No, let's not swear an oath. If the expression on men's faces,
The suffering of our souls, the corruption (by Caesar) in these days –
Are not enough motivation for us, let us break it off at once,
And each of us return to his unslept- in bed;
Then we will allow this high-flying tyrant to proceed unchallenged
Until each one of us dies according to his chance displeasure. But if these reasons,
As I am convinced they do, carry enough fire
To ignite cowards to action and inspire, with great courage,
The weakening spirits of women, then, countrymen,
Why do we need any encouragement, other than our own reasons
To spur us into action? What bond do we need other
Than the fact that we are Romans who, once we have given our word, can be trusted to hold our tongues.
And will not deceive? And what oath do we need other
Than words of honour exchanged
That this shall happen, or we shall die trying?

45

Swear priests and cowards and men cautelous,	Swearing is for priests and cowards and deceitful men,
Old feeble carrions and such suffering souls	Feeble old people and those long- suffering sorts
That welcome wrongs; unto bad causes swear	Who welcome ill-treatment; for wrong reasons
Such creatures as men doubt; but do not stain	Such untrustworthy people swear oaths; but do not spoil
The even virtue of our enterprise,	The steadfast virtue of our mission,
Nor the insuppressive mettle of our spirits,	Nor the indomitable resilience of our spirits,
To think that or our cause or our performance	By thinking that our cause or our performance
Did need an oath; when every drop of blood	Need a binding oath; when every drop of blood
That every Roman bears, and nobly bears,	That every noble Roman has within him,
Is guilty of a several bastardy,	Would be proven to be bastard's blood,
If he do break the smallest particle	If he broke the smallest part
Of any promise that hath pass'd from him.	Of any promise that he had made.
CASSIUS	**CASSIUS**
But what of Cicero? Shall we sound him?	But what about Cicero? Shall we find out what he thinks about this matter?
I think he will stand very strong with us.	I think he will agree wholeheartedly with us.
CASCA	**CASCA**
Let us not leave him out.	Let's not leave him out.
CINNA	**CINNA**
No, by no means.	No, by no means.
METELLUS CIMBER	**METELLUS CIMBER**
O, let us have him, for his silver hairs	Oh, let's have him on board, because his grey-headed wisdom
Will purchase us a good opinion	Will earn us a good reputation
And buy men's voices to commend our deeds.	And cause men to speak out in support of our actions.
It shall be said his judgment ruled our hands;	It will be assumed that it was his wise decision-making that ordered our actions;
Our youths and wildness shall no whit appear,	Our youthful, wild ways will not be at all apparent,
But all be buried in his gravity.	But will be concealed by his solemn dignity.
BRUTUS	**BRUTUS**
O, name him not; let us not break with him,	Oh, don't talk about him; let's not broach the matter with him,
For he will never follow any thing	Because he will never follow anything
That other men begin.	That other men have started.
CASSIUS	**CASSIUS**
Then leave him out.	Then leave him out.
CASCA	**CASCA**
Indeed he is not fit.	Indeed, he is not right for this.

DECIUS BRUTUS
Shall no man else be touch'd but only Caesar?

CASSIUS
Decius, well urged. I think it is not meet

Mark Antony, so well beloved of Caesar,
Should outlive Caesar. We shall find of him
A shrewd contriver; and you know his means,

If he improve them, may well stretch so far
As to annoy us all; which to prevent,
Let Antony and Caesar fall together.

BRUTUS
Our course will seem too bloody, Caius Cassius,
To cut the head off and then hack the limbs,

Like wrath in death and envy afterwards;

For Antony is but a limb of Caesar.
Let us be sacrificers, but not butchers, Caius.
We all stand up against the spirit of Caesar,

And in the spirit of men there is no blood.
O, that we then could come by Caesar's spirit,

And not dismember Caesar! But, alas,
Caesar must bleed for it. And, gentle friends,
Let's kill him boldly, but not wrathfully;
Let's carve him as a dish fit for the gods,

Not hew him as a carcass fit for hounds.
And let our hearts, as subtle masters do,
Stir up their servants to an act of rage,
And after seem to chide 'em. This shall make

Our purpose necessary and not envious;

Which so appearing to the common eyes,

We shall be call'd purgers, not murderers.
And for Mark Antony, think not of him;

For he can do no more than Caesar's arm

When Caesar's head is off.

DECIUS BRUTUS
Are we going after any other men or is it just Caesar?

CASSIUS
Well said, Decius. I don't think it would be proper if
Mark Antony, who is so loved by Caesar,
Outlived Caesar. We would find him to be
A cunning plotter; and you know his connections,
If he made good use of them, may well go as far
As harming us all; to forestall this,
Antony and Caesar should die together.

BRUTUS
Our actions will seem too bloody, Caius Cassius,
If we cut off Caesar's head and then hack at his limbs too,
It will look like rage when we kill Caesar and like malice when we kill Antony afterwards;
Because Antony is just one of Caesar's limbs.
Let's be sacrificers, but not butchers, Caius.
We all stand up against the spirit of what Caesar represents,
And in the spirit of men there is no blood.
Oh, how I wish that we could overcome Caesar's over-ambitious spirit,
And not have to dismember Caesar! But alas,
Caesar must bleed. And, noble friends,
Let us kill him boldly, but not with anger;
Let us carve him ceremoniously like a dish fit for the gods,
Not chop him up like a carcass fit for dogs.
And let our hearts, as cunning masters do,
Stir up our emotions to an act of rage,
And afterwards seem to rebuke them. This will make it plain
That our reason is one of political necessity and not personal malice;
Which will make us appear to the common people,
As surgeons, and not murderers.
And as for Mark Antony, don't worry about him;
Because he won't be able to do anything as Caesar's arm
After Caesar's head has been cut off.

CASSIUS Yet I fear him; For in the ingrafted love he bears to Caesar –	**CASSIUS** But I am afraid of him; Because the deep-rooted love he has for Caesar
BRUTUS Alas, good Cassius, do not think of him. If he love Caesar, all that he can do Is to himself: take thought and die for Caesar; And that were much he should; for he is given To sports, to wildness and much company.	**BRUTUS** Alas, good Cassius, don't worry about him. If he loves Caesar, all the injury he can inflict Is on himself: by succumbing to grief and dying for Caesar; And that would be far too much to expect from someone like him; because he prefers Sports, wildness, fun and many friends.
TREBONIUS There is no fear in him; let him not die; For he will live, and laugh at this hereafter.	**TREBONIUS** There is nothing to worry about as far as he is concerned; let's not kill him; Because he will live and laugh at this in the future.
Clock strikes	*Clock strikes*
BRUTUS Peace, count the clock.	**BRUTUS** Be quiet and count how many times the clock chimes.
CASSIUS The clock hath stricken three.	**CASSIUS** The clock struck three.
TREBONIUS 'Tis time to part.	**TREBONIUS** It is time to leave.
CASSIUS But it is doubtful yet Whether Caesar will come forth to-day or no; For he is superstitious grown of late, Quite from the main opinion he held once Of fantasy, of dreams and ceremonies. It may be these apparent prodigies, The unaccustom'd terror of this night, And the persuasion of his augurers May hold him from the Capitol to-day.	**CASSIUS** But as yet, we are unsure Whether Caesar will come out into a public place today or not; Because he has become superstitious recently, Quite opposite from the strong opinions he once held against Imaginings, dreams and omens. It may be that these manifest, out of the ordinary occurrences, The exceptional terror of this night, And the persuasion of his fortune tellers Will keep him away from the Capitol today.
DECIUS BRUTUS Never fear that. If he be so resolved, I can o'ersway him; for he loves to hear	**DECIUS BRUTUS** Don't worry about that. If that is what he has decided, I can convince him to change his mind; because he loves to hear

That unicorns may be betray'd with trees, And bears with glasses, elephants with holes,	How unicorns can be captured with trees, And bears with mirrors, elephants with holes,
Lions with toils and men with flatterers. But when I tell him he hates flatterers, He says he does, being then most flattered. Let me work; For I can give his humour the true bent,	Lions with traps and men with flattery. But when I tell him that he hates flatterers, He agrees, just as I am flattering him the most. Let me work on him; Because I can influence him in the right direction,
And I will bring him to the Capitol.	And I will bring him to the Capitol.
CASSIUS Nay, we will all of us be there to fetch him.	**CASSIUS** No, we will all go there to bring him.
BRUTUS By the eighth hour; is that the uttermost?	**BRUTUS** By eight o'clock; Is that the latest that we can do it?
CINNA Be that the uttermost, and fail not then.	**CINNA** That is the latest, and don't be any later than that.
METELLUS CIMBER Caius Ligarius doth bear Caesar hard, Who rated him for speaking well of Pompey; I wonder none of you have thought of him.	**METELLUS CIMBER** Caius Ligarius feels enmity towards Caesar, Who rebuked him for speaking well of Pompey; I am wondering why none of you have thought of enlisting his support.
BRUTUS Now, good Metellus, go along by him; He loves me well, and I have given him reasons. Send him but hither, and I'll fashion him.	**BRUTUS** Now, good Metellus, go and call at his house; He genuinely likes me very much, and I have given him good reason to do so. Just send him here and I will persuade him to join our party.
CASSIUS The morning comes upon 's; we'll leave you, Brutus. And, friends, disperse yourselves; but all remember What you have said, and show yourselves true Romans.	**CASSIUS** The morning is fast approaching; we shall leave you, Brutus. And, friends, go your separate ways; but be sure to remember What you have said and prove yourselves to be true Romans.
BRUTUS Good gentlemen, look fresh and merrily; Let not our looks put on our purposes, But bear it as our Roman actors do, With untired spirits and formal constancy. And so good morrow to you every one.	**BRUTUS** Good gentlemen, look fresh-faced and happy; Don't let our facial expressions betray our plans, But carry it off as our Roman actors do, With alert spirits and dignified composure. And so, good morning to each and every one of you.

(Exeunt all but BRUTUS)

Boy! Lucius! Fast asleep? It is no matter.

Enjoy the honey-heavy dew of slumber;
Thou hast no figures nor no fantasies,
Which busy care draws in the brains of men;

Therefore thou sleep'st so sound.

Enter PORTIA

PORTIA
Brutus, my lord.

BRUTUS
Portia! What mean you? Wherefore rise you now?
It is not for your health thus to commit
Your weak condition to the raw cold morning.

PORTIA
Nor for yours neither. You've ungently, Brutus,

Stole from my bed; and yesternight at supper
You suddenly arose and walk'd about,
Musing and sighing, with your arms across;
And when I ask'd you what the matter was,

You stared upon me with ungentle looks.
I urged you further; then you scratch'd your head,
And too impatiently stamp'd with your foot;
Yet I insisted, yet you answer'd not,
But with an angry wafture of your hand
Gave sign for me to leave you. So I did,

Fearing to strengthen that impatience
Which seem'd too much enkindled, and withal

Hoping it was but an effect of humour,
Which sometime hath his hour with every man.
It will not let you eat, nor talk, nor sleep;
And could it work so much upon your shape,

As it hath much prevail'd on your condition,
I should not know you, Brutus. Dear my lord,

Make me acquainted with your cause of grief.

(Exeunt all but BRUTUS)

Boy! Lucius! Are you fast sleep? It doesn't matter.
Enjoy the honey sweetness of deep sleep;
You have no strange imaginings,
Which overwhelming worries deposit in men's brains;
That is why you sleep so soundly.

Enter PORTIA

PORTIA
Brutus, my lord.

BRUTUS
Portia! What are you doing? Why are you up so early?
It is not good for your health to expose
Your weak condition to the raw, cold morning air.

PORTIA
It is not good for your health either. Brutus, you disrespectfully,
Crept out of bed; and last night at supper
You suddenly got up and walked to and fro,
Musing and sighing in a melancholy way, with your arms crossed;
And when I asked you what the matter was,
You glared at me angrily.
I urged you to tell me; then you scratched your head,
And stamped your foot impatiently;
Still I persisted, still you wouldn't answer me,
But with an angry waving gesture of your hand
You signalled that I should leave you alone. So I did,
Afraid to increase that impatience
Which was already aroused in you, and moreover
Hoping it was a passing moment of moodiness,
Which affects everyone once in a while.
Your mood won't let you eat, talk or sleep;
And if it could have as much effect on your body,
As it has had on your frame of mind,
I would not be able to recognise you, Brutus. My dear lord,
Tell me what is causing your grief.

BRUTUS

I am not well in health, and that is all.

PORTIA

Brutus is wise, and, were he not in health,

He would embrace the means to come by it.

BRUTUS

Why, so I do. Good Portia, go to bed.

PORTIA

Is Brutus sick? And is it physical
To walk unbraced and suck up the humours

Of the dank morning? What, is Brutus sick?
And will he steal out of his wholesome bed
To dare the vile contagion of the night,
And tempt the rheumy and unpurged air,
To add unto his sickness? No, my Brutus;
You have some sick offence within your mind,

Which, by the right and virtue of my place,
I ought to know of; and, upon my knees,
I charm you, by my once-commended beauty,
By all your vows of love and that great vow

Which did incorporate and make us one,
That you unfold to me, yourself, your half,
Why you are heavy, and what men to-night
Have had to resort to you; for here have been

Some six or seven, who did hide their faces

Even from darkness.

BRUTUS

Kneel not, gentle Portia.

PORTIA

I should not need, if you were gentle Brutus.

Within the bond of marriage, tell me, Brutus,
Is it excepted I should know no secrets

That appertain to you? Am I yourself
But, as it were, in sort or limitation,
To keep with you at meals, comfort your bed,
And talk to you sometimes? Dwell I but in the suburbs

BRUTUS

I am not feeling well, that's all.

PORTIA

Brutus, you're wise, and if you were not in good health,
You would take whatever was needed to obtain it.

BRUTUS

Well, I am doing so. Good Portia, go to bed.

PORTIA

Are you ill, Brutus? And is it healthy
To walk around, buttons undone, breathing in the dampness
Of the dank morning? Well, are you ill, Brutus?
And did you sneak out of your warm, cosy bed
To brave the vile, infectious night,
And tempt the watery and unclean air,
To add to your illness? No, my Brutus;
You have some harmful sickness within your mind,

Which, by virtue of my position as your wife,
I ought to be told about; and on my knees,
I entreat you, by my once-praised beauty,
By all your vows of love and that great vow of marriage
Which joined us and made us one,
That you reveal to me, yourself, your wife,
Why you are downhearted, and what men,
Have to come to see you tonight; because there were
About six or seven men here who hid their faces
Even in the darkness.

BRUTUS

Don't kneel, noble Portia.

PORTIA

I would not need to, if you were behaving nobly, Brutus.
Within the bond of marriage, Brutus, tell me,
Is it expected that I should not be told any secrets
That concern you? Am I one with you
But only in a limited way,
Eating meals with you, sleeping with you,
And talking to you sometimes? Do I live only in the outskirts

Of your good pleasure? If it be no more,
Portia is Brutus' harlot, not his wife.

BRUTUS
You are my true and honourable wife,
As dear to me as are the ruddy drops
That visit my sad heart.

PORTIA
If this were true, then should I know this secret.

I grant I am a woman; but withal

A woman that Lord Brutus took to wife;
I grant I am a woman; but withal

A woman well-reputed, Cato's daughter.

Think you I am no stronger than my sex,

Being so father'd, and so husbanded?

Tell me your counsels, I will not disclose 'em.
I have made strong proof of my constancy,

Giving myself a voluntary wound
Here, in the thigh; can I bear that with patience,

And not my husband's secrets?

BRUTUS
O ye gods,
Render me worthy of this noble wife!

Knocking within

Hark, hark! One knocks. Portia, go in awhile;

And by and by thy bosom shall partake
The secrets of my heart.
All my engagements I will construe to thee,
All the charactery of my sad brows.

Leave me with haste.

Exit PORTIA

Lucius, who's that knocks?

Re-enter LUCIUS with LIGARIUS

Of your happiness? If I am no more than that,
Then I am your whore and not your wife.

BRUTUS
You are my true and honourable wife,
As dear to me as the red drops of blood
That flow through my sad heart.

PORTIA:
If that were true, then I would know what this secret is.

I grant you that I am a woman; but you must consider
I am the woman Lord Brutus took for his wife;
I grant you that I am a woman; but you must consider
I am a woman from a reputable family, Cato's daughter.
Do you honestly think that I am no stronger than other women,
Having such men as yourselves for my father and my husband?
Tell me these things you're deliberating over,
I will not betray them.
I have proved my faithful endurance,
By giving myself a voluntary wound
Here, in my thigh; if I can bear that with patience,
Can't I bear my husband's secrets?

BRUTUS
Oh, ye gods,
Make me worthy of this noble wife!

A knocking sound offstage

Listen! Someone is knocking. Portia, go inside for a while;
And before long your heart shall share in
The secrets of my heart.
All my assignations I will explain to you,
Everything that is written in my sad facial expression.
Leave me quickly.

Exit PORTIA

Lucius, who's that knocking?

Re-enter LUCIUS with LIGARIUS.

Original	Modern
LUCIUS He is a sick man that would speak with you.	**LUCIUS** Here is a sick man who wants to speak with you.
BRUTUS Caius Ligarius, that Metellus spake of. Boy, stand aside. Caius Ligarius, how?	**BRUTUS** It's Caius Ligarius, who Metellus was talking about. Boy, stand aside. Caius Ligarius, how are you?
LIGARIUS Vouchsafe good morrow from a feeble tongue.	**LIGARIUS** Please accept my feeble good morning.
BRUTUS O, what a time have you chose out, brave Caius, To wear a kerchief! Would you were not sick!	**BRUTUS** Oh, what a time you have chosen to be unavailable, brave Caius, Wearing a cloth around your head, showing that you're sick! I wish you weren't ill!
LIGARIUS I am not sick if Brutus have in hand Any exploit worthy the name of honour.	**LIGARIUS** I am not ill if Brutus is ready with An honourable exploit for me.
BRUTUS Such an exploit have I in hand, Ligarius, Had you a healthful ear to hear of it.	**BRUTUS** I do have such an exploit ready, Ligarius, If you're well enough to hear about it.
LIGARIUS By all the gods that Romans bow before, I here discard my sickness. (*He throws off the cloth*) Soul of Rome! Brave son, derived from honourable loins! Thou, like an exorcist, hast conjured up My mortified spirit. Now bid me run, And I will strive with things impossible, Yea, get the better of them. What's to do?	**LIGARIUS** By all the gods that Romans worship, I throw off my sickness here. (*He throws off the cloth*) Soul of Rome! Noble son, of honourable parents! You, like an exorcist, have conjured up My spirit which was dead. Now give me the go ahead, And I will attempt to do impossible things, Yes, and succeed too. What needs to be done?
BRUTUS A piece of work that will make sick men whole.	**BRUTUS** A deed which will make sick men healthy.
LIGARIUS But are not some whole that we must make sick?	**LIGARIUS** But aren't there some healthy men whom we have to kill?
BRUTUS That must we also. What it is, my Caius, I shall unfold to thee, as we are going To whom it must be done.	**BRUTUS** That too. The deed, dear Caius, I shall explain to you, as we are on our way To the dwelling of him to whom it must be done.

LIGARIUS Set on your foot, And with a heart new-fired I follow you, To do I know not what; but it sufficeth That Brutus leads me on. **BRUTUS** Follow me then. *Exeunt*	**LIGARIUS** Advance on foot, And with a heart rekindled with life and courage I will follow you, To do what, I do not know; but it is enough for me That Brutus leads the way. **BRUTUS** Follow me then. *Exeunt*

Part 10: Analysing Act 2 Scene 1

It is still night-time, which is appropriate for a conspiracy with masked plotters. At the beginning of the scene, Shakespeare draws attention to the darkness, which serves as pathetic fallacy: Brutus has supressed his feelings of friendship towards Caesar and has decided to join the conspiracy to murder Caesar. The busy Lucius, whose name derives from *lux*, Latin for *light*, brings a candle to Brutus. The ironic contrast between Lucius the light-bringer and Brutus, brooding in darkness and solitude, emphasises the setting and the latter's violent thoughts.

The theme of ignoring private feelings for the benefit of the public good dominates this scene. Brutus's soliloquy provides the opportunity for the audience to learn his thoughts and feelings:

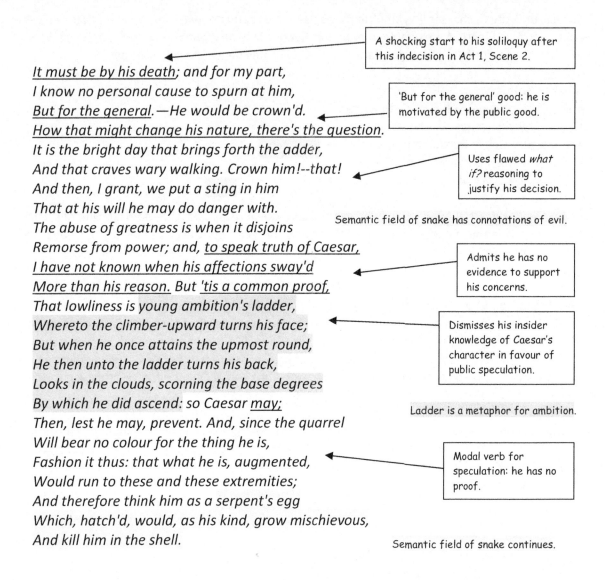

It must be by his death; and for my part,
I know no personal cause to spurn at him,
But for the general.—He would be crown'd.
How that might change his nature, there's the question.
It is the bright day that brings forth the adder,
And that craves wary walking. Crown him!--that!
And then, I grant, we put a sting in him
That at his will he may do danger with.
The abuse of greatness is when it disjoins
Remorse from power; and, to speak truth of Caesar,
I have not known when his affections sway'd
More than his reason. But 'tis a common proof,
That lowliness is young ambition's ladder,
Whereto the climber-upward turns his face;
But when he once attains the upmost round,
He then unto the ladder turns his back,
Looks in the clouds, scorning the base degrees
By which he did ascend: so Caesar may;
Then, lest he may, prevent. And, since the quarrel
Will bear no colour for the thing he is,
Fashion it thus: that what he is, augmented,
Would run to these and these extremities;
And therefore think him as a serpent's egg
Which, hatch'd, would, as his kind, grow mischievous,
And kill him in the shell.

A shocking start to his soliloquy after this indecision in Act 1, Scene 2.

'But for the general' good: he is motivated by the public good.

Uses flawed *what if?* reasoning to justify his decision.

Semantic field of snake has connotations of evil.

Admits he has no evidence to support his concerns.

Dismisses his insider knowledge of Caesar's character in favour of public speculation.

Ladder is a metaphor for ambition.

Modal verb for speculation: he has no proof.

Semantic field of snake continues.

We have already learnt that Brutus is a Stoic, and this might explain why he focuses on speculative—but flawed—reasoning when he decides that Caesar must die. Poignantly, Brutus ignores his knowledge of his friend's character; indeed, he has no evidence that Caesar's personality will even change after he has been crowned. Brutus's decision that Caesar must die is based on what he perceives to be the best thing for Rome. This is the first time in the play that we explicitly hear that Caesar must die, and it is ironic that it does not come from one of the conspirators but from the mouth of Caesar's friend.

We see more evidence of Brutus's sense of honour influencing his thoughts for the public good through the device of Cassius's forged letter. By referencing his 'ancestors', who drove out King Tarquin, Brutus seems to be saying that it is his fate to save Rome: this example centuries ago compels him to act similarly now. The letter also contains references to Rome ('Shall Rome, etc.') which appeal to Brutus's sense of public responsibility. After he has reflected upon the contents of the letter, he exclaims 'O Rome, I make thee promise,/If the redress will follow, thou receives/Thy full petition at the hand of Brutus'. The long vowel sound in 'O' turns the declaration that he will 'redress' into a formal, solemn moment, which is emphasised when Brutus refers to himself in the third person. The use of this moment therefore signifies Brutus's mistaken belief that his decision to kill Caesar is at the request of the Roman citizens.

Aspects of Brutus's character symbolise Rome itself, illustrating how closely he aligns himself to the public good. We learn, for example, that he has been awake all night and wishes that he could 'sleep soundly'. The soft sibilance is a gentle sound that connotes peace. Portia later says:

What, is Brutus sick?
And will he steal out of his wholesome bed
To dare the vile contagion of the night,
And tempt the rheumy and unpurged air,
To add unto his sickness? No, my Brutus;
You have some sick offence within your mind,

Imagery of illness and infections.

In the above extract, the adjective 'wholesome' connotes Brutus's private, domestic life of security and peace while the imagery of illness and infections provides contrast. His inability to sleep is the opposite of peace: he is being infected by the words of others, and the metaphor of illness symbolises the spreading rebellion.

Once Brutus joins the conspiracy, the balance of power amongst the conspirators shifts as he begins to make important decisions and overrules Cassius. For example, Brutus rejects Cassius's suggestion of recruiting Cicero, saying 'he will never follow any thing/That other men begin'. He also tells Metellus to call at the house of Ligarius to recruit him: 'Just send him here and I will persuade him to join our party'. This ability to take control, make decisions and act symbolises another aspect of Roman society: the manoeuvring of political powers.

Now that Brutus has reached a decision, we see the full extent to which he is influenced by public opinion when he insists that the assassination of Caesar is honourable. He is moved to act by the purest of motives—the retention of the Republic. The merits of that are so self-evident (he thinks) that an oath is unnecessary and demeaning:

> Do not stain
> The even virtue of our enterprise,
> Nor the insuppressive mettle of our spirits,
> To think that or our cause or our performance
> Did need an oath

Brutus does not see the need to swear an oath because he believes this insults the integrity of the conspirators. The connotations of the nouns 'virtue' and 'enterprise' illustrate his conviction that they are acting for the greater good. He characterises the conspirators with 'insuppressive mettle of our spirits' (indomitable resilience of our spirits) as heroes. It is at this point that the audience perceives the irony of the situation: Brutus's belief in the public good determines his view of the assassination plot—yet he has, unlike a man of virtue, rejected his previous loyalties to his friend Caesar. Moreover, the juxtaposition of the verb 'stain' with the noun 'virtue' connotes blood. Brutus is asking them not to stain the virtue of the scheme with unnecessary promises. However, Brutus has already stained his own virtue as he will betray Caesar, whose blood will be on his hands.

At this moment in the play, blood imagery starts to dominate, replacing earlier light and fire imagery. Brutus reiterates that there is no need to swear an oath, saying 'every drop of blood/That every Roman bears, and nobly bears, /Is guilty of a several bastardy' if they break the promise to murder Caesar. He uses the imagery of noble Roman blood to appeal to the conspirators' sense of honour. The repetition of 'bears' emphasises the adjective 'nobly', highlighting his belief that they are acting for the public good. Blood is therefore used to rationalise spilling more blood--Caesar's blood. Brutus's belief that they will act in the public good can also be seen when he declares 'Let us be sacrificers, but not butchers', as it would be 'too bloody' to dismember Caesar, but he 'must bleed'. In other words, kill him but do not mutilate the body. The sacrifice and blood imagery implies the murder has a religious context, again illustrating that he believes his decision is for the greater good.

When prioritising the public good over the men's personal safety, Brutus does not expect that there will be any danger from allowing Antony to live. Consequently, he overrules Cassius, who wants Antony dead. Brutus, like Caesar, does not always listen to the views of others. Naïvely, he fails to consider that Antony's love for Caesar will lead him to reject Brutus's reasons for the assassination.

We see the extent to which private beliefs are compromised by public obligations when we meet Brutus's wife, Portia, who symbolises his domestic life. By refusing to tell her what is troubling him, Brutus either does not want Portia to be involved, or he is troubled by his conscience and still has doubts. Whatever his reason, he refuses to confide in his wife in favour of his duty to the Republic. There is an interesting intermingling between Brutus's public and private thoughts of blood and honour when he calls Portia his 'true and honourable wife, /As dear […] as are the ruddy drops/That visit my sad heart'. With Caesar and Portia, blood is associated with honour, but with Caesar, it justifies murder while with Portia, the blood simile emphasises love.

Portia also represents the strong Roman woman, the noble daughter of the Republic. Her strength of character can be seen despite her exploitation of contemporary ideas about femininity:

> *…should I know this secret.*
> *I grant I am a woman; but withal*
> *A woman that Lord Brutus took to wife;*
> *I grant I am a woman; but withal*
> *A woman well-reputed, Cato's daughter.*

Her use of repetition (or anaphora because it is at the beginning of a sentence) with 'I grant that I am a woman; but withal' is an effective persuasive device: she belittles herself and then continues these phrases by reminding Brutus of her status as his 'wife' and 'Cato's daughter'. Cato the Younger, 95 BC - 46 BC, was a politician, statesman and skilled orator, who followed Stoic philosophy. He was respected for being obstinate, persistent, honest and incorruptible. In many ways, he was seen as the conscience of Rome. Portia defines herself through her relationship with great men, basing her reasoning on the commonly accepted idea that women were weaker than men.

Portia's self-inflicted wound is an honourable act, being proof to her husband of her ability to bear pain as a man would. It is important to stress that this is not an example of self-harm, but in Roman eyes an example of physical courage. Shakespeare is here evoking a parallel between Portia and Athena, the Greek goddess of war and wisdom, who is said to have been born out of Zeus's thigh. The wound therefore elevates Portia's status and illustrates that she is worthy of her husband's trust. We have already seen that Romans equate suicide with honour and masculine strength of will when Caesar offered to take his life in Act 1, Scene 2; sadly, Portia's wound also provides evidence to the audience of Portia's strength of character, a strength sufficient for her later suicide. The wound therefore links to Roman ideas about sacrificing life in the face of dishonour.

As we have seen, Brutus's decisions are based on a skewed logic and his belief that by assassinating Caesar he is helping the citizens of Rome. In contrast, Ligarius's decision to join the conspiracy is based on loyalty to Brutus. Ligarius hero-worships Brutus so much that he is prepared to kill for him: 'But are not some whole that we must make sick?' With this statement, he implies that he is willing to harm others, despite not knowing any of the details. Moreover, the sick Ligarius now feels better:

> And with a heart new-fired I follow you,
> To do I know not what; but it sufficeth
> That Brutus leads me on.

Brutus makes Ligarius's 'heart new-fired'; this has invigorating, energetic, life-giving connotations which emphasise that, in Ligarius's eyes, Brutus is inspirational.

Shakespeare deliberately places this conversation at the end of the scene so that the audience can reflect on the advisability of blindly following inspirational leaders such as Brutus or Caesar. This is supported by the stage direction '[t]hunder' at the end of the scene, which suggests divine disapproval.

Freytag's Pyramid
Let's remind ourselves of Gustav Freytag's pyramid:

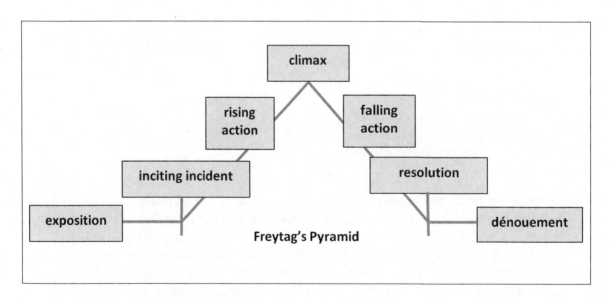

In this scene, we have seen the **inciting incident** of Brutus's decision to join the conspiracy and assume a leadership position. From this moment onwards, the consequences of his decision will unfold in the **rising action**.

Part 11: Translating Act 2 Scene 2

ORIGINAL TEXT	MODERN TRANSLATION
CAESAR's house.	*CAESAR's house.*
Thunder and lightning. Enter CAESAR, in his night-gown.	*Thunder and lightning. Enter CAESAR, in his night-gown.*
CAESAR Nor heaven nor earth have been at peace tonight; Thrice hath Calpurnia in her sleep cried out, 'Help, ho! They murder Caesar!' Who's within?	**CAESAR** Neither heaven nor earth have been at peace tonight; Three times Calpurnia cried out in her sleep, 'Help, help! They are murdering Caesar!' Who's there?
Enter a Servant	*Enter a Servant*
SERVANT My lord?	**SERVANT** My lord?
CAESAR Go bid the priests do present sacrifice, And bring me their opinions of success.	**CAESAR** Go and tell the priests to perform a sacrifice immediately, And bring me their judgements on the outcome.
SERVANT I will, my lord.	**SERVANT** I will, my lord.
Exit servant. Enter CALPURNIA	*Exit servant. Enter CALPURNIA*
CALPURNIA What mean you, Caesar? Think you to walk forth? You shall not stir out of your house to-day.	**CALPURNIA** What do you intend to do, Caesar? Are you planning to go out? You are not to leave the house today.
CAESAR Caesar shall forth. The things that threaten'd me Ne'er look'd but on my back; when they shall see The face of Caesar, they are vanished.	**CAESAR** Caesar shall go forth. The things that threatened me Have only seen my back; when they see The face of Caesar, they will vanish.
CALPURNIA Caesar, I never stood on ceremonies, Yet now they fright me. There is one within, Besides the things that we have heard and seen,	**CALPURNIA** Caesar, I have never attached much importance to omens, But now they frighten me. A servant here, Besides the things that we have seen and heard ourselves,

Recounts most horrid sights seen by the watch.	Has told me of horrid things which the night watchman saw.
A lioness hath whelped in the streets,	A lioness has given birth to her cubs in the streets,
And graves have yawn'd, and yielded up their dead;	And graves have opened wide and given up their dead;
Fierce fiery warriors fought upon the clouds	Fierce fiery warriors fought in the clouds
In ranks and squadrons and right form of war,	In ranks and squadrons and in regular battle order,
Which drizzled blood upon the Capitol;	Until blood drizzled onto the Capitol;
The noise of battle hurtled in the air,	The noise of battle clashed in the air,
Horses did neigh, and dying men did groan,	Horses neighed and dying men groaned,
And ghosts did shriek and squeal about the streets.	And ghosts shrieked and squealed in the streets.
O Caesar, these things are beyond all use,	Oh Caesar, these things are outside all normal experience,
And I do fear them.	And they frighten me.
CAESAR	**CAESAR**
What can be avoided	How can we avoid
Whose end is purposed by the mighty gods?	That which is ordained by the mighty gods to happen?
Yet Caesar shall go forth; for these predictions	But Caesar will go out today; because these predictions
Are to the world in general as to Caesar.	Apply to the world in general, just as much as they apply to me.
CALPURNIA	**CALPURNIA**
When beggars die, there are no comets seen;	When beggars die, no comets are seen in the sky;
The heavens themselves blaze forth the death of princes.	The heavens themselves proclaim the deaths of princes.
CAESAR	**CAESAR**
Cowards die many times before their deaths;	Cowards die many times before their deaths;
The valiant never taste of death but once.	The fearless experience death only once.
Of all the wonders that I yet have heard,	Of all the curious things that I have ever heard,
It seems to me most strange that men should fear,	It seems to me that the strangest is that men fear death,
Seeing that death, a necessary end,	Given that death, inevitable for us all,
Will come when it will come.	Will come whenever it wants to.
Re-enter Servant	Re-enter Servant
What say the augurers?	What do the priests foretell?
SERVANT	**SERVANT**
They would not have you to stir forth to-day.	They don't want you to go out today.
Plucking the entrails of an offering forth,	When they pulled out the vital organs of the sacrificed animal,
They could not find a heart within the beast.	They found that the beast didn't have a heart.

CAESAR
The gods do this in shame of cowardice:

Caesar should be a beast without a heart
If he should stay at home to-day for fear.
No, Caesar shall not. Danger knows full well

That Caesar is more dangerous than he.
We are two lions litter'd in one day,

And I the elder and more terrible;
And Caesar shall go forth.

CALPURNIA
Alas, my lord,
Your wisdom is consumed in confidence.
Do not go forth to-day: call it my fear
That keeps you in the house, and not your own.

We'll send Mark Antony to the Senate-House,
And he shall say you are not well to-day.
Let me, upon my knee, prevail in this.

CAESAR
Mark Antony shall say I am not well,
And for thy humour I will stay at home.

Enter DECIUS BRUTUS

Here's Decius Brutus; he shall tell them so.

DECIUS BRUTUS
Caesar, all hail! Good morrow, worthy Caesar;
I come to fetch you to the Senate-House.

CAESAR
And you are come in very happy time

To bear my greeting to the senators,
And tell them that I will not come to-day:
Cannot, is false; and that I dare not, falser;

I will not come to-day. Tell them so, Decius.

CALPURNIA
Say he is sick.

CAESAR
The gods are doing this to discover whether I
am a coward:
Caesar would be a beast without a heart
If he were to stay at home today out of fear.
No, Caesar shall not stay at home. Danger
knows full well
That Caesar is more dangerous than he is.
We are like two lions born in the same litter on
the same day,
And I am the older and more terrible;
And Caesar shall go out.

CALPURNIA
Alas, my lord,
Your wisdom is destroyed by overconfidence.
Do not go out today: say that it is my fear
Which keeps you in the house, and not your
own.
We'll send Mark Antony to the Senate House,
And he shall say that you are not well today.
Let me, on my knees, persuade you to do this.

CAESAR
Mark Antony shall say that I am not well,
And to please you I will stay at home.

Enter DECIUS BRUTUS

Here's Decius Brutus; he shall tell them so.

DECIUS BRUTUS
Hail, Caesar! Good morning, worthy Caesar;
I have come to accompany you to the Senate
House.

CAESAR
And you have come at a very opportune
moment
To convey my greeting to the senators,
And to tell them that I will not come today:
To say that I cannot, wouldn't be true; and to
say that I don't dare to come would be even less
true;
I simply will not come today. Tell them so,
Decius.

CALPURNIA
Say that he is ill.

CAESAR Shall Caesar send a lie? Have I in conquest stretch'd mine arm so far, To be afraid to tell greybeards the truth? Decius, go tell them Caesar will not come.	**CAESAR** Should Caesar send a lie? Have I achieved so much in battle, That now I am afraid to tell old men the truth? Decius, just tell them that Caesar will not come.
DECIUS BRUTUS Most mighty Caesar, let me know some cause, Lest I be laugh'd at when I tell them so.	**DECIUS BRUTUS** Most mighty Caesar, give me a reason, Otherwise I will be laughed at when I tell them this.
CAESAR The cause is in my will: I will not come; That is enough to satisfy the Senate. But for your private satisfaction, Because I love you, I will let you know: Calpurnia here, my wife, stays me at home. She dreamt to-night she saw my statue, Which, like a fountain with an hundred spouts, Did run pure blood; and many lusty Romans Came smiling, and did bathe their hands in it. And these does she apply for warnings and portents And evils imminent; and on her knee Hath begg'd that I will stay at home to-day.	**CAESAR** The reason is that it is what I want: I don't want to come; That is enough for the Senate to know. But for your private information, Because I love you, I will tell you: Calpurnia, my wife, is keeping me at home. Last night she dreamt that she saw a statue of me, Which, like a fountain with a hundred spouts, Flowed with pure blood; and many brawny Romans Came smiling, and washed their hands in it. And she interprets these as warnings and predictions Of imminent disaster; and on her knees She has begged me to stay at home today.
DECIUS BRUTUS This dream is all amiss interpreted; It was a vision fair and fortunate: Your statue spouting blood in many pipes, In which so many smiling Romans bathed, Signifies that from you great Rome shall suck Reviving blood, and that great men shall press For tinctures, stains, relics and cognizance. This by Calpurnia's dream is signified.	**DECIUS BRUTUS** This dream has been misinterpreted; It was a good and favourable vision: Your statue spouting blood through many pipes, In which so many smiling Romans bathed, Signifies that from you great Rome shall draw Reviving blood, and that great men shall crowd around To obtain tokens of recognition from your holy blood. This is what Calpurnia's dream means.
CAESAR And this way have you well expounded it.	**CAESAR** You have explained the interpretation well.
DECIUS BRUTUS I have, when you have heard what I can say: And know it now. The Senate have concluded To give this day a crown to mighty Caesar. If you shall send them word you will not come,	**DECIUS BRUTUS** I will have, when you have heard everything I have to say: And please listen. The Senate have decided To give mighty Caesar a crown today. If you send them word that you won't come,

Their minds may change. Besides, it were a mock Apt to be render'd, for some one to say, 'Break up the Senate till another time, When Caesar's wife shall meet with better dreams.' If Caesar hide himself, shall they not whisper, 'Lo, Caesar is afraid'? Pardon me, Caesar, for my dear dear love To your proceeding bids me tell you this, And reason to my love is liable.	They might change their minds. Besides, it would be a sarcastic remark Likely to be passed for someone to say, 'Postpone the Senate until some other time, When Caesar's wife has had better dreams.' If you hide yourself, won't they whisper, 'Caesar is afraid'? Forgive me, Caesar, because my deep, genuine concern For your career's advancement prompts me to say this to you, And my affection overcomes what my reason tells me is too outspoken to utter.
CAESAR How foolish do your fears seem now, Calpurnia! I am ashamed I did yield to them. Give me my robe, for I will go.	**CAESAR** How foolish your fears seem now, Calpurnia! I am ashamed that I gave in to them. Give me my robe, because I am going.
Enter PUBLIUS, BRUTUS, LIGARIUS, METELLUS, CASCA, TREBONIUS, and CINNA	Enter PUBLIUS, BRUTUS, LIGARIUS, METELLUS, CASCA, TREBONIUS, and CINNA
And look where Publius is come to fetch me.	And look, Publius has come to fetch me.
PUBLIUS Good morrow, Caesar.	**PUBLIUS** Good morning, Caesar.
CAESAR Welcome, Publius. What, Brutus, are you stirr'd so early too? Good morrow, Casca. Caius Ligarius, Caesar was ne'er so much your enemy As that same ague which hath made you lean. What is 't o'clock?	**CAESAR** Welcome, Publius. What, Brutus, are you awake this early too? Good morning, Casca. Caius Ligarius, I was never your enemy so much As that shivering fever which has made you so thin. What is the time?
BRUTUS Caesar, 'tis strucken eight.	**BRUTUS** Caesar, the clock has struck eight times.
CAESAR I thank you for your pains and courtesy.	**CAESAR** Thank you for your trouble and courtesy.
Enter ANTONY	Enter ANTONY
See! Antony, that revels long o' nights, Is notwithstanding up. Good morrow, Antony.	Look! Antony, who likes to party the night away, Is nevertheless awake. Good morning, Antony.
ANTONY So to most noble Caesar.	**ANTONY** And to you also, most noble Caesar.

CAESAR
Bid them prepare within.
I am to blame to be thus waited for.
Now, Cinna; now, Metellus; what, Trebonius;
I have an hour's talk in store for you;
Remember that you call on me to-day;
Be near me, that I may remember you.

TREBONIUS
Caesar, I will.
(Aside) And so near will I be
That your best friends shall wish I had been further.

CAESAR
Good friends, go in, and taste some wine with me;
And we, like friends, will straightway go together.

BRUTUS
(Aside) That every like is not the same, O Caesar,
The heart of Brutus yearns to think upon.

Exeunt

CAESAR
Ask the servants to set out the wine.
I am to blame for the delay.
Now, Cinna; now, Metellus; now Trebonius;
I need to talk with you for an hour;
Remember to come and see me today;
Stay close to me, so that I will remember.

TREBONIUS
Caesar, I will.
(Aside) And I will be so near
That your best friends will wish that I had been further away.

CAESAR
Good friends, go in and drink some wine with me;
And we will all go together like friends.

BRUTUS
(Aside) That we are now only 'like' friends, oh Caesar,
Grieves my heart when I think about it.

Exeunt

Part 12: Analysing Act 2 Scene 2

The opening stage directions '[t]hunder and lightning' indicate that Shakespeare is continuing with a storm as an extended metaphor (or pathetic fallacy) for the workings of fate, omens and portents. As the conspirators' powers increase, there are more warnings from the gods. About six years after 'Julius Caesar' was performed, Shakespeare again used the pathetic fallacy of a storm in the play 'King Lear' to suggest the king's breakdown was mirrored by disturbance in the heavens. Shakespeare uses thunderstorms as a device illustrate a divine or supernatural response, particularly relevant as a king or queen was believed to be God's representative on earth. Although 'Julius Caesar' is set in pre-Christian Rome, its Elizabethan audience will have lived through plots to assassinate Queen Elizabeth I. Shakespeare uses the thunderstorms as a device to hold up to critical gaze those who plot against Caesar and, by implication, Queen Elizabeth I.

In contrast to Portia, Calpurnia is associated with the supernatural. She reports more portents: 'a lioness hath whelped in the streets'; graves have 'yielded up their dead'; rain has 'drizzled blood'; and 'ghosts did shriek and squeal about the streets'. The list of vivid visual images combine with the onomatopoeic verbs 'drizzled', 'shrieked' and 'squeal' to build momentum and tension, creating a horrifying apocalyptic vision of a world turned upside down, as the natural order of society (a class system in which Caesar is at the top) is challenged by humans to the wrath of the gods. These are all terrifying, unnatural events that a modern audience might associate with a horror film.

Shakespeare deliberately includes a reference to a comet when Calpurnia says 'When beggars die, there are no comets seen;/The heavens themselves blaze forth the death of princes'. The historical Julius Caesar was deified (turned into a god) by the Roman citizens in 42 BC, two years after he died. This was because a comet, which they believed to be his soul, blazed over Rome for seven days and nights—and it was so bright that it could be seen in the daytime. Shakespeare's inclusion of the comet in the play reminds the audience of the historical comet that preceded Caesar's deification. It also suggests that for Caesar to ignore the omen is to ignore it at his peril.

When Caesar orders an animal to be sacrificed, he is following the accepted belief system of the day, as he would have been expected to consult the omens at this important moment in time. In the religions of Ancient Rome, specialists (called *haruspices* in Latin) were trained to predict the future, based on readings of the entrails of sacrificed animals. Whether Caesar believes in the power of prophecy or not is open to question. What cannot be disputed, however, is that by gambling with his fate, he is expecting a positive outcome. In this case, Shakespeare makes the gamble fail. Historic *haruspices* mainly inspected the livers of animals, but in the play, Shakespeare deliberately references the animal not having a 'heart'; this is more difficult to interpret and thereby increases dramatic tension:

> Caesar should be a beast without a heart
> If he should stay at home to-day for fear.
> No, Caesar shall not. Danger knows full well
> That Caesar is more dangerous than he.
> We are two lions litter'd in one day,
> And I the elder and more terrible;
> And Caesar shall go forth.

The lack of heart might signify a warning or, as Caesar prefers to believe, he will be 'a beast without a heart' if he stays at home. A lack of heart, juxtaposed with 'fear' implies cowardice, which is not how a public figure of Caesar's standing would wish to be perceived. He personifies 'Danger' to imply that danger is more afraid of him. He compares himself and Danger, using the metaphor of 'two lions litter'd'. The alliteration emphasises the imagery of lion cubs and their potential to grow into full powers. Their birth rank symbolises strength, authority and command. We then have the comparative adjective with Caesar being 'more terrible', which elevates his character to having almost supernatural abilities. The use of the lion cub metaphor therefore establishes his potential to be a fearless ruler.

In the above quotation, Caesar seems to demonstrate an air of grandeur by referring to himself in the third person. Shakespeare may have borrowed Julius Caesar's own writing style in his classic 'Commentaries on the Gallic War' which brilliantly describes (and justifies) his own leadership. It is written in the third person ('When Caesar, who had addressed the tenth legion, reached the right wing, he found his troops under severe pressure') to present subjective facts as if they are objective facts. His rhetorical re-interpretation of 'a beast without a heart' further indicates the lengths to which Caesar will go to maintain his public image. However, ignoring the result of the animal sacrifice illustrates that he is a gambler.

Does Caesar die because he is destined to do so or because he ignores the omens? As a great public figure, Caesar's response to the portents is complex. He must realise that these omens predict his death, but he dismisses the idea: He says 'What can be avoided/Whose end is purposed by the mighty gods?'. In other words, there is nothing he can do to alter fate so, he must accept that death 'Will come when it will come'. Caesar therefore must ignore the omens because—keenly aware of his public persona—he is aware that should people see that be believes the omens, they will conclude that he is afraid.

The ambiguity of the omens (and Caesar's response to them) increases dramatic tension, as the audience wonders whether Caesar will heed them and stay at home. There is therefore a sense of relief when he decides not to go to the Capitol. It is at this moment in the play that we see parallels in the plot: he has more empathy for the distress of his wife than Brutus has for Portia, indicating perhaps that Caesar is the better man of the two. It also implies that temporarily at least, his private life is more important than his public life. However, he then changes his mind at the behest of Decius Brutus; ultimately, his ambition and concern about his public self are more important than domestic concerns.

Caesar does not want to be seen as a weak man who listens to omens or—of greater significance in a patriarchal society—listens to his wife. He agrees to stay at home, but he manufactures a reason: 'Mark Antony shall say I am not well'. He then changes his mind (ironically enough, this was understood in a patriarchal society to be behaviour typical of women) and decides not to provide a reason for his absence: 'The cause is in my will: I will not come;/That is enough to satisfy the Senate'. By deciding not to give a reason, he is positioning himself as a man of power who does not have to justify his decisions or actions to anyone. He places himself above the Senate, and this reinforces the fear that Brutus and others have about him as a potential tyrant.

After lulling the audience into a sense of security when Caesar agrees to stay at home, tension escalates when Caesar reports Calpurnia's dream to justify his decision. Firstly, we have the motif (a recurring theme or idea) of blood with the symbolism of the bleeding statue. Caesar states that it:

> ...like a fountain with an hundred spouts,
> Did run pure blood; and many lusty Romans
> Came smiling, and did bathe their hands in it.

The audience is not slow to realise that the statue symbolises Caesar's body and the simile of the 'fountain' with 'spouts' of 'blood' foreshadows his blood running from his many stab wounds. The 'lusty Romans' full of life and vitality, contrast with the deathly fountain: they are the conspirators who are 'smiling' and bathing their hands in the blood of Caesar as they celebrate the success of their 'enterprise'. The conspirators will literally and metaphorically have blood on their hands, foreshadowing their guilt.

As we have seen, omens and portents can be interpreted in different ways, and Decius Brutus deliberately misinterprets the dream, suggesting that in the dream Caesar's blood is 'reviving' the citizens of Rome. The audience feels the power of Decius Brutus's rhetoric as, in a dramatically tense speech, he persuades Caesar to go out:

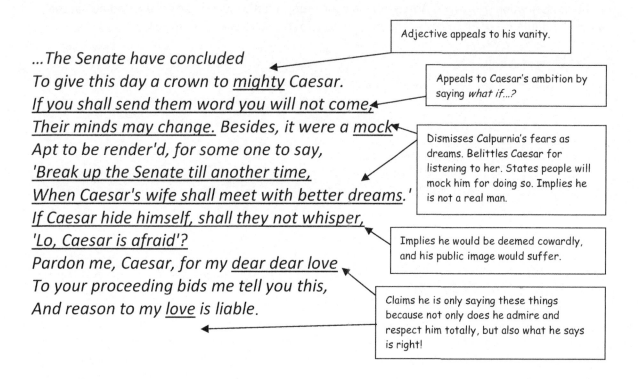

...The Senate have concluded
To give this day a crown to <u>mighty</u> Caesar.
<u>If you shall send them word you will not come,</u>
<u>Their minds may change.</u> Besides, it were a <u>mock</u>
Apt to be render'd, for some one to say,
<u>'Break up the Senate till another time,</u>
<u>When Caesar's wife shall meet with better dreams.'</u>
<u>If Caesar hide himself, shall they not whisper,</u>
<u>'Lo, Caesar is afraid'?</u>
Pardon me, Caesar, for my <u>dear dear love</u>
To your proceeding bids me tell you this,
And reason to my <u>love</u> is liable.

Annotations:
- Adjective appeals to his vanity.
- Appeals to Caesar's ambition by saying *what if...?*
- Dismisses Calpurnia's fears as dreams. Belittles Caesar for listening to her. States people will mock him for doing so. Implies he is not a real man.
- Implies he would be deemed cowardly, and his public image would suffer.
- Claims he is only saying these things because not only does he admire and respect him totally, but also what he says is right!

Decius Brutus appeals to Caesar's ambition and public image, justifying his blunt speaking by saying that he loves Caesar so much that he wants what is best for him.

Caesar's private ambition comes to the fore in this scene, contrasting with his behaviour in Act 1, Scene 2. At the beginning of the play, we heard that he refused the crown three times; Casca's opinion was that, when he returned the crown, 'he was very loath to lay his fingers off it'. The double adjectives of 'very loath' imply that it was a struggle for Caesar to return the crown and the noun 'fingers' connotes a desire to touch and caress the crown, suggesting the strength of Caesar's temptation. While Casca may have been biased, his opinion prepares the audience for Caesar's change of mind in this scene, which represents a time shift of just one day. It is, of course, the public perception that he wants the crown that leads the conspirators to his assassination.

At the end of the scene, the tone changes when Caesar relaxes with the people he believes to be his friends—Publius, Brutus, Ligarius, Metellus, Casca, Trebonius and Cinna. Ostensibly, Caesar is chatty, apologetic for keeping them waiting, and offers them refreshments: 'Good friends, go in, and taste some wine with me;/And we, like friends, will straightway go together'. The repetition of 'friends' stresses that he is completely trusting and unaware of their plot, heightening the dramatic irony. The preposition 'with', the pronoun 'we' and the adverb 'together' emphasise his feelings of trust and unity as he offers them his wine. Red wine, however, is the colour of blood, and this might be a symbol of the consequence of their friendship. The audience sees the assassins gathering for the kill and even hears Trebonius uttering as an aside his threat to stay dangerously close to Caesar. Predictably, the only one who appears to have doubts about the rightness of the action is Brutus, whose heart at this late stage still 'yearns' to think about the assassination. Brutus's comment is at the very end of the scene, raising faint hopes that the murder will not take place.

There is a sense of inevitability, however: nothing can stop fate. Brutus's comments about Antony being harmless appear to be confirmed by Caesar's observation about hard-partying Antony, who 'revels long o' nights'. This comment suggests Antony will not be sufficiently effective or powerful to stop the assassination. However, Antony's sole contribution to the scene ('So to most noble Caesar') reminds the audience of his loyalties and prepares us for his actions later in the play.

SCENE III. A street near the Capitol.
Enter ARTEMIDORUS, reading a paper

ARTEMIDORUS
Caesar, beware of Brutus; take heed of Cassius;
come not near Casca; have an eye to Cinna; trust
not Trebonius; mark well Metellus Cimber; Decius
Brutus loves thee not; thou hast wronged Caius
Ligarius. There is but one mind in all these men, and
it is bent against Caesar. If thou beest not immortal,
look about you: security gives way to conspiracy.
The mighty gods defend thee!
Thy lover,

Artemidorus.

Here will I stand till Caesar pass along,
And as a suitor will I give him this.

My heart laments that virtue cannot live
Out of the teeth of emulation.
If thou read this, O Caesar, thou mayst live;
If not, the Fates with traitors do contrive.

Exit

SCENE III. A street near the Capitol.
Enter ARTEMIDORUS, reading aloud from a letter

ARTEMIDORUS
Caesar, beware of Brutus; pay close attention to
Cassius; don't go near Casca; keep an eye on Cinna;
don't trust Trebonius; pay attention to Metellus
Cimber; Decius Brutus is not your loving friend; you
have wronged Caius Ligarius. There is one purpose
that all these men have in common, and it is
directed against Caesar. If you are not immortal,
stay alert and watchful: overconfidence gives
opportunity for treason. May the mighty gods
defend you!
Your devoted friend,
Artemidorus.

I shall stand here until Caesar passes by,
And pretending to be a petitioner, I will give him
this.
My heart is sad that virtuous men can't live
Beyond the reach of envious rivalry.
If you read this, oh Caesar, you might live;
If not, the Fates are conspiring with the traitors.

Exit

Part 14: Analysing Act 2 Scene 3

This scene, part of the rising action, is deliberately short to quicken the pace and create tension. Using the plot device of a letter is a convenient way for Shakespeare to summarise who is responsible for what and to establish Artemidorus's position as a loyal subject of Caesar. The audience does not know how Artemidorus has managed to uncover the plot, but news of the private conspiracy has become public knowledge, and this adds to the tension. It also prepares us for Popilius Lena's good luck comment in Act 3, Scene 1.

We have seen many instances so far of the power of rhetoric in the play as a persuasive tool; none of this is present in Artemidorus's letter, which is written in prose and contains only facts. This is ironic as Artemidorus teaches rhetoric. Shakespeare is therefore alerting the audience to the unlikelihood of his letter (if it is read) having any effect.

Tension is created when the audience learns through Artemidorus's soliloquy that he plans to hand the warning letter to Caesar, so the assassination might yet be stopped. The tension rises when Artemidorus worries that, after handing Caesar the letter, he might not read it:

> *If thou read this, O Caesar, thou mayst live;*
> *If not, the Fates with traitors do contrive.*

The exclamatory 'O Caesar' implies pleading and anguish: Caesar's life hangs by the slenderest of threads. The repetition of 'If' emphasises the precariousness of the situation.

In Artemidorus's opinion, the Fates will determine whether Caesar reads the letter. The juxtaposition of 'Fates' with 'traitors do contrive' implies that, if Caesar is fated not to read the warning letter, Artemidorus is resigned to this, knowing that there is nothing he can do.

Shakespeare's placement of 'the Fates' in the last line of the scene is significant. In Roman mythology, the Fates (Parcae) were three goddesses who controlled the lives of humans by spinning a web of destiny. Nona spun the thread of a human life; Decuma measured it; and Morta cut it, choosing how the person would die. Ending the scene with this reference therefore concentrates the attention of the audience: is Caesar fated to die, or can his assassination be prevented by the letter? Once more, the tension rises.

Part 15: Translating Act 2 Scene 4

ORIGINAL TEXT	MODERN TRANSLATION
Another part of the same street, before the house of BRUTUS.	**Another part of the same street, in front of the house of BRUTUS.**
Enter PORTIA and LUCIUS	*Enter PORTIA and LUCIUS*
PORTIA I prithee, boy, run to the Senate House. Stay not to answer me, but get thee gone. Why dost thou stay?	**PORTIA** Please, boy, run to the Senate House. Don't stay to answer me, but go quickly. Why are you still here?
LUCIUS To know my errand, madam.	**LUCIUS** To find out what I should do there, madam.
PORTIA I would have had thee there and here again Ere I can tell thee what thou shouldst do there.	**PORTIA** I wanted you to go there and back again Before I had a chance to tell you what you should do there.
(To herself, so that no-one can hear her)	*(To herself, so that no-one can hear her)*
O constancy, be strong upon my side; Set a huge mountain 'tween my heart and tongue!	Oh self-control, don't leave my side; Put a huge mountain between my heart and my tongue!
I have a man's mind, but a woman's might. How hard it is for women to keep counsel! *(To Lucius)* Art thou here yet?	I have a man's mind, but only a woman's strength. How hard it is for women to keep a secret! *(To Lucius)* Are you still here?
LUCIUS Madam, what should I do? Run to the Capitol and nothing else? And so return to you, and nothing else?	**LUCIUS** Madam, what do you want me to do? To just run to the Capitol and nothing else? And then return to you and nothing else?
PORTIA Yes, bring me word, boy, if thy lord look well, For he went sickly forth; and take good note	**PORTIA** Yes, bring me news, boy, if your master looks well, Because he was ill when he left here; and observe closely
What Caesar doth, what suitors press to him.	What Caesar is doing, which members of his retinue are keeping close to him.
Hark, boy, what noise is that?	Listen, boy, what is that noise?
LUCIUS I hear none, madam.	**LUCIUS** I can't hear anything, madam.
PORTIA Prithee, listen well. I heard a bustling rumour like a fray, And the wind brings it from the Capitol.	**PORTIA** Please, listen carefully. I heard a confused noise like a riot, And it is carried on the wind from the Capitol.
LUCIUS Sooth, madam, I hear nothing.	**LUCIUS** Truly, madam, I can't hear anything.
Enter the Soothsayer	*Enter the Soothsayer*

PORTIA
Come hither, fellow. Which way hast thou been?

SOOTHSAYER
At mine own house, good lady.

PORTIA
What is't o'clock?

SOOTHSAYER
About the ninth hour, lady.

PORTIA
Is Caesar yet gone to the Capitol?

SOOTHSAYER
Madam, not yet; I go to take my stand,
To see him pass on to the Capitol.

PORTIA
Thou hast some suit to Caesar, hast thou not?

SOOTHSAYER
That I have, lady, if it will please Caesar
To be so good to Caesar as to hear me:

I shall beseech him to befriend himself.

PORTIA
Why, know'st thou any harm's intended towards him?

SOOTHSAYER
None that I know will be, much that I fear may chance.
Good morrow to you. Here the street is narrow;
The throng that follows Caesar at the heels,
Of senators, of praetors, common suitors,
Will crowd a feeble man almost to death;
I'll get me to a place more void, and there
Speak to great Caesar as he comes along.

Exit

PORTIA
I must go in. Ay me, how weak a thing
The heart of woman is! O Brutus,
The heavens speed thee in thine enterprise!
(Aside) Sure, the boy heard me. *(To Lucius)* Brutus hath a suit
That Caesar will not grant. *(Aside)* O, I grow faint.
Run, Lucius, and commend me to my lord;
Say I am merry; come to me again,
And bring me word what he doth say to thee.

PORTIA
Come here, man. Which direction have you come from?

SOOTHSAYER
My own house, good lady.

PORTIA
What is the time?

SOOTHSAYER
About nine o'clock, madam.

PORTIA
Has Caesar gone to the Capitol yet?

SOOTHSAYER
Not yet, madam; I am going to stand in a position
Where I can see him pass by on his way to the Capitol.

PORTIA
You have something to say to Caesar, don't you?

SOOTHSAYER
Yes, I do, madam, if Caesar is willing
To be good to himself and to listen to what I must say:
I shall plead with him to do what is best for him.

PORTIA
Why, do you know if someone intends to harm him?

SOOTHSAYER
I don't know anything for sure, but there is a lot that I fear may happen.
Good morning to you. The street is narrow here;
The crowd that follows Caesar at his heels,
Senators, Roman judges, common petitioners,
Will crush a weak man almost to death;
I will go to a less crowded place and there
Speak to great Caesar as he walks past.

Exit

PORTIA
I must go in. Oh dear, what a weak thing
The heart of a woman is! Oh Brutus,
May the gods assist you in your mission!
(Aside) Surely, the boy heard me. *(To Lucius)* Brutus has a request
That Caesar will not grant. *(Aside)* Oh, I feel faint.
Run, Lucius, and speak well of me to my lord;

Say that I am in good spirits; then come back to me,

Exeunt severally	And tell me what he says to you.
	Exeunt severally

Part 16: Analysing Act 2 Scene 4

This scene is another short one to quicken the pace and increase tension. Shakespeare keeps the audience in suspense because, by changing the focus of the act to Portia, we are forced to wait to see if Caesar will read Artemidorus's letter of warning.

This scene contrasts with Act 2, Scene 1, in which we saw a strong, determined, persuasive Portia; we now see contemporary attitudes to women confirmed when the previously rational Portia is depicted as an irrational, indecisive, hysterical female, moaning about female weakness: 'Ay me, how weak a thing/The heart of woman is!'. This pandering to contemporary beliefs about women is likely to be problematic to a modern audience.

Tension rises when we see the soothsayer for the second time and we are reminded of the theme of fate. In response to Portia's question about whether anything bad will happen, he confirms that he does not know: 'None that I know will be, much that I fear may chance'. In other words, he cannot know the future for certain as it has not happened yet. This suggests that Caesar's assassination is not inevitable, just probable. Moreover, the fact that the Soothsayer is here to warn Caesar a second time indicates his opinion that the assassination might yet be averted, further developing tension. We have death imagery in the Soothsayer's speech, however: talking about himself, he states that '[t]he throng…/Will crowd a feeble man almost to death'. The Soothsayer is commenting on his own lack of physical strength, but we are reminded of Caesar's physical weaknesses and the manner in which the crowding 'throng' of assassins will kill him.

Portia's mental fragility in this scene can be seen through a range of actions and words. She tells Lucius to run to the Capitol, but he has to ask her twice for the purpose of his errand; she appears to hallucinate ('Hark, boy, what noise is that?'), imagining she can hear a riot and Lucius has to repeat that he hears nothing; she is close to collapse ('O, I grow faint'); and she finally states that she is 'merry' when clearly, she is very far from this—this merriness is probably her rising hysteria. It is perfectly obvious that Portia, who cannot control herself, cannot support Brutus, thereby adding tension to the end of this act. Her behaviour also prepares the audience for her final breakdown when, later in the play, she commits suicide.

ORIGINAL TEXT	MODERN TRANSLATION
Rome. Before the Capitol; the Senate sitting above.	**Rome. Before the Capitol; the Senate sitting above.**
A crowd of people; among them ARTEMIDORUS and the Soothsayer. Flourish. Enter CAESAR, BRUTUS, CASSIUS, CASCA, DECIUS BRUTUS, METELLUS CIMBER, TREBONIUS, CINNA, ANTONY, LEPIDUS, POPILIUS, PUBLIUS, and others	*A crowd of people; among them ARTEMIDORUS and the Soothsayer. Flourish. Enter CAESAR, BRUTUS, CASSIUS, CASCA, DECIUS BRUTUS, METELLUS CIMBER, TREBONIUS, CINNA, ANTONY, LEPIDUS, POPILIUS, PUBLIUS, and others*
CAESAR *(To the Soothsayer)* The ides of March are come.	**CAESAR** *(To the Soothsayer)* The 15th March has come.
SOOTHSAYER Ay, Caesar, but not gone.	**SOOTHSAYER** Yes, Caesar, but it has not gone yet.
ARTEMIDORUS *(Offering his letter)* Hail, Caesar! Read this schedule.	**ARTEMIDORUS** *(Offering his letter)* Hail, Caesar! Read this document.
DECIUS BRUTUS *(Offering Caesar another document)* Trebonius doth desire you to o'er-read, At your best leisure, this his humble suit.	**DECIUS BRUTUS** *(Offering Caesar another document)* Trebonius would like you to read through, At your leisure, this his humble petition.
ARTEMIDORUS O Caesar, read mine first; for mine's a suit That touches Caesar nearer. Read it, great Caesar.	**ARTEMIDORUS** Oh Caesar, read mine first; because mine is a petition Which affects you directly. Read it, great Caesar.
CAESAR What touches us ourself shall be last served.	**CAESAR** The things which concern me personally will be dealt with last.
ARTEMIDORUS Delay not, Caesar. Read it instantly.	**ARTEMIDORUS** Don't delay, Caesar. Read it straight away.
CAESAR What, is the fellow mad?	**CAESAR** Is this man insane?
PUBLIUS *(To Artemidorus)* Sirrah, give place.	**PUBLIUS** *(To Artemidorus)* Get out of the way, man.
CASSIUS *(To Artemidorus)* What, urge you your petitions in the street? Come to the Capitol.	**CASSIUS** *(To Artemidorus)* Are you presenting your petition in the street? Come to the Capitol.
CAESAR goes up to the Senate-House, the rest following	*CAESAR goes up to the Senate-House, the rest following*
POPILIUS	**POPILIUS**

(To Cassius) I wish your enterprise to-day may thrive.	*(To Cassius)* I hope your mission today goes well.
CASSIUS What enterprise, Popilius?	**CASSIUS** What mission, Popilius?
POPILIUS Fare you well.	**POPILIUS** Good luck.
Advances to CAESAR	*Advances to CAESAR*
BRUTUS *(To Cassius)* What said Popilius Lena?	**BRUTUS** *(To Cassius)* What did Popilius Lena say?
CASSIUS *(Aside to Brutus)* He wish'd to-day our enterprise might thrive. I fear our purpose is discovered.	**CASSIUS** *(Aside to Brutus)* He wished that our mission would go well today. I am afraid that our plan has been discovered.
BRUTUS Look how he makes to Caesar: mark him.	**BRUTUS** Look, he is going towards Caesar: watch him.
CASSIUS Casca, be sudden, for we fear prevention. Brutus, what shall be done? If this be known, Cassius or Caesar never shall turn back, For I will slay myself.	**CASSIUS** Casca, be quick, because we're afraid of being forestalled. Brutus, what shall we do? If our plan has been discovered, Either Caesar or I will not return alive, Because I will kill myself.
BRUTUS Cassius, be constant: Popilius Lena speaks not of our purposes; For look, he smiles, and Caesar doth not change.	**BRUTUS** Cassius, be resolute: Popilius Lena is not discussing our plans; Because look, he is smiling and Caesar's expression has not changed.
CASSIUS Trebonius knows his time; for look you, Brutus, He draws Mark Antony out of the way.	**CASSIUS** Trebonius knows when to act; because look, Brutus, He is taking Mark Antony to one side.
Exeunt ANTONY and TREBONIUS	*Exeunt ANTONY and TREBONIUS*
DECIUS BRUTUS Where is Metellus Cimber? Let him go, And presently prefer his suit to Caesar.	**DECIUS BRUTUS** Where is Metellus Cimber? He should go, And present his petition to Caesar immediately.
BRUTUS He is address'd. Press near and second him.	**BRUTUS** He is ready to do so. Stay close to him and second his petition.
CINNA Casca, you are the first that rears your hand.	**CINNA** Casca, you will be the first one to raise your hand.
CAESAR Are we all ready? What is now amiss That Caesar and his senate must redress?	**CAESAR** Are we all ready? What is the problem That Caesar and his senate must put right?

METELLUS CIMBER	METELLUS CIMBER
(Kneeling) Most high, most mighty, and most puissant Caesar, Metellus Cimber throws before thy seat An humble heart -	*(Kneeling)* Most high, most mighty, and most powerful Caesar, Metellus Cimber kneels before you With a humble heart –
CAESAR I must prevent thee, Cimber; These couchings and these lowly courtesies Might fire the blood of ordinary men, And turn pre-ordinance and first decree Into the law of children. Be not fond, To think that Caesar bears such rebel blood That will be thaw'd from the true quality With that which melteth fools - I mean sweet words, Low-crooked court'sies and base spaniel-fawning. Thy brother by decree is banished: If thou dost bend and pray and fawn for him, I spurn thee like a cur out of my way. Know, Caesar doth not wrong, nor without cause Will he be satisfied.	**CAESAR** I must forestall you, Cimber; These bowings and these humble good manners May impress ordinary men, And alter what has been decreed by time-honoured and pre-ordained law Into children's games. Don't be so stupid, As to believe that Caesar has such uncontrollable passions Which can be swayed from true stability In the way that fools can be swayed – I mean sweet flattery, Low, crooked curtsies and shameless puppy-dog fawning. Your brother has been banished as the law decrees: If you kneel and pray and flatter for him, I will kick you out of my way as if you were a dog. Know that I am not unjust and neither will I, without a genuine reason, Grant him a pardon.
METELLUS CIMBER Is there no voice more worthy than my own, To sound more sweetly in great Caesar's ear For the repealing of my banish'd brother?	**METELLUS CIMBER** Is there no voice worthier than mine, To appeal gently in great Caesar's ear For the recalling from banishment of my brother?
BRUTUS *(Kneeling)* I kiss thy hand, but not in flattery, Caesar, Desiring thee that Publius Cimber may Have an immediate freedom of repeal.	**BRUTUS** *(Kneeling)* I kiss your hand, but not to flatter you, Caesar, Asking you that Publius Cimber may Have immediate permission for his sentence of banishment to be overruled.
CAESAR What, Brutus?	**CAESAR** What, even you, Brutus?
CASSIUS *(Kneeling)* Pardon, Caesar; Caesar, pardon; As low as to thy foot doth Cassius fall, To beg enfranchisement for Publius Cimber.	**CASSIUS** *(Kneeling)* Pardon him, Caesar; Caesar, pardon him; I fall at your feet, To beg you to restore Publius Cimber to citizenship.
CAESAR I could be well moved, if I were as you; If I could pray to move, prayers would move me; But I am constant as the northern star, Of whose true-fix'd and resting quality There is no fellow in the firmament. The skies are painted with unnumber'd sparks,	**CAESAR** I could be persuaded to change my decision, if I were like you; If I were capable of begging other people to change their minds, then begging would change my mind too; But I am as unchanging as the pole star, Whose immovable and unchanging character Is unequalled in the sky. The skies are decorated with countless stars,

They are all fire and every one doth shine;

But there's but one in all doth hold his place.

So in the world: 'tis furnish'd well with men,
And men are flesh and blood, and apprehensive;
Yet in the number I do know but one
That unassailable holds on his rank,
Unshaked of motion; and that I am he,
Let me a little show it, even in this:
That I was constant Cimber should be banish'd,
And constant do remain to keep him so.

CINNA
(Kneeling) O Caesar -

CAESAR
Hence! Wilt thou lift up Olympus?

DECIUS BRUTUS
(Kneeling) Great Caesar –

CAESAR
Doth not Brutus bootless kneel?

CASCA
Speak hands for me!

CASCA first, then the other Conspirators and BRUTUS stab CAESAR

CAESAR
Et tu, Brute? - Then fall, Caesar!

CAESAR dies

CINNA
Liberty! Freedom! Tyranny is dead!
Run hence, proclaim, cry it about the streets.

CASSIUS
Some to the common pulpits, and cry out,

'Liberty, freedom, and enfranchisement!'

Confusion. Exit some citizens and Senators

BRUTUS
People and senators, be not affrighted.
Fly not; stand still; ambition's debt is paid.

CASCA
Go to the pulpit, Brutus.

They are all made of fire and every one of them shines;
But there is only one amongst them that retains its position.
It is the same on earth: the earth has many men,
And men are flesh and blood and capable of reason;
Yet, of all of them, I know only one
Who, invincible, retains his position,
Unshaken and unmoved; and as I am that one,
Let me demonstrate it a little, in this case:
I was resolute that Cimber should be banished,
And I remain resolute that he should be kept banished.

CINNA
(Kneeling) Oh Caesar -

CAESAR
Be gone! Would you try to lift Mount Olympus?

DECIUS BRUTUS
(Kneeling) Great Caesar -

CAESAR
Hasn't Brutus knelt before me, to no avail?

CASCA
Let the actions of my hands speak for me!

CASCA first, then the other Conspirators and BRUTUS stab CAESAR

CAESAR
And you too, Brutus? In that case, die, Caesar!

CAESAR dies

CINNA
Liberty! Freedom! Tyranny is dead!
Run and proclaim it, shouting it out loud in the streets.

CASSIUS
Some of you go to the rostra in the Forum and proclaim,
'Liberty, freedom, and democracy!'

Confusion. Exit some citizens and Senators

BRUTUS
People and senators, do not be afraid.
Do not run away; stand still; the debt that was due to Caesar's ambition has been paid.

CASCA
Go to the rostrum, Brutus.

DECIUS BRUTUS And Cassius too.	**DECIUS BRUTUS** And Cassius too.
BRUTUS Where's Publius?	**BRUTUS** Where is Publius?
CINNA Here, quite confounded with this mutiny.	**CINNA** Here, quite astonished by this mutiny.
METELLUS CIMBER Stand fast together, lest some friend of Caesar's Should chance -	**METELLUS CIMBER** Stand close together, in case a loyal friend of Caesar Should try -
BRUTUS Talk not of standing. Publius, good cheer; There is no harm intended to your person, Nor to no Roman else. So tell them, Publius.	**BRUTUS** Don't talk about organising resistance. Publius, cheer up; We do not intend to harm you, Nor any other Roman. Tell them this, Publius.
CASSIUS And leave us, Publius, lest that the people, Rushing on us, should do your age some mischief.	**CASSIUS** And leave us, Publius, in case the people, Rushing towards us, should cause you, as an old man, some harm.
BRUTUS Do so; and let no man abide this deed But we the doers.	**BRUTUS** Do so; and let no one pay the penalty for this deed Except us, the perpetrators.
Enter TREBONIUS	*Enter TREBONIUS*
CASSIUS Where is Antony?	**CASSIUS** Where is Antony?
TREBONIUS Fled to his house amazed. Men, wives, and children stare, cry out, and run, As it were doomsday.	**TREBONIUS** He ran to his house bewildered. Men, wives, and children are staring, crying out, and running, As if it were doomsday.
BRUTUS Fates, we will know your pleasures. That we shall die, we know; 'tis but the time And drawing days out, that men stand upon.	**BRUTUS** Fate, we will find out what your plans are for us. That we shall die, is certain; it's just the time we don't know And extending our life span is what men set great store by.
CASSIUS Why, he that cuts off twenty years of life Cuts off so many years of fearing death.	**CASSIUS** Well, the man who shortens his life by twenty years Cuts off that many years of fearing death.
BRUTUS Grant that, and then is death a benefit: So are we Caesar's friends, that have abridged His time of fearing death. Stoop, Romans, stoop, And let us bathe our hands in Caesar's blood Up to the elbows, and besmear our swords;	**BRUTUS** We agree on that, and so death is an advantage: So, we are Caesar's friends, who have shortened His time spent fearing death. Bend down, Romans, bend down, And let's wash our hands in Caesar's blood Up to our elbows, and smear it on our swords;

Then walk we forth, even to the market-place, And, waving our red weapons o'er our heads, Let's all cry, 'Peace, freedom, and liberty!'	Then we will walk out into the Roman Forum, And, waving our red weapons over our heads, Let's all shout, 'Peace, freedom, and liberty!'
CASSIUS Stoop then, and wash.	**CASSIUS** Bend down then, and wash.
The conspirators smear their hands and swords with Caesar's blood	*The conspirators smear their hands and swords with Caesar's blood*
How many ages hence Shall this our lofty scene be acted over, In states unborn, and accents yet unknown!	How many years from now Will this our noble scene be re-enacted, In countries that don't yet exist, and in languages not yet known!
BRUTUS How many times shall Caesar bleed in sport, That now on Pompey's basis lies along, No worthier than the dust!	**BRUTUS** How many times in the future shall Caesar be killed for entertainment in plays, He who now lies stretched out at the pedestal of Pompey's statue, Worth no more than dust!
CASSIUS So oft as that shall be, So often shall the knot of us be call'd The men that gave their country liberty.	**CASSIUS** As often as it is re-enacted, Our party of men who united in conspiracy will be hailed as The men who gave their country freedom.
DECIUS BRUTUS What, shall we forth?	**DECIUS BRUTUS** Well, shall we go out?
CASSIUS Ay, every man away. Brutus shall lead, and we will grace his heels With the most boldest and best hearts of Rome.	**CASSIUS** Yes, every man shall go forward. Brutus will lead, and we will do honour to him, following behind With the boldest and best hearts of Rome.
Enter Antony's servant	*Enter Antony's servant*
BRUTUS Soft, who comes here? A friend of Antony's.	**BRUTUS** Wait a moment, who's this coming? It is a friend of Antony's.
ANTONY'S SERVANT *(Kneeling)* Thus, Brutus, did my master bid me kneel; Thus did Mark Antony bid me fall down; And, being prostrate, thus he bade me say: Brutus is noble, wise, valiant, and honest; Caesar was mighty, bold, royal, and loving: Say I love Brutus, and I honour him; Say I fear'd Caesar, honour'd him and loved him. If Brutus will vouchsafe that Antony May safely come to him, and be resolved How Caesar hath deserved to lie in death, Mark Antony shall not love Caesar dead So well as Brutus living; but will follow	**ANTONY'S SERVANT** *(Kneeling)* Brutus, my master told me to kneel like this; Mark Antony told me to bow low like this; And he told me to lie prostrate like this and say: Brutus is noble, wise, brave and honest; Caesar was mighty, bold, royal and loving: Antony loves Brutus and honours him; Antony feared Caesar, honoured him and loved him. If Brutus will grant that Antony May come to him safely, and conclude That Caesar deserved to die, Mark Antony will love dead Caesar not nearly As much as living Brutus; but will follow

The fortunes and affairs of noble Brutus
Thorough the hazards of this untrod state,

With all true faith. So says my master Antony.

BRUTUS
Thy master is a wise and valiant Roman;
I never thought him worse.
Tell him, so please him come unto this place,
He shall be satisfied; and, by my honour,

Depart untouch'd.

ANTONY'S SERVANT
I'll fetch him presently.

Exit

BRUTUS
I know that we shall have him well to friend.

CASSIUS
I wish we may: but yet have I a mind
That fears him much; and my misgiving still
Falls shrewdly to the purpose.

Enter Antony

BRUTUS
But here comes Antony.
Welcome, Mark Antony.

ANTONY
O mighty Caesar! Dost thou lie so low?
Are all thy conquests, glories, triumphs, spoils

Shrunk to this little measure? Fare thee well.
I know not, gentlemen, what you intend,
Who else must be let blood, who else is rank:

If I myself, there is no hour so fit
As Caesar's death hour; nor no instrument
Of half that worth as those your swords, made rich
With the most noble blood of all this world.
I do beseech ye, if you bear me hard,
Now, whilst your purpled hands do reek and smoke,

Fulfil your pleasure. Live a thousand years,

I shall not find myself so apt to die;
No place will please me so, no mean of death,

As here by Caesar, and by you cut off,
The choice and master spirits of this age.

The fortunes and affairs of noble Brutus
Through the difficulties of this still unknown set of circumstances,
With all true faith. That is what my master Antony says.

BRUTUS
Your master is a wise and valiant Roman;
I have never thought of him any differently.
Tell him, if it should please him to come here,
He will be satisfied by my explanation; and, on my word,
He will leave unharmed.

ANTONY'S SERVANT
I'll go and get him at once.

Exit

BRUTUS
I know that we shall have him as a friend.

CASSIUS
I hope that we will: but I have a sense of foreboding
And fear him; and my reservations always
Turn out to be uncomfortably close to what happens.

Enter Antony

BRUTUS
But here comes Antony.
Welcome, Mark Antony.

ANTONY
Oh, mighty Caesar! Do you lie so low?
Have all your conquests, glories, triumphs, and plunder
Been reduced to this? Farewell.
I don't know, gentlemen, what you intend to do,
Who else must be put to death, who else you consider corrupt:
If it is me, there is no hour as fitting
As the hour of Caesar's death; nor no weapon
Worth even half as much as your swords, enriched
With the noblest blood in the whole world.
I beg you, if you have a grudge against me,
Then, now, whilst your hands are reddened with the smell of steaming blood,
Go ahead and kill me. If I should live a thousand years,
I would not find myself any readier to die;
No place would please me so much, no manner of dying more,
Than here beside Caesar, my life ended by you,
The chosen masters of this new era.

BRUTUS

O Antony, beg not your death of us.
Though now we must appear bloody and cruel,

As by our hands and this our present act
You see we do, yet see you but our hands

And this the bleeding business they have done.
Our hearts you see not; they are pitiful;

And pity to the general wrong of Rome-
As fire drives out fire, so pity, pity -
Hath done this deed on Caesar. For your part,

To you our swords have leaden points, Mark Antony;
Our arms in strength of malice, and our hearts

Of brothers' temper, do receive you in
With all kind love, good thoughts, and reverence.

CASSIUS

Your voice shall be as strong as any man's
In the disposing of new dignities.

BRUTUS

Only be patient till we have appeased
The multitude, beside themselves with fear,
And then we will deliver you the cause
Why I, that did love Caesar when I struck him,
Have thus proceeded.

ANTONY

I doubt not of your wisdom.
Let each man render me his bloody hand.
First, Marcus Brutus, will I shake with you;
Next, Caius Cassius, do I take your hand;
Now, Decius Brutus, yours; now yours, Metellus;
Yours, Cinna; and, my valiant Casca, yours;
Though last, not least in love, yours, good Trebonius.
Gentlemen all - alas, what shall I say?
My credit now stands on such slippery ground,

That one of two bad ways you must conceit me,
Either a coward, or a flatterer.
That I did love thee, Caesar, O, 'tis true!
If then thy spirit look upon us now,
Shall it not grieve thee dearer than thy death,

To see thy Antony making his peace,
Shaking the bloody fingers of thy foes,
Most noble, in the presence of thy corse?

Had I as many eyes as thou hast wounds,
Weeping as fast as they stream forth thy blood,

BRUTUS

Oh Antony, do not beg us to kill you.
Although now we must appear to you to be bloody and cruel,
Because of our hands and the deed
You see we have just done, you are seeing only our hands
And the bloody business they have carried out.
You don't see our hearts; they are full of pity for Caesar;
But pity for the wrongs committed against Rome –
Just as fire drives out fire, so pity for Rome has driven out our pity for Caesar –
And led us to kill him. But for you,
Our swords have dull, blunt blades, Mark Antony;

Our arms, whose strength appears cruel, and our hearts
Full of brotherly love, embrace you
With only kind love, good thoughts, and reverence.

CASSIUS

Your vote will be as strong as any man's
In the assembling of a new government.

BRUTUS

Just be patient until we have calmed down
The crowd, who are beside themselves with fear,
And then we will explain to you the reason
Why I, who loved Caesar, even as I stabbed him,
Have taken this course of action.

ANTONY

I do not doubt your wisdom.
Each one of you men, give me your bloody hand.
First, Marcus Brutus, I will shake your hand;
Next, Caius Cassius, I take your hand;
Now, Decius Brutus, yours; now yours, Metellus;
Yours, Cinna; and, my courageous Casca, yours;
Last but not least, yours, good Trebonius.
All of you are gentleman – alas, what can I say?
My credibility is now standing on such slippery ground,
That you must judge me in one of two bad ways,
As either a coward, or a flatterer.
Oh, it is true that I did love you, Caesar!
If your spirit is looking down on us now,
It must cause you even more anguish than your death,
To see your Antony making his peace,
Shaking the bloody hands of your enemies,
Most honourable, in the presence of your dead body?

If I had as many eyes as you have wounds,
Weeping as fast as your wounds stream with your blood,

It would become me better than to close	It would be more fitting than it would be for me to arrive at an agreement
In terms of friendship with thine enemies.	In terms of friendship with your enemies.
Pardon me, Julius! Here wast thou bay'd, brave hart;	Forgive me, Julius! At this place you were hunted down, brave deer;
Here didst thou fall; and here thy hunters stand,	It is here that you fell; and it is here that your hunters are standing,
Sign'd in thy spoil, and crimson'd in thy lethe.	Bearing the evidence of your slaughter, and reddened with your life-blood.
O world, thou wast the forest to this hart;	Oh world, you were the forest to this deer;
And this indeed, O world, the heart of thee.	And indeed, this deer, oh world, was your dear.
How like a deer, strucken by many princes,	How you look like a deer who has been stabbed by many princes,
Dost thou here lie!	Lying here!
CASSIUS	**CASSIUS**
Mark Antony –	Mark Antony –
ANTONY	**ANTONY**
Pardon me, Caius Cassius;	Forgive me, Caius Cassius;
The enemies of Caesar shall say this;	Even the enemies of Caesar would say this;
Then, in a friend, it is cold modesty.	So, from a friend, it is merely common decency.
CASSIUS	**CASSIUS**
I blame you not for praising Caesar so;	I do not blame you for praising Caesar like that;
But what compact mean you to have with us?	But what agreement do you intend to have with us?
Will you be prick'd in number of our friends,	Will you be numbered as one of our friends,
Or shall we on, and not depend on you?	Or shall we proceed, and not depend on you?
ANTONY	**ANTONY**
Therefore I took your hands, but was indeed	I shook you all by the hand, but was indeed
Sway'd from the point by looking down on Caesar.	Distracted from what I was doing when I looked down at Caesar.
Friends am I with you all, and love you all,	I am friends with you all, and I love you all,
Upon this hope, that you shall give me reasons	On condition that you will give me reasons
Why, and wherein, Caesar was dangerous.	Why, and in what respect, you considered Caesar to be dangerous.
BRUTUS	**BRUTUS**
Or else were this a savage spectacle.	Without those reasons this would have been a savage sight.
Our reasons are so full of good regard,	Our reasons are so full of sound considerations,
That were you, Antony, the son of Caesar,	That even if you, Antony, were the son of Caesar,
You should be satisfied.	You would be satisfied with them.
ANTONY	**ANTONY**
That's all I seek,	That is all I ask,
And am moreover suitor that I may	And I am furthermore asking that I may
Produce his body to the market-place,	Take his body to the market-place,
And in the pulpit, as becomes a friend,	And in the rostrum in the Forum, as befits a friend,
Speak in the order of his funeral.	Speak in the ceremonies arranged for his funeral.
BRUTUS	**BRUTUS**
You shall, Mark Antony.	You may, Mark Antony.
CASSIUS	**CASSIUS**
Brutus, a word with you.	Brutus, may I have a word with you.

(Aside to BRUTUS) You know not what you do; do not consent That Antony speak in his funeral. Know you how much the people may be moved By that which he will utter?	*(Aside to BRUTUS)* You don't know what you are doing; do not allow Antony to speak at his funeral. Do you realise how much the people could be influenced By the things that he will say?
BRUTUS *(Aside to Cassius)* By your pardon: I will myself into the pulpit first, And show the reason of our Caesar's death. What Antony shall speak, I will protest He speaks by leave and by permission; And that we are contented Caesar shall Have all true rites and lawful ceremonies, It shall advantage more than do us wrong.	**BRUTUS** *(Aside to Cassius)* With your permission: I will go to the rostrum first, And explain the reason for our Caesar's death. Whatever Antony says, I will proclaim That he is speaking with our permission; And that we are satisfied that Caesar should Have all proper tradition and lawful ceremonies, Will be more to our advantage than to our detriment.
CASSIUS *(Aside to BRUTUS)* I know not what may fall; I like it not.	**CASSIUS** *(Aside to BRUTUS)* I don't know what might happen; I do not like it.
BRUTUS Mark Antony, here take you Caesar's body. You shall not in your funeral speech blame us, But speak all good you can devise of Caesar, And say you do't by our permission; Else shall you not have any hand at all About his funeral. And you shall speak In the same pulpit whereto I am going, After my speech is ended.	**BRUTUS** Mark Antony, you take Caesar's body. You must not blame us in your funeral speech, But can say all the good you can think of about Caesar, And tell them that you do so with our permission; Otherwise, you will not have any role at all In his funeral. And you will speak At the same rostrum as I do, After I have finished my speech.
ANTONY Be it so; I do desire no more.	**ANTONY** May it be so; That is all I wish for.
BRUTUS Prepare the body, then, and follow us.	**BRUTUS** Prepare the body, then, and follow us.
Exeunt all but ANTONY	*Exeunt everyone except ANTONY*
ANTONY O, pardon me, thou bleeding piece of earth, That I am meek and gentle with these butchers. Thou art the ruins of the noblest man That ever lived in the tide of times. Woe to the hand that shed this costly blood! Over thy wounds now do I prophesy - Which like dumb mouths do ope their ruby lips, To beg the voice and utterance of my tongue - A curse shall light upon the limbs of men; Domestic fury and fierce civil strife Shall cumber all the parts of Italy; Blood and destruction shall be so in use, And dreadful objects so familiar,	**ANTONY** Oh, forgive me, you bleeding corpse, For being meek and gentle towards these butchers. You are the remains of the noblest man That ever lived in the course of history. Woe to the hand that shed this precious blood! Over your wounds I prophesy – Wounds which like speechless mouths open their red lips, To beg me to use my tongue and voice to speak – A curse will fall upon the lives of men; Domestic curses and fierce civil war Shall burden all of Italy; Blood and destruction will be so common, And dreadful things so familiar,

That mothers shall but smile when they behold
Their infants quarter'd with the hands of war,
All pity choked with custom of fell deeds;

And Caesar's spirit, ranging for revenge,
With Ate by his side, come hot from hell,

Shall in these confines with a monarch's voice
Cry havoc and let slip the dogs of war,
That this foul deed shall smell above the earth
With carrion men, groaning for burial.

Enter a Servant

You serve Octavius Caesar, do you not?

SERVANT
I do, Mark Antony.

ANTONY
Caesar did write for him to come to Rome.

SERVANT
He did receive his letters, and is coming,
And bid me say to you by word of mouth – *(Sees Caesar's body)*
O Caesar!

ANTONY
Thy heart is big; get thee apart and weep.

Passion, I see, is catching, for mine eyes,
Seeing those beads of sorrow stand in thine,
Began to water. Is thy master coming?

SERVANT
He lies to-night within seven leagues of Rome.

ANTONY
Post back with speed, and tell him what hath chanced.
Here is a mourning Rome, a dangerous Rome,
No Rome of safety for Octavius yet.
Hie hence, and tell him so. Yet stay awhile;
Thou shalt not back till I have borne this corse
Into the market-place; there shall I try,
In my oration, how the people take
The cruel issue of these bloody men;
According to the which, thou shalt discourse

To young Octavius of the state of things.
Lend me your hand.

Exeunt with CAESAR's body

That mothers will merely smile when they witness
Their children hacked to pieces by the hands of war,
All sympathy squeezed out of them because of the commonness of cruel actions;
And Caesar's ghost, searching for revenge,
With the goddess Ate by his side, come straight from hell,
Shall in these regions, with a king's voice
Cry havoc and unleash the dogs of war,
So that this foul deed will stink to the heavens
With rotting men, groaning to be buried.

Enter a Servant

You serve Octavius Caesar, don't you?

SERVANT
I do, Mark Antony.

ANTONY
Caesar wrote, asking him to come to Rome.

SERVANT
He received his letters, and he is coming,
And he asked me to tell you this message – *(Sees Caesar's body)*
Oh, Caesar!

ANTONY
Your heart is big with sorrow; take yourself aside and weep.
Sorrow, I see, is contagious, because my eyes,
Seeing those tears in your eyes,
Began to overflow. Is your master coming?

SERVANT
He is lodging tonight within twenty-one miles of Rome.

ANTONY
Report back to him quickly, and tell him what has happened.
Rome is now a mourning Rome, a dangerous Rome,
Not a Rome of safety for Octavius yet.
Away with you, and tell him so. But stay a while;
Don't leave until I have carried this corpse
Into the marketplace; There I shall test,
Through my speech, how the people react
To the cruel actions of these bloody men;
You shall communicate the result of my experiment accordingly
To young Octavius.
Help me, please.

Exeunt with CAESAR's body

Part 18: Analysing Act 3 Scene 1

At the very beginning of the scene, the importance of fate is stated once again: Caesar tells the soothsayer 'The ides of March are come', implying the soothsayer's prophesy is wrong because Caesar is still alive. The warning tone in the response 'Ay, Caesar, but not gone' reminds the audience of fate's all powerful influence and hence Caesar's mortality.

Not only fate, but also the theme of a person's public self in relation to their private life makes a very early re-appearance. Caesar refuses to read Artemidorus's warning letter, saying 'What touches us ourself shall be last served'. In other words, anything to do with his private life is of the lowest priority, as his duties to the public come first. His use of 'us ourself' links to the royal 'we' or majestic plural, which is the first-person plural. By using the royal 'we' in a public situation, Caesar is creating the impression that he is speaking in the official capacity of a great leader. This suggests that he has so much confidence in his public self that he believes he cannot be harmed.

A few lines later, Shakespeare creates further tension when Popilius wishes the conspirators luck ('I wish your enterprise to-day may thrive'). A private secret appears to be in the public domain, and the audience members are inevitably caught up in the increasing suspense.

The tension mounts further when Metellus Cimber makes a public request about a personal matter: the repeal of his brother's banishment. The co-conspirators appear to be within touching distance of Caesar (Brutus says 'I kiss thy hand' and Cassius says 'As low as to thy foot doth Cassius fall'), evidence that the assassins are closing in for the kill. The request is a cover to get close enough to stab Caesar and to keep away those who might help him.

Caesar's formal response to Cimber's request creates dramatic irony when he uses celestial imagery to describe himself with the simile of the North Star. He states that he is as:

> ... constant as the northern star,
> Of whose true-fix'd and resting quality
> There is no fellow in the firmament.

The North Star, says Caesar, is 'constant', and the comparison implies that his own views are resolute and firm. Two further points of comparison are suggested: the North Star was used to guide ships, as Caesar suggests he now guides his people; and, says Caesar, it has 'no fellow' in the heavens, implying he himself has no equal. This brief speech confirms the conspirators in the rightness of their course of action. One further dramatic irony is that, although Caesar may see himself as all-powerful, decisive and of singular importance, the audience knows he will shortly be brought back down to earth in the most brutal and literal fashion.

Caesar's use of star imagery alienates him from the other characters, as his arrogance makes him less likeable. Like a star, he is cold and distant, and the audience takes a step back to judge him. However, the audience also understands now that Brutus's logic is flawed because he bases his decision to kill Caesar on the premise that Caesar will change upon coming to power, comparing him to a 'serpent's egg/Which, hatch'd, would, as his kind, grow mischievous, /And kill him in the shell' (Act 2, Scene 1). Caesar's bragging about constancy contradicts this premise and proves that Brutus is wrong.

The North Star speech, brief though it is, suggests Caesar may well believe in his own divinity. We have more irony because four months after he was assassinated, the Great Comet of 44 BC, shone for seven days and nights. The Romans believed that it was Caesar's soul en route to the heavens, so they deified him and gave him the title 'The Divine Julius' in 42 BC. Caesar's North Star imagery therefore foreshadows this.

A few lines later, Caesar describes himself as 'Olympus' i.e. Mount Olympus. Like an immovable mountain, Caesar cannot be persuaded to change his mind. Mount Olympus is the highest mountain in Greece, so it is an effective metaphor for his social status. In addition, it is reputed to be the home of the Greek gods, so we have more imagery associated with his belief in his own deity and the holiness of his words; this anticipates his imminent death and subsequent deification.

Freytag's Pyramid

Since the **inciting incident** of Brutus's decision to join the conspiracy, we have seen the play become more exciting as conflicts have built with the **rising action**:

- Act 2, Scene 2. Calpurnia's dream and subsequent attempts to persuade Caesar to stay at home. His agreement and then change of mind.
- Act 2, Scene 3. Artemidorus's decision to warn Caesar of the conspiracy.
- Act 2, Scene 4. Portia's anxiety and hysteria.
- Act 3, Scene 1. Caesar's refusal to read Artemidorus 's letter
- Act 3, Scene 1. The ambiguity of Popilius wishing the conspirators luck
- Act 3, Scene 1. Metellus Cimber's request for repeal of his brother's banishment and the conspirators closing in for the kill.

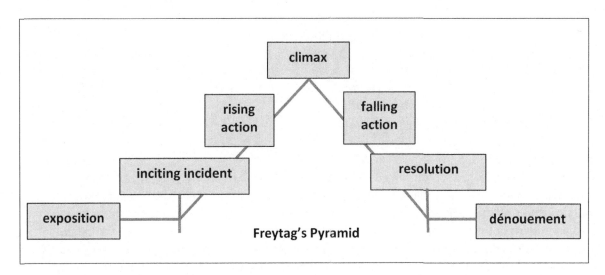

Freytag's Pyramid

The next part of this scene is the **climax** in which the conspirators murder Caesar. This draws the attention of the audience to the themes of love, friendship, politics and morals when Caesar realises that Brutus has betrayed him. According to the Greek biographer Plutarch, Caesar stopped defending himself when he saw Brutus and realised the extent of his betrayal. Plutarch gave Caesar his final words 'Et tu, Brute?' (*And you, Brutus?*), which Shakespeare keeps. The Latin phrase illustrates Caesar's heartbreak about being betrayed by his friend. Shakespeare probably decided to keep the Latin expression because even then, it was famous so the audience would have enjoyed anticipating it.

After the climax of Caesar's assassination begins the **falling action** of its aftermath. We begin with imagery from the world of the theatre when Cassius states 'How many ages hence/Shall this our lofty scene be acted over, /In states unborn, and accents yet unknown!', suggesting that the assassination will be performed by future generations time and time again. The adjective 'lofty' implies that future audiences will feel awe at this moment of murder. The repetition of adjectives with the prefix -un with 'states unborn' and 'accents yet unknown' underlines his conviction that this story will be told in countries yet undiscovered and performed in languages yet unknown. Of course, the audience will understand that this play itself is one of those enactments. A compelling dramatic irony will be that Cassius will not be the hero of the story.

Rather than feeling awe, it is more likely that the audience will be repelled by the murder, as it sees that Calpurnia's dream about the fountain spurting blood and people washing their hands in it has come true. The conspirators' decision to 'wash' in Caesar's blood is a macabre and repulsive image. Proposed by Caesar's erstwhile best friend Brutus, it is even more revolting. The assassins transform themselves into bloody-handed red devils, suggesting that they have cast off their humanity. Cassius's earlier use of stage imagery therefore creates dramatic irony as, instead of feeling awe at this momentous event in history, the audience is revolted.

The motif of blood soaks through the scene when Antony asks to shake the 'bloody hand' of each of the conspirators. This is a symbolic act in which he appears to align himself with them, but there is another layer to the symbolism: he is marking each man for his later revenge. The adjective 'bloody' focuses the attention of the audience on the hands that committed the act of murder. The transference of Caesar's blood from the assassins to Antony is also like war paint, signifying his intention to avenge Caesar's murder.

Antony is distracted by the sight of Caesar's bleeding corpse and in front of the conspirators veers dangerously off message. He declares:

> Pardon me, Julius! Here wast thou bay'd, brave hart;
> Here didst thou fall; and here thy hunters stand,
> Sign'd in thy spoil, and crimson'd in thy lethe.
> O world, thou wast the forest to this hart;
> And this indeed, O world, the heart of thee.
> How like a deer, strucken by many princes,
> Dost thou here lie!

Hunting imagery

The colour crimson is most commonly used as an adjective or a noun. By using it as a verb, Shakespeare is focusing the audience's attention on the act of murder and the imagery of the assassins covering themselves in his lifeblood. The hunting imagery also positions Caesar as a victim, emphasising his betrayal at the hands of his friends. There is a pun with 'hart', a deer, and *heart* which suggests Antony's love. This also reminds the audience of the animal that was sacrificed and had no heart—we see that the hart/heart is now lying dead in front of them. Finally, the repetition of 'here' implies that Antony is marking the spot, fixing the place that Caesar was murdered in his heart for his later revenge.

The theme of love and friendship continues when Antony requests permission to speak over Caesar's body at his funeral 'as becomes a friend'. This is an ambiguous phrase, as Brutus believes that Antony will be a grieving friend whilst still supporting the assassination. But Cassius is suspicious of Antony's motives. This moment in the play reveals the relative political acumen of Cassius and Brutus, and the differences in their ability to understand Antony:

CASSIUS

Know you how much the people may be moved
By that which he will utter?

Alliteration emphasises much mistrust and cynicism.

BRUTUS

(Aside to Cassius) By your pardon:
I will myself into the pulpit first,
And show the reason of our Caesar's

Logical, rational response. Because he is logical, he mistakenly believes that everyone else will listen to reason.

We associate Cassius with envy, suspicion and distrust—in short, he is ruled by his emotions. Brutus, on the other hand, uses reason not emotion, so the idea of Antony's friendship with Caesar fuelling his desire for an avenging funeral oration is alien to him. Brutus allows Antony to speak because he is confident that the Roman citizens will respect Brutus's sacrifice of the life of his friend for the greater public good—their good. We must remember that his reasoning is based on flawed evidence: his original decision to join the conspirators was confirmed by a forged letter, so he misjudges the reception that the crowd will give Antony's speech. Brutus, unlike Cassius, completely underestimates Antony's oratorical skills. His decision to allow Antony to speak signals the beginning of the end for the conspirators.

Antony's soliloquy at the end of this scene proves that Cassius's suspicions are founded. It reminds the audience of the power of rhetoric and the fickleness of the crowd that we saw in Act 1, Scene 1. Without a ruler or government, it is 'a dangerous Rome', Antony observes, and there is likely to be civil unrest. As mentioned earlier, this parallels contemporary anxieties about the consequences of Queen Elizabeth I dying without naming an heir. It is at this moment in the play that the theatre audience anticipates with excitement Antony's opportunity to manipulate public opinion through the power of oration.

Part 19: Translating Act 3 Scene 2

ORIGINAL TEXT	MODERN TRANSLATION
The Forum.	**The Forum.**
Enter BRUTUS and CASSIUS, and a throng of Citizens	*Enter BRUTUS and CASSIUS, and a throng of Citizens*
CITIZENS We will be satisfied: let us be satisfied.	**CITIZENS** We demand a satisfactory explanation: Give us an explanation.
BRUTUS Then follow me, and give me audience, friends. Cassius, go you into the other street, And part the numbers. Those that will hear me speak, let 'em stay here; Those that will follow Cassius, go with him; And public reasons shall be rendered Of Caesar's death.	**BRUTUS** Then follow me, and give me a hearing, friends. Cassius, you go into the other street, And divide the crowd. Those who want to hear me speak, let them stay here; Those who want to hear Cassius, go with him; And, in public, reasons shall be given For Caesar's death.
FIRST CITIZEN I will hear Brutus speak.	**FIRST CITIZEN** I want to hear Brutus speak.
SECOND CITIZEN I will hear Cassius, and compare their reasons, When severally we hear them rendered.	**SECOND CITIZEN** I want to hear Cassius, and we will compare their reasons, When we have heard them given separately.
Exit CASSIUS, with some of the Citizens. BRUTUS goes into the pulpit.	*Exit CASSIUS, with some of the Citizens. BRUTUS goes into the pulpit.*
THIRD CITIZEN The noble Brutus is ascended. Silence!	**THIRD CITIZEN** Noble Brutus has gone up to the rostrum. Silence!
BRUTUS Be patient till the last. Romans, countrymen, and lovers, hear me for my cause, and be silent, that you may hear. Believe me for mine honour, and have respect to mine honour, that you may believe. Censure me in your wisdom, and awake your senses, that you may the better judge. If there be any in this assembly, any dear friend of Caesar's, to him I say that Brutus' love to Caesar was no less than his. If then that friend demand why Brutus rose against Caesar, this is my answer: not that I loved Caesar less, but that I loved Rome more. Had you rather Caesar were living, and die all slaves, than that Caesar were dead, to live all free men? As Caesar loved me, I weep for him; as he was fortunate, I rejoice at it; as he was valiant, I honour him; but, as he was ambitious, I slew him. There is tears for his love; joy for his fortune; honour for his valour; and death for his ambition. Who is here so	**BRUTUS** Be patient until the end of my address. Romans, countrymen, and dear friends, listen to me for my reasons, and be silent, so that you can hear. Believe in my integrity, and accept me as an honourable man, so you may believe me. Judge me in your wisdom, and be alert in your reasoning, so that you can judge me fairly. If there is anyone in this assembly, any dear friend of Caesar's, I would say to him that my love for Caesar was no less than his. If then, that friend demands to know why I, Brutus, rose up against Caesar, this is my reply: it is not that I loved Caesar less, but that I loved Rome more. Would you rather that Caesar were alive, and we all die as slaves, or that Caesar were dead, and we all live as free men? As Caesar was a dear friend to me, I mourn him; as he had good fortune, I rejoice in it; as he was courageous, I honour him; but, as he was ambitious, I killed him. There are tears for his love; joy for his fortune; honour for his

base that would be a bondman? If any, speak; for him have I offended. Who is here so rude that would not be a Roman? If any, speak; for him have I offended. Who is here so vile that will not love his country? If any, speak; for him have I offended. I pause for a reply.

ALL
None, Brutus, none.

BRUTUS
Then none have I offended. I have done no more to Caesar than you shall do to Brutus. The question of his death is enrolled in the Capitol; his glory not extenuated, wherein he was worthy; nor his offences enforced, for which he suffered death.

Enter ANTONY and others, with CAESAR's body.

Here comes his body, mourned by Mark Antony, who, though he had no hand in his death, shall receive the benefit of his dying, a place in the commonwealth, as which of you shall not? With this I depart, that, as I slew my best lover for the good of Rome, I have the same dagger for myself, when it shall please my country to need my death.

ALL
Live, Brutus! Live! Live!

FIRST CITIZEN
Bring him with triumph home unto his house.

SECOND CITIZEN
Give him a statue with his ancestors.

THIRD CITIZEN
Let him be Caesar.

FOURTH CITIZEN
Caesar's better parts
Shall be crown'd in Brutus.

FIRST CITIZEN
We'll bring him to his house with shouts and clamours.

BRUTUS
My countrymen -

SECOND CITIZEN
Peace! Silence! Brutus speaks.

---

courage; and death for his ambition. Who here is so low that he wants to be a slave? If there are any, speak; because it is he whom I have offended. Who here is so barbarous that he doesn't want to be a Roman? If there are any, speak; because it is he whom I have offended. Who here is so vile that he doesn't love his country? If there are any, speak; because it is he whom I have offended. I am pausing for a reply.

ALL
No one, Brutus, no one.

BRUTUS
Then I have not offended anyone. I have done no more to Caesar than you will do to me. The considerations which led to his death are recorded in the archives in the Capitol; his greatness has not been devalued, where he earned it; nor have his offences, for which he was killed, been unduly stressed.

Enter ANTONY and others, with CAESAR's body.

Here comes his body, mourned by Mark Antony, who, though he played no part in killing him, shall receive the benefit of his death, a position in the commonwealth, as you all will. With these words I depart, that in the same way that I killed my best friend for the good of Rome, I have the same dagger to kill myself, if my country requires my death.

ALL
Live, Brutus! Live! Live!

FIRST CITIZEN
Bring him triumphantly home to his house!

SECOND CITIZEN
Let's put a statue of him with those of his ancestors.

THIRD CITIZEN
Let him become Caesar.

FOURTH CITIZEN
Caesar's best qualities
Are evident in Brutus and so we will crown him.

FIRST CITIZEN
We'll bring him to his house with shouts and loud voices.

BRUTUS
My countrymen –

SECOND CITIZEN
Be quiet! Be silent! Brutus is speaking.

FIRST CITIZEN
Peace, ho!

BRUTUS
Good countrymen, let me depart alone,
And, for my sake, stay here with Antony.
Do grace to Caesar's corpse, and grace his speech

Tending to Caesar's glories, which Mark Antony,
By our permission, is allow'd to make.
I do entreat you, not a man depart,
Save I alone, till Antony have spoke.

Exit

FIRST CITIZEN
Stay, ho! and let us hear Mark Antony.

THIRD CITIZEN
Let him go up into the public chair;
We'll hear him. Noble Antony, go up.

ANTONY
For Brutus' sake, I am beholding to you.

Goes into the pulpit

FOURTH CITIZEN
What does he say of Brutus?

THIRD CITIZEN
He says, for Brutus' sake
He finds himself beholding to us all.

FOURTH CITIZEN
'Twere best he speak no harm of Brutus here!

FIRST CITIZEN
This Caesar was a tyrant.

THIRD CITIZEN
Nay, that's certain.
We are blest that Rome is rid of him.

SECOND CITIZEN
Peace! Let us hear what Antony can say.

ANTONY
You gentle Romans –

CITIZENS
Peace, ho! Let us hear him.

FIRST CITIZEN
Be quiet, over there!

BRUTUS
Good countrymen, let me leave alone,
And, for my sake, stay here with Antony.
Show due respect to Caesar's body, and listen with
courtesy to Antony's speech
Relating to Caesar's glories, which Mark Antony,
Is allowed to make, with our permission.
I request that no one leaves,
Except myself, until Antony has finished speaking.

Exit

FIRST CITIZEN
Let us stay and listen to Mark Antony.

THIRD CITIZEN
Let him go up into the pulpit for speeches;
We shall listen to him. Noble Antony, go up into the
rostrum.

ANTONY
In Brutus' name, I am indebted to you.

Goes into the rostrum.

FOURTH CITIZEN
What is he saying about Brutus?

THIRD CITIZEN
He is saying that for Brutus' sake
He finds himself indebted to us all.

FOURTH CITIZEN
He had better not say anything bad about Brutus
here!

FIRST CITIZEN
Caesar was a tyrant.

THIRD CITIZEN
That's definitely true.
We are fortunate that Rome is rid of him.

SECOND CITIZEN
Be quiet! Let's hear what Antony has to say.

ANTONY
Noble Romans –

CITIZENS
Everyone be quiet! Let's listen to him.

ANTONY

Friends, Romans, countrymen, lend me your ears;

I come to bury Caesar, not to praise him.
The evil that men do lives after them,
The good is oft interred with their bones;
So let it be with Caesar. The noble Brutus
Hath told you Caesar was ambitious.
If it were so, it was a grievous fault,
And grievously hath Caesar answer'd it.
Here, under leave of Brutus and the rest -
For Brutus is an honourable man;
So are they all, all honourable men -
Come I to speak in Caesar's funeral.
He was my friend, faithful and just to me;
But Brutus says he was ambitious,
And Brutus is an honourable man.
He hath brought many captives home to Rome,
Whose ransoms did the general coffers fill:
Did this in Caesar seem ambitious?
When that the poor have cried, Caesar hath wept;
Ambition should be made of sterner stuff:

Yet Brutus says he was ambitious,
And Brutus is an honourable man.
You all did see that on the Lupercal
I thrice presented him a kingly crown,
Which he did thrice refuse. Was this ambition?

Yet Brutus says he was ambitious,
And sure he is an honourable man.

I speak not to disprove what Brutus spoke,
But here I am to speak what I do know.
You all did love him once, not without cause;
What cause withholds you then to mourn for him?

O judgment! Thou art fled to brutish beasts,
And men have lost their reason. Bear with me;

My heart is in the coffin there with Caesar,
And I must pause till it come back to me. *(He weeps)*

FIRST CITIZEN
Methinks there is much reason in his sayings.

SECOND CITIZEN
If thou consider rightly of the matter,
Caesar has had great wrong.

THIRD CITIZEN
Has he, masters?
I fear there will a worse come in his place.

ANTONY

Friends, Romans, countrymen, give me your attention;

I have come here to bury Caesar, not to praise him.
The evil that men do is remembered after they die,
The good that men do is often buried with them;
Let it be so with Caesar. The noble Brutus
Has told you that Caesar was ambitious.
If that was true, it was a severe fault,
And Caesar has paid a severe price for it.
With the permission of Brutus and all the others –
Because Brutus is an honourable man;
They are all honourable men –
I have come to speak at Caesar's funeral.
He was my friend, faithful and just to me;
But Brutus says he was ambitious,
And Brutus is an honourable man.
He brought many captives home to Rome,
Whose ransoms brought wealth to our city:
Did this make Caesar appear ambitious?
When the poor cried, Caesar wept too;
Someone who's ambitious should be made of sterner stuff:

Yet Brutus says he was ambitious,
And Brutus is an honourable man.
You all saw that on the Lupercal feast day
I presented him with a king's crown three times,
And, three times he refused it. Was that an ambitious man?

Yet Brutus says he was ambitious,
And I do not question that Brutus is an honourable man.
I am not speaking to disprove what Brutus has said,
But I am here to speak of what I know.
You all loved him once, and not without reason;
Then what is the reason that is holding you back from mourning for him?

Oh, common sense! You have fled to brutish beasts,
And men have lost all rational thought. Bear with me;

My heart is in the coffin there with Caesar,
And I need to pause until it returns to me. *(He weeps)*

FIRST CITIZEN
I think there is a lot of sense in what he is saying.

SECOND CITIZEN
If you think carefully about it,
Caesar has been greatly wronged.

THIRD CITIZEN
Has he, gentlemen?
I am worried that there will be someone worse replacing him.

FOURTH CITIZEN Mark'd ye his words? He would not take the crown; Therefore 'tis certain he was not ambitious.	**FOURTH CITIZEN** Did you pay attention to what Antony said? Caesar refused the crown; So, he definitely was not ambitious.
FIRST CITIZEN If it be found so, some will dear abide it.	**FIRST CITIZEN** If that turns out to be the case, someone will dearly pay the penalty for it.
SECOND CITIZEN Poor soul! His eyes are red as fire with weeping.	**SECOND CITIZEN** Poor soul! Antony's eyes are as red as fire from weeping.
THIRD CITIZEN There's not a nobler man in Rome than Antony.	**THIRD CITIZEN** There is not a nobler man in all of Rome than Antony.
FOURTH CITIZEN Now mark him; he begins again to speak.	**FOURTH CITIZEN** Now listen to him; he's starting to speak again.
ANTONY But yesterday the word of Caesar might Have stood against the world; now lies he there, And none so poor to do him reverence. O masters! If I were disposed to stir Your hearts and minds to mutiny and rage, I should do Brutus wrong, and Cassius wrong, Who, you all know, are honourable men. I will not do them wrong; I rather choose To wrong the dead, to wrong myself and you, Than I will wrong such honourable men. But here's a parchment with the seal of Caesar; I found it in his closet; 'tis his will. Let but the commons hear this testament, Which, pardon me, I do not mean to read, And they would go and kiss dead Caesar's wounds, And dip their napkins in his sacred blood, Yea, beg a hair of him for memory, And, dying, mention it within their wills, Bequeathing it as a rich legacy Unto their issue.	**ANTONY** Only yesterday the word of Caesar might Have stood against the world; now he is lying there, And the lowest member of society is too high to pay his respects to Caesar. Oh gentlemen! If I were inclined to provoke Your hearts and minds to riot and rage, I would offend Brutus and Cassius, Who, as you all know, are honourable men. I will not offend them; I would prefer To offend the dead, to offend myself and you, Than to offend such honourable men. But here's a paper with Caesar's seal on it; I found it in his study; it is his will. If only the ordinary people could hear this testament, Which, forgive me, I do not intend to read aloud, They would go and kiss dead Caesar's wounds, And dip their handkerchiefs in his sacred blood, And beg for a lock of his hair to remember him by, And, when they died, they'd mention these items in their wills, Bequeathing them as a rich legacy To their offspring.
FOURTH CITIZEN We'll hear the will. Read it, Mark Antony.	**FOURTH CITIZEN** We want to hear the will. Read it, Mark Antony.
ALL The will, the will! We will hear Caesar's will!	**ALL** The will, the will! We want to hear Caesar's will!
ANTONY Have patience, gentle friends; I must not read it. It is not meet you know how Caesar loved you. You are not wood, you are not stones, but men; And being men, hearing the will of Caesar,	**ANTONY** Be patient, noble friends; I cannot read it. It is not fitting that you should know how much Caesar loved you. You are not wood, you are not stones, you are men; And because you are men, if you hear Caesar's will,

It will inflame you, it will make you mad. 'Tis good you know not that you are his heirs; For if you should, O, what would come of it?	It will enrage you, and make you distraught. It's a good thing that you don't know you are his heirs; Because if you did know, oh, what would come of it?
FOURTH CITIZEN Read the will! We'll hear it, Antony! You shall read us the will, Caesar's will!	**FOURTH CITIZEN** Read the will! We want to hear it, Antony! You must read us the will, Caesar's will!
ANTONY Will you be patient? Will you stay awhile? I have o'ershot myself to tell you of it. I fear I wrong the honourable men Whose daggers have stabb'd Caesar; I do fear it.	**ANTONY** Will you be patient? Will you wait a while? I have said more than I intended by telling you about it. I'm afraid I am wronging the honourable men Whose daggers have stabbed Caesar; I am afraid of that.
FOURTH CITIZEN They were traitors. Honourable men!	**FOURTH CITIZEN** They were traitors. Honourable men!
ALL The will! The testament!	**ALL** The will! The testament!
SECOND CITIZEN They were villains, murderers! The will! Read the will!	**SECOND CITIZEN** They were villains, murderers! The will! Read the will!
ANTONY You will compel me then to read the will? Then make a ring about the corpse of Caesar, And let me show you him that made the will. Shall I descend? And will you give me leave?	**ANTONY** You are forcing me to read the will, then? Then form a circle around Caesar's body, And allow me to show you the man who wrote this will. Shall I come down? And will you give me your permission?
SEVERAL CITIZENS Come down.	**SEVERAL CITIZENS** Come down.
SECOND CITIZEN Descend.	**SECOND CITIZEN** Descend.
THIRD CITIZEN You shall have leave.	**THIRD CITIZEN** You have permission.
ANTONY comes down	*ANTONY comes down from the rostrum*
FOURTH CITIZEN A ring! Stand round.	**FOURTH CITIZEN** Form a circle! Stand around him.
FIRST CITIZEN Stand from the hearse! Stand from the body!	**FIRST CITIZEN** Stand away from the hearse! Stand away from the body!
SECOND CITIZEN Room for Antony, most noble Antony!	**SECOND CITIZEN** Make room for Antony, most noble Antony!

ANTONY
Nay, press not so upon me; stand far off.

SEVERAL CITIZENS
Stand back! Room! Bear back!

ANTONY
If you have tears, prepare to shed them now.
You all do know this mantle. I remember
The first time ever Caesar put it on;
'Twas on a summer's evening in his tent,
That day he overcame the Nervii.
Look, in this place ran Cassius' dagger through;

See what a rent the envious Casca made;
Through this, the well-beloved Brutus stabb'd,
And as he pluck'd his cursed steel away,
Mark how the blood of Caesar follow'd it,
As rushing out of doors, to be resolved
If Brutus so unkindly knock'd, or no;

For Brutus, as you know, was Caesar's angel.
Judge, O you gods, how dearly Caesar loved him!
This was the most unkindest cut of all;
For when the noble Caesar saw him stab,
Ingratitude, more strong than traitors' arms,
Quite vanquish'd him: then burst his mighty heart;
And in his mantle muffling up his face,
Even at the base of Pompey's statue,
Which all the while ran blood, great Caesar fell.
O, what a fall was there, my countrymen!
Then I, and you, and all of us fell down,
Whilst bloody treason flourish'd over us.
O, now you weep, and I perceive you feel

The dint of pity. These are gracious drops.
Kind souls, what weep you when you but behold
Our Caesar's vesture wounded? Look you here,

Here is himself, marr'd, as you see, with traitors.

FIRST CITIZEN
O piteous spectacle!

SECOND CITIZEN
O noble Caesar!

THIRD CITIZEN
O woeful day!

FOURTH CITIZEN
O traitors! Villains!

FIRST CITIZEN
O most bloody sight!

ANTONY
No, don't crowd me; stand back a bit.

SEVERAL CITIZENS
Stand back! Make room! Move back!

ANTONY
If you have tears, prepare to shed them now.
You all recognise this cloak. I remember
The first time ever that Caesar put it on;
It was on a summer's evening in his tent,
On the day he overcame the Nervii warriors.
Look, this is the part where Cassius' dagger pierced it;
See what a tear the spiteful Casca made;
Through this part, the dearly loved Brutus stabbed,
And as he pulled out his cursed dagger,
See how Caesar's blood followed it,
As if rushing out of a door, to learn for certain
Whether it was Brutus who so cruelly knocked, or not;

For Brutus, as you know, was Caesar's favourite.
Judge, oh you gods, how dearly Caesar loved him!
This was the unkindest cut of all;
Because when noble Caesar saw Brutus stab,
The ingratitude, stronger than traitors' arms,
Overwhelmed him: and then burst his mighty heart;
And with his cloak covering his face,
At the base of Pompey's statue,
Bleeding profusely, great Caesar fell.
Oh, what a fall it was, my countrymen!
Then I and you and all of us fell down,
Whilst bloody treason triumphed over us.
Oh, now you are weeping, and I am aware that you feel
The stroke of pity. These are compassionate tears.
Kind souls, how you weep when you observe
Merely our Caesar's wounded clothing? Look here, at this,
Here is the man himself, mangled, as you see, by traitors.

FIRST CITIZEN
Oh, what a pitiful sight!

SECOND CITIZEN
Oh, noble Caesar!

THIRD CITIZEN
Oh, sad day!

FOURTH CITIZEN
Oh, traitors! Villains!

FIRST CITIZEN
Oh, what a bloody sight!

SECOND CITIZEN We will be revenged.	**SECOND CITIZEN** We will take revenge.
ALL Revenge! About! Seek! Burn! Fire! Kill! Slay! Let not a traitor live!	**ALL** Let's take revenge! To work! Seek! Burn! Set fire! Kill! Put to death! Leave not even one traitor alive!
ANTONY Stay, countrymen.	**ANTONY** Wait, countrymen.
FIRST CITIZEN Peace there! Hear the noble Antony!	**FIRST CITIZEN** Be quiet! Listen to the noble Antony!
SECOND CITIZEN We'll hear him, we'll follow him, we'll die with him.	**SECOND CITIZEN** We'll listen to him, we'll follow him, we'll die with him.
ANTONY Good friends, sweet friends, let me not stir you up To such a sudden flood of mutiny. They that have done this deed are honourable. What private griefs they have, alas, I know not, That made them do it. They are wise and honourable, And will, no doubt, with reasons answer you. I come not, friends, to steal away your hearts; I am no orator, as Brutus is, But, as you know me all, a plain blunt man, That love my friend; and that they know full well That gave me public leave to speak of him. For I have neither wit, nor words, nor worth, Action, nor utterance, nor the power of speech To stir men's blood; I only speak right on. I tell you that which you yourselves do know, Show you sweet Caesar's wounds, poor poor dumb mouths, And bid them speak for me. But were I Brutus, And Brutus Antony, there were an Antony Would ruffle up your spirits, and put a tongue In every wound of Caesar that should move The stones of Rome to rise and mutiny.	**ANTONY** Good friends, sweet friends, don't let me stir you up To such a sudden outburst of mutiny. Those who have carried out this act are honourable men. What personal grievances they have, however, I do not know, That caused them to do this. They are wise and honourable, And will, no doubt, explain to you the reasons. I haven't come, friends, to steal your loyalty; I am not an eloquent public speaker like Brutus, But, as you all know, I am a plain speaking, blunt man, Who loved my friend; and fully aware of this fact Are the men who gave me permission to speak publicly about him. For I have neither intellectual brilliance, nor fluency, nor weight of authority, Gesture and bearing, nor delivery, nor the power of speech To stir men to action; I only say what I think. I tell you what you already know, Show you sweet Caesar's wounds, poor, poor speechless mouths, And ask them to speak for me. But if I were Brutus, And if Brutus were me, there would be an Antony Who would stir you up to anger, and put a tongue In each of Caesar's wounds which would inspire Even the stones of Rome to rise in mutiny.
ALL We'll mutiny.	**ALL** We'll mutiny.
FIRST CITIZEN We'll burn the house of Brutus.	**FIRST CITIZEN** We'll set fire to Brutus' house.
THIRD CITIZEN Away then! Come, seek the conspirators.	**THIRD CITIZEN** Let's go then! Come and look for the conspirators.

ANTONY
Yet hear me, countrymen; yet hear me speak.

ALL
Peace, ho! Hear Antony, most noble Antony!

ANTONY
Why, friends, you go to do you know not what.

Wherein hath Caesar thus deserved your loves?
Alas, you know not! I must tell you then:
You have forgot the will I told you of.

ALL
Most true. The will! Let's stay and hear the will.

ANTONY
Here is the will, and under Caesar's seal.
To every Roman citizen he gives,
To every several man, seventy-five drachmas.

SECOND CITIZEN
Most noble Caesar! We'll revenge his death.

THIRD CITIZEN
O royal Caesar!

ANTONY
Hear me with patience.

ALL
Peace, ho!

ANTONY
Moreover, he hath left you all his walks,
His private arbours, and new-planted orchards,
On this side Tiber; he hath left them you,

And to your heirs for ever: common pleasures,
To walk abroad and recreate yourselves.
Here was a Caesar! When comes such another?

FIRST CITIZEN
Never, never! Come, away, away!
We'll burn his body in the holy place,
And with the brands fire the traitors' houses.

Take up the body.

SECOND CITIZEN
Go fetch fire.

THIRD CITIZEN
Pluck down benches.

ANTONY
Wait and listen to me, countrymen; listen to what I have to say.

ALL
All be quiet! Listen to Antony, most noble Antony!

ANTONY
Why, friends, you don't even know what you are doing yet.
In what respect has Caesar earned your love?
Alas, you don't know! So, I must tell you:
You have forgotten the will I told you about.

ALL
That is true. The will! Let's stay and hear the will.

ANTONY
Here is the will, with Caesar's seal on it.
To every Roman citizen he gives,
To every individual man, seventy-five drachmas.

SECOND CITIZEN
Most noble Caesar! We shall avenge his death.

THIRD CITIZEN
Oh, royal Caesar!

ANTONY
Listen patiently to me.

ALL
Everyone, be quiet!

ANTONY
Furthermore, he has left you all his walkways,
His private lawns, and newly planted orchards,
On this side of the river Tiber; he has left them to you,
And to your heirs forever: public parks,
Where you can all go for a relaxing stroll.
This was Caesar! When will there be another like him?

FIRST CITIZEN
Never, never! Come on, let's go!
We'll burn his body in the holy place,
And, with the fire brands, we'll set fire to the traitors' houses.
Take up his body.

SECOND CITIZEN
Let's go and start a fire.

THIRD CITIZEN
Tear loose the benches.

FOURTH CITIZEN Pluck down forms, windows, any- thing. *Exeunt Citizens with the body* **ANTONY** Now let it work. Mischief, thou art afoot, Take thou what course thou wilt. *Enter a Servant* How now, fellow? **SERVANT** Sir, Octavius is already come to Rome. **ANTONY** Where is he? **SERVANT** He and Lepidus are at Caesar's house. **ANTONY** And thither will I straight to visit him. He comes upon a wish. Fortune is merry, A nd in this mood will give us anything. **SERVANT** I heard him say Brutus and Cassius Are rid like madmen through the gates of Rome. **ANTONY** Belike they had some notice of the people, How I had moved them. Bring me to Octavius. *Exeunt*	**FOURTH CITIZEN** Tear loose windowsills, shutters, anything. *Exeunt Citizens with the body* **ANTONY** Now let it work. Trouble, you are about to begin, Take whatever course you choose. *Enter a Servant* What news, man? **SERVANT** Sir, Octavius has already arrived in Rome. **ANTONY** Where is he? **SERVANT** He and Lepidus are at Caesar's house. **ANTONY** And I will go there at once to visit him. He has come exactly as I desired. Fortune is favouring us, And in this mood will give us anything we want. **SERVANT** I heard Octavius say that Brutus and Cassius Have ridden like madmen through the gates of Rome. **ANTONY** Probably, they had some information about the people, And how I had stirred them up. Take me to Octavius. *Exeunt*

Part 20: Analysing Act 3 Scene 2

The power of rhetoric to influence the fickle-minded crowd features strongly in this scene. From Shakespeare's crafting of language, we have evidence of his education: grammar and rhetoric played an important role in the Elizabethan curriculum, in which students studied Cato (Portia's great-great-grandfather), Horace, Virgil, Cicero and other classical authors. Grammar and rhetoric were highly esteemed in Elizabethan England as tools for moving people's feelings. This chapter contains detailed analysis of Shakespeare's rhetoric; for those of you who are particularly interested, advanced rhetorical terminology is in brackets.

When Brutus speaks to the crowd, he employs prose, usually spoken by low-status characters. This suggests that the high-status Brutus is deliberately adapting his speech to that of the crowd to appeal to their feelings. He employs a rhetorical question with his first reason for killing Caesar: 'Had you rather Caesar were living, and die all slaves, than that Caesar were dead, to live all free men?' This device focuses the attention of the crowd on the contrasting nouns of 'slaves' and 'free men' to emphasise his belief that he, Brutus, acted for the public good. A thoughtful listener might notice that he presents his opinion as a fact: he assumes the Romans would be 'slaves' to Caesar but, as Caesar never survived to support this theory, his reasoning is flawed.

Brutus's second justification for killing Caesar is that he was too ambitious. Brutus uses grammatically parallel clauses (called isocolon) to position himself as someone working for the public good. He begins as follows:

> *As Caesar loved me, I weep for him; as he was fortunate, I rejoice at it; as he was valiant, I honour him; but, as he was ambitious, I slew him.*

Brutus lists Caesar's honourable qualities and Brutus's own responses, starting with his position as Caesar's friend: 'As Caesar loved me, I weep for him'. The words are all positive to describe Caesar and Brutus's responses to him: 'fortunate...rejoice', 'valiant...honour'. There is the build-up of the three strong positives leading into the resoundingly negative: 'as he was ambitious, I slew him'. The use of parallel clauses creates surprise and forces the crowd to focus on Brutus's reasons for killing Caesar, emphasising his belief that he is doing his public duty.

The second set of parallel clauses continues in the next sentence, precisely developing the pattern of the first sentence:

> *There is tears for his love; joy for his fortune; honour for his valour; and death for his ambition.*

Interestingly, the first three nouns 'tears...love; joy' link to feelings and emotions, again emphasising that Brutus loved Caesar. The next nouns 'fortune; honour...valour' connote being blessed by fate to have qualities linked to contemporary ideas of manhood. The final parallel clause 'death for his ambition' suggests that Brutus overcame his emotions and, like any reasonable man, took the law into his own hands to kill Caesar. So, we see how parallel clauses are used to hoodwink the crowd, creating the impression that Brutus is acting out of concern for the people, but once again he presents no evidence to support his reasons.

This conscious crafting continues with Brutus's direct appeal to the crowd and the rule of three with the pattern of rhetorical question, followed by an imperative and repetition:

> *Who is here so base that would be a bondman? If any, speak; for him have I offended.*
> *Who is here so rude that would not be a Roman? If any, speak; for him have I offended.*
> *Who is here so vile that will not love his country? If any, speak; for him have I offended.*

The parallel rhetorical question/imperative structure is full of loaded language to influence the crowd. The alliteration of 'base' and 'bondsman' emphasises his question of who would want to demean themselves to be a slave. Similarly, he employs alliteration with 'rude' and 'Roman' to stress that anyone who does not want to be a Roman is barbarous. In his last rhetorical question, Brutus suggests that anyone who does 'not love his country' is 'vile'. The combination of emotive vocabulary, alliteration and pattern of question/answer persuades the crowd to believe that anyone who disagrees with Brutus's reasons for killing Caesar, would (1) want to be a slave; (2) be primitive and uncivilized (unlike Romans) and (3) does not love their country. The repetition of 'If any, speak; for him have I offended' challenges them to admit to these faults, which of course no-one will do. Of course, once more we see Brutus's opinions presented as facts. He therefore proves himself to be an expert manipulator of people's thoughts and feelings.

However, some modern audience members might argue that Brutus's speech is so consciously crafted that it suggests a lack of sincerity and spontaneity. Furthermore, some might say that his use of rhetorical devices draws the listeners' attention to the style of communication (i.e. *look at me: see how clever I am!*) at the expense of engaging the listeners with the content.

Nevertheless, the citizens are receptive to the point of wanting to crown Brutus; the meaning of Caesar's name changes and becomes synonymous with *king*:

THIRD CITIZEN
Let him [Brutus] be Caesar.

FOURTH CITIZEN
Caesar's better parts
Shall be crown'd in Brutus.

With the third citizen's comment 'Let him be Caesar', we see the rabble's lack of logic: their thought process at this moment in the play is that Brutus has correctly killed Caesar because no-one wants a king; therefore, let Brutus be king! Perhaps Shakespeare includes this reaction to invite us to compare two different types of illogicality: that of the educated Brutus and the other of the third citizen. Perhaps we are being invited to draw the conclusion that both thought processes appear to be attractive but, in reality, they are both of little value.

The audience also sees that the crowd accepts Brutus's argument: no-one challenges him, suggesting that they are easily swayed. Of course, this means that they can also be influenced against him, as we will see with Antony. In addition, their response contradicts Brutus's assumption that having a king is wrong, as some of the citizens would quite obviously be happy to crown Brutus. Interestingly, Brutus ignores the comments, as he cannot be seen to aspire to a crown when he has just killed the previous aspirant.

In contrast to Brutus, Antony speaks in blank verse, suggesting that he is not attempting to adapt his language in such an obvious way as Brutus. Antony also uses a range of rhetorical devices to influence the crowd. The first is the rule of three with his term of address 'Friends, Romans, countrymen'. We see from the first item on the list that he appeals to friendship first. This contrasts with Brutus's similar three-part address 'Romans, countrymen, and lovers' in which he appeals to their sense of Roman identity first and friendship last. Antony from the start intends to appeal to people's hearts while Stoic Brutus appeals to facts and logic.

Antony from the beginning knows how to work the crowd and create a spectacle, so he enters with a visual aid—Caesar's body, which he will reference in his oration. First, Antony positions himself as being on the side of the Brutus and the crowd by declaring: 'I come to bury Caesar, not to praise him'. The carefully chosen verbs 'bury' (links to dead body) and 'praise' (links to pathos) support the visual aid of the body and ensure that the citizens are receptive to his words. This of course is ironic, as it is the exact opposite of what he is planning to do.

His rhetorical skills include flattering Brutus, praising Caesar by presenting facts about him, and using repetition and rhetorical questions. An example can be seen with this extract:

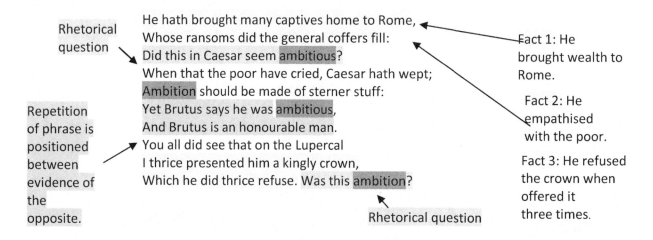

Repetition increasingly weakens Brutus's argument.

Antony frequently employs repetition with 'Brutus says he was ambitious, /And Brutus is an honourable man' to openly flatter Brutus. But the facts that he provides to support this statement all contradict Brutus's point about ambition, thereby weakening Brutus's argument. Antony also repeats Brutus's name to hammer home the connection between Brutus and Caesar's death, making sure the crowd knows whom to blame. We have a considerable amount of irony because, although on the surface Antony appears respect Caesar's murderers, his use of repetition and rhetorical questions indicates that he is questioning Brutus's honour and, by default, encouraging the crowd to do the same.

Another rhetorical device that Shakespeare uses is to deliberately become silent (this is called aposiopesis):

> My heart is in the coffin there with Caesar,
> And I must pause till it come back to me. (He weeps)

By showing the crowd that he is too upset to speak, Antony appeals to the crowd's emotions and gives the citizens time to think about his words. This has the desired effect of rousing them to rebellion. This is also a traditional stage technique that, Shakespeare well knew, could look contrived. In 'Antony and Cleopatra', Enobarbus accuses Antony of having play-acted at this very moment, calling Antony's tears 'rheum', a watery discharge from his eyes.

Next, Antony deliberately dismisses a point in order to draw attention to it (this is called paralipsis). To encourage the crowd to beg him to read Caesar's will, he deliberately dismisses the idea of reading it because it will upset them too much to hear the details:

> *Have patience, gentle friends; I must not read it.*
> *It is not meet you know how Caesar loved you.*
> *You are not wood, you are not stones, but men;*
> *And being men, hearing the will of Caesar,*
> *It will inflame you, it will make you mad.*
> *'Tis good you know not that you are his heirs;*
> *For if you should, O, what would come of it?*

By withholding information about what they will inherit, Antony manipulates the crowd, who respond by begging him to read the will ('Read the will! We'll hear it, Antony!'). Sandwiched between his dismissal of reading the will, Antony pretends that he wants to stop the crowd becoming angry, employing repetition ('You are not wood, you are not stones). This is imagery of hardness contrasts with the noun 'men', which is repeated for emphasis and juxtaposed with imagery of warmth and emotion ('inflame', 'mad'). This use of contrasting imagery depicts Antony as caring for the citizens in a paternalistic way. By pretending that he does not want them to become angry, he is hinting that they should in fact become angry which, of course, is exactly the reaction that he wants. By making them wait before he eventually reads the will, he whips them up into a bigger frenzy.

There is conscious visual symbolism in the embedded stage direction when the citizens give Antony permission to '[c]ome down' so he can talk to the crowd on their level. In contrast to Brutus, who addressed the crowd in prose to imply he was one of the people, Antony physically descends to their level, symbolising his affinity with the citizens; this is not, however, at the expense of his rhetoric, which, continuing in blank verse, lends authority to his words and suggests that he is being genuine.

Antony, still making the crowd wait to hear the contents of the will, cleverly changes the subject by focusing on the pathos of Caesar's cloak. He employs emotive language to describe the stabbing of Caesar, using Caesar's cloak ('mantle') as another visual aid. Then he appeals to shared knowledge and appears to reminisce:

> If *you have tears, prepare to shed them now.*
> *You all do know this mantle. I remember*
> *The first time ever Caesar put it on;*
> *'Twas on a summer's evening in his tent,*
> *That day he overcame the Nervii.*

Shared knowledge of cloak leads to an anecdote, creating a conversational tone as if reminiscing with friends.

By using the determiner 'that' with the noun 'day', Antonio is assuming that everyone knows when Caesar 'overcame the Nervii'. This would be the case, as it was a heroic day for Caesar who, in 57 BC, defeated the Nervians (or Nervii) in Northern France. His skill, determination and knowledge of tactics, coupled with the arrival of reinforcements, turned an apparently lost cause into a celebrated victory for the Romans. Antony reminds the crowd that Julius Caesar was a war hero and charismatic leader of men, appealing to their sense of national pride and loyalty.

Then Antony encourages the crowd to examine where the cloak has been damaged by the daggers. This arouses pathos and emphasises Brutus's betrayal:

> *Look, in this place ran Cassius' dagger through* (Violent vocabulary to recreate the murder in the minds of the crowd and encourage empathy);
> *See what a rent the envious* (Emotive adjective to prejudice crowd against Casca) *Casca made;*
> *Through this, the well-beloved* (Positive compound adjective contrasts with previous adjective to describe Casca. Also emphasises how much Caesar loved Brutus, stressing the degree of his betrayal.) *Brutus stabb'd,*
> *And as he pluck'd his cursed steel away, Mark how the blood of Caesar follow'd it,*
> *As rushing out of doors,* (Motif of blood imagery. Blood is personified and juxtaposed with onomatopoeic verb 'rushing' to convey the quantity of it.) *to be resolved*
> *If Brutus so unkindly knock'd, or no;*
> *For Brutus, as you know, was Caesar's angel.*
> *Judge, O you gods, how dearly Caesar loved him!* (Noun 'angel' and appeal to heavens 'you gods' to stress how much Caesar loved the traitor Brutus.)
> *This was the most unkindest cut of all; For when the noble Caesar* (motive adjectives to emphasise Caesar's greatness. The personification of '[i]ngratitude' in conjunction with the metaphor of the bursting of his mighty heart emphasises the extent of Brutus's betrayal) *saw him stab,*
> *Ingratitude, more strong than traitors' arms,*
> *Quite vanquish'd him: then burst his mighty heart;*
> *And in his mantle muffling up his face,*
> *Even at the base of Pompey's statue,*
> *Which all the while ran blood,* (Blood is personified with 'bloody treason flourish'd over') *great Caesar fell.*
> *O, what a fall was there, my countrymen!*
> *Then I, and you, and all of us* (us'. Use of pronouns I/you/us to include crowd and imply that the citizens were also betrayed.) *fell down,*
> *Whilst bloody treason flourish'd over us.*
> *O, now you weep,* (Emotive vocabulary to praise the empathy of the crowd.) *and I perceive you feel*
> *The dint of pity. These are gracious drops.*
> *Kind souls, what weep you when you but behold*
> *Our Caesar's vesture wounded?* (Speech comes around in a full circle. It started with the cloak and ends with the cloak.) *Look you here,*
> *Here is himself, marr'd, as you see, with traitors.* (Invites the crowd to turn their attention away from the cloak to Caesar's body. The emotive noun is positioned at the end of the speech to rouse the crowd).

The description of Caesar's murder followed by the invitation to view his cloak and body at the end of the speech invites empathy and anger from the crowd. Caesar's body is the most compelling and terrible evidence of all, and the bloody wounds speak more powerfully than any rhetorical device—an image is worth more than a word. Inevitably, the citizens now want revenge; however, Antony stalls them, because he wants to rouse their passions still further.

Once more, Antony deliberately dismisses a point to draw attention to it (paralipsis). He pretends that he does not want to influence the crowd and that he is not as good an orator as Brutus:

> *I come not, friends, to steal away your hearts;* (He dismisses this point to draw attention to it. This is exactly why he is there!)
> *I am no orator, as Brutus is,* (False modesty: simile of Brutus being a better orator helps the crowd to draw a comparison)
> *But, as you know me all, a plain blunt man,*
> *That love my friend; and that they know full well*

> *That gave me public leave to speak of him.* (Plain language to match his description of himself. Use of mostly monosyllabic words at this point makes it easier for the crowd to relate to him)
> *For I have neither wit, nor words, nor worth,* (Alliteration with the rule of three contradicts those ideas to prove that he is an expert orator. This develops into a list on the next line)
> *Action, nor utterance, nor the power of speech* (Repetition of coordinating conjunctions (polysyndeton) adds rhythm to the list, building momentum and passion. Once again, we see oration at its best)
> *To stir men's blood*

In the above extract, we see that, despite his professed modesty of being a 'plain blunt man', Antony is entirely the reverse. He is a great orator, a sophisticated manipulator. By saying that he is not, he wants to 'stir men's blood'.

Let's pause for a moment and reflect upon how Antony has structured his speech so far with his references to Caesar's will. Each reference has been carefully planned to whip the crowd into a passion. He has pretended to raise the subject of the will to attract the interest of the crowd, stating that he does not mean to read it ('pardon me, I do not mean to read'), which of course makes them want to hear it. He has excited their curiosity by intimating that Caesar has left 'a rich legacy' for them to inherit. Once he has hooked the crowd, he has refused to read the will ('I must not read it') to arouse their curiosity further. He has made them wait to hear its contents by changing the subject and reminiscing about Caesar, using the bloody cloak as a prop and then showing them the best visual aid of all, Caesar's wounds. Finally, Antony has appealed to the crowd's emotions even more by forcing them to compare Brutus with him. Now that the crowd is whipped into a passion and he is sure they are on his side, he finally reads the will.

Antony now employs hard facts from the will to prove to the crowd how they will benefit from Caesar's legacy: every Roman citizen will receive 'seventy-five drachmas', and Caesar has left them 'all his walks, /His private arbours, and new-planted orchards, /On this side Tiber'. By using evidence of Caesar's generosity to illustrate that he loved the citizens, Antony is inflaming the crowd's feelings of injustice. Consequently, in complete contrast to the beginning of his oration, the citizens are completely on his side and ready to riot.

Shakespeare manipulates the time frame of the play to develop tension and to keep the pace fast moving and exciting. For example, in the play, the assassination of Caesar, his funeral, Antony's speech, the reading of the will and Octavius's arrival all take place on the same day. In reality, the historical Caesar was assassinated on March the 15th; his will was published on the 18th; his funeral was on 20th; and Octavius's arrival was in May. Had Shakespeare been faithful to the original timeframe, the dramatic impact of these actions would have been greatly lessened.

This scene is considered by many to be one of the most dramatic that Shakespeare ever wrote. You might want to experiment with some of the rhetorical devices that Antony has used when you are practising for your GCSE English language exams.

Part 21: Translating Act 3 Scene 3

ORIGINAL TEXT	MODERN TRANSLATION
A street.	**A street.**
Enter CINNA the poet	*Enter CINNA the poet*
CINNA THE POET I dreamt to-night that I did feast with Caesar, And things unlucky charge my fantasy; I have no will to wander forth of doors, Yet something leads me forth.	**CINNA THE POET** I dreamt last night that I feasted with Caesar, And something loads my imaginings with bad omens; I have no desire to go outside, And yet something is leading me outside.
Enter Citizens	*Enter Citizens*
FIRST CITIZEN What is your name?	**FIRST CITIZEN** What is your name?
SECOND CITIZEN Whither are you going?	**SECOND CITIZEN** Where are you going?
THIRD CITIZEN Where do you dwell?	**THIRD CITIZEN** Where do you live?
FOURTH CITIZEN Are you a married man or a bachelor?	**FOURTH CITIZEN** Are you a married man or a bachelor?
SECOND CITIZEN Answer every man directly.	**SECOND CITIZEN** Answer every man straightforwardly.
FIRST CITIZEN Ay, and briefly.	**FIRST CITIZEN** Yes, and briefly.
FOURTH CITIZEN Ay, and wisely.	**FOURTH CITIZEN** Yes, and wisely.
THIRD CITIZEN Ay, and truly, you were best.	**THIRD CITIZEN** Yes, and truthfully, if you know what's best for you.
CINNA THE POET What is my name? Whither am I going? Where do I dwell? Am I a married man or a bachelor? Then to answer every man directly and briefly, wisely and truly; wisely I say, I am a bachelor.	**CINNA THE POET** What is my name? Where am I going? Where do I live? Am I a married man or a bachelor? Then to answer every man straightforwardly and briefly, wisely and truthfully; wisely I say, I am a bachelor.
SECOND CITIZEN That's as much as to say they are fools that marry. You'll bear me a bang for that, I fear. Proceed, directly.	**SECOND CITIZEN** That's as good as saying that men who marry are fools. I shall strike you for saying that, I'm afraid. Proceed with what you were saying, straightforwardly.
CINNA THE POET Directly, I am going to Caesar's funeral.	**CINNA THE POET** Straightforwardly, I am going to Caesar's funeral.

FIRST CITIZEN As a friend or an enemy? **CINNA THE POET** As a friend. **SECOND CITIZEN** That matter is answered directly. **FOURTH CITIZEN** For your dwelling, briefly. **CINNA THE POET** Briefly, I dwell by the Capitol. **THIRD CITIZEN** Your name, sir, truly. **CINNA THE POET** Truly, my name is Cinna. **FIRST CITIZEN** Tear him to pieces! He's a conspirator. **CINNA THE POET** I am Cinna the poet, I am Cinna the poet. **FOURTH CITIZEN** Tear him for his bad verses, tear him for his bad verses! **CINNA THE POET** I am not Cinna the conspirator. **FOURTH CITIZEN** It is no matter, his name's Cinna; pluck but his name out of his heart, and turn him going. **THIRD CITIZEN** Tear him, tear him! *They attack Cinna.* Come, brands, ho, fire-brands! To Brutus', to Cassius'; burn all! Some to Decius' house, and some to Casca's; some to Ligarius'. Away, go! *Exeunt all the citizens with Cinna's body.*	**FIRST CITIZEN** As a friend or an enemy? **CINNA THE POET** As a friend. **SECOND CITIZEN** That question has been answered straightforwardly. **FOURTH CITIZEN** Where you are living, in brief. **CINNA THE POET** In brief, I live near the Capitol. **THIRD CITIZEN** Your name, sir, truthfully. **CINNA THE POET** Truthfully, my name is Cinna. **FIRST CITIZEN** Tear him to pieces! He's a conspirator. **CINNA THE POET** I am Cinna the poet, I am Cinna the poet. **FOURTH CITIZEN** Tear him apart for his bad verses, tear him apart for his bad verses! **CINNA THE POET** I am not Cinna the conspirator. **FOURTH CITIZEN** It does not matter, his name is Cinna; remove only his name from his heart, and send him packing. **THIRD CITIZEN** Tear him apart, tear him apart! *They attack Cinna.* Come on, firebrands, over here, firebrands! To Brutus', to Cassius'; let's burn them all! Some of you go to Decius' house, and some to Casca's; some to Ligarius'. Go now! *Exeunt all the citizens with Cinna's body.*

Part 22: Analysing Act 3 Scene 3

This scene can be interpreted in two ways, depending upon the production. One interpretation is that it contains the last comic moment in the play and, following the oracy in the previous scene, it breaks the tension, providing the audience with the opportunity to relax before the tension rises again in the next act. Another interpretation is that the tension escalates, as the audience watches an innocent man being beaten to death by a baying mob.

Shakespeare deliberately includes some humour at the beginning of this scene using the device of a pun, but whether the humour develops or stops is open to interpretation. Cinna makes a punning comment: 'wisely I say, I am a bachelor. He is answering 'wisely' but he comically suggests it is wise to be a bachelor i.e. unmarried. This has the effect of relaxing the audience before the confusion surrounding his name. The crowd initially mistakes the poet for a conspirator called Cinna and, when they discover he is not Cinna the conspirator but Cinna the poet, they kill him for his bad verses. This could be enacted as a comic moment, thereby extending the comedy, or be interpreted as a serious moment, thereby being an unexpected shock after the previous humour.

However this scene is interpreted, it clearly shows the audience the danger of mob rule. We saw in the previous scene how easily the citizens can be swayed by rhetoric; in this scene, the inflamed mob descends into anarchy and murders an innocent man. When writing this scene, Shakespeare might well have had in mind the angry mob of Roman citizens who attacked Cassius's and Brutus's homes after Caesar's funeral.

Finally, there are parallels between this scene and the murder of Caesar: Cinna, like Caesar, ignored the omens, and both men were murdered. Perhaps Shakespeare is trying to say that fate influences the lives of everyone, not just the great figures of history. Furthermore, the mob murdered the wrong Cinna in a case of literal mistaken identity; the conspirators have murdered Caesar literally but, metaphorically speaking, they have been unable to kill his reputation, his influence and his impact on the Republic—which will inevitably turn into a kingdom or an empire.

Part 23: Translating Act 4 Scene 1

ORIGINAL TEXT	MODERN TRANSLATION
A house in Rome.	**A house in Rome.**
ANTONY, OCTAVIUS, and LEPIDUS, seated at a table.	*ANTONY, OCTAVIUS, and LEPIDUS, seated at a table.*
ANTONY These many then shall die; their names are prick'd.	**ANTONY** These are the ones then who will die; their names are marked on the list.
OCTAVIUS *(To Lepidus)* Your brother too must die; consent you, Lepidus?	**OCTAVIUS** *(To Lepidus)* Your brother too must die; do you agree, Lepidus?
LEPIDUS I do consent.	**LEPIDUS** I do agree.
OCTAVIUS Prick him down, Antony.	**OCTAVIUS** Mark him on the list, Antony.
LEPIDUS Upon condition Publius shall not live, Who is your sister's son, Mark Antony.	**LEPIDUS** On condition that Publius dies too, Publius, who is your sister's son, Mark Antony.
ANTONY He shall not live. Look, with a spot I damn him. But, Lepidus, go you to Caesar's house; Fetch the will hither, and we shall determine How to cut off some charge in legacies.	**ANTONY** He shall die. Look, with a mark against his name I condemn him to death. But, Lepidus, go to Caesar's house; Bring the will here, and we will decide How we can reduce some of the expenditure of his legacies.
LEPIDUS *(To Octavius)* What, shall I find you here?	**LEPIDUS** *(To Octavius)* Will you still be here when I get back?
OCTAVIUS Or here or at the Capitol.	**OCTAVIUS** Either here or at the Capitol.
Exit LEPIDUS	*Exit LEPIDUS*
ANTONY This is a slight unmeritable man, Meet to be sent on errands. Is it fit, The three-fold world divided, he should stand One of the three to share it?	**ANTONY** He is an insignificant man, not worthy of consideration, Fit only to be sent on errands. Is it right, That when we have divided the world into three parts, he should be One of the three who share rulership?
OCTAVIUS So you thought him, And took his voice who should be prick'd to die In our black sentence and proscription.	**OCTAVIUS** You thought that he should be, And you listened to his opinion regarding who should be marked to die In our death sentence and condemnation.

ANTONY
Octavius, I have seen more days than you;
And though we lay these honours on this man,

To ease ourselves of divers slanderous loads,

He shall but bear them as the ass bears gold,
To groan and sweat under the business,
Either led or driven, as we point the way;
And having brought our treasure where we will,

Then take we down his load, and turn him off,

Like to the empty ass, to shake his ears
And graze in commons.

OCTAVIUS
You may do your will;
But he's a tried and valiant soldier.

ANTONY
So is my horse, Octavius, and for that
I do appoint him store of provender.
It is a creature that I teach to fight,
To wind, to stop, to run directly on,
His corporal motion govern'd by my spirit.
And, in some taste, is Lepidus but so:
He must be taught, and train'd, and bid go forth:

A barren-spirited fellow; one that feeds
On objects, arts, and imitations,
Which, out of use and staled by other men,

Begins his fashion. Do not talk of him

But as a property. And now, Octavius,

Listen great things. Brutus and Cassius
Are levying powers; we must straight make head.

Therefore let our alliance be combined,
Our best friends made, our means stretch'd;

And let us presently go sit in council,

How covert matters may be best disclosed,
And open perils surest answered.

OCTAVIUS
Let us do so; for we are at the stake,
And bay'd about with many enemies;
And some that smile have in their hearts, I fear,
Millions of mischiefs.

Exeunt

ANTONY
Octavius, I am older than you;
And although we're giving these honours to this man,
To relieve ourselves of some of the blame that may be laid upon us,
He will carry these honours like an ass carries gold,
Groaning and sweating under the heavy load,
Either led or driven, as we direct him;
And when he has carried our treasure to where we want it,
Then we shall relieve him of his load, and turn him loose,
Like an unburdened ass, to shake his ears
And graze on public pasture lands.

OCTAVIUS
You can do what you want;
But he's an experienced and courageous soldier.

ANTONY
So is my horse, Octavius, and for that reason
I give him a supply of hay.
My horse is a creature that I teach to fight,
To turn, to stop, to run straight ahead,
His bodily movements controlled by my mind.
And, to some degree, Lepidus is like that:
He must be taught, and trained, and told to go forward:
A man lacking in initiative; one that takes on
Wonders, ways of thinking, and second-hand ideas,
Which, although out-dated and made common by other men,
Are for him at the height of fashion. Do not talk about Lepidus
Except as a mere tool for cleverer men to use. And now, Octavius,
Hear important things. Brutus and Cassius
Are raising armies; we must raise our own immediately.
So, let our allies join forces,
Our best friends rallied, our resources used to their fullest extent;
And let's immediately go and sit in council to discuss,
How hidden plans may be brought into the open,
And open dangers safely dealt with.

OCTAVIUS
Let's do that; because we are tied to a stake,
And surrounded by many enemies;
And some of those who smile at us, carry in their hearts, I'm afraid,
Many schemes to harm us.

Exeunt

Part 24: Analysing Act 4 Scene 1

In this scene, we meet the Second Triumvirate, formed to defeat Caesar's assassins. Its three members are Mark Antony, Marcus Lepidus and Octavius. When his great-uncle Julius Caesar's will was read, the historical Octavius learnt that Caesar had named him not only his adopted son but also his heir. Octavius later became Augustus and would rule as the first Roman emperor in 27 BC, seventeen years after the death of Caesar. Each man in theory rules a third of the Roman Empire but, as we see in this scene, tensions have arisen amongst them, and the relationships are unequal.

The ugliness and brutality of politics is made very clear from the beginning of the scene, as the three men examine a list of supposed traitors (called the 'order of proscription' in Act 4, Scene 3) and coldly barter away the lives even of family members. Octavius tells Lepidus 'Your brother too must die', to which Lepidus consents upon the condition that Antony's 'sister's son' shall die. Antony agrees and says 'Look, with a spot I damn him'. Through this interaction, we see three ruthless men who are prepared to barter the lives of their relatives for the sake of political power. Astute audience members might also observe that the great men of the Triumvirate are behaving exactly as the little men of the mob behaved in the previous scene: randomly selecting people to die.

The focus on the immorality of politics continues with Antony's desire to save money for his own military purposes by not honouring the terms of Caesar's will. He tells Lepidus 'Fetch the will hither, and we shall determine/How to cut off some charge in legacies'. This is despite having manipulated the funeral crowd with a promise that legacies from Caesar's will should be rapidly distributed. The audience therefore sees a ruthless, unsentimental and treacherous side to Antony's character, as he attempts to divert these funds away from the Roman people to his pockets.

Politically, the Triumvirate is a successful alliance, but the audience learns that there is no moral obligation for its members to respect each other. The audience's opinion of Antony will fall further when, after he has sent Lepidus on an errand, he compares him to a 'horse':

> He must be taught, and train'd, and bid go forth:
> A barren-spirited fellow; one that feeds
> On objects, arts, and imitations,
> Which, out of use and staled by other men,
> Begins his fashion. Do not talk of him
> But as a property.

By comparing Lepidus to a horse who 'must be taught, and train'd', we see how little respect Antony has for him. Lepidus, in Antony's opinion, is a mere drudge or slave to be told what to do and is only useful for menial tasks. Antony's use of the noun 'property' to describe Lepidus extends this idea and suggests Lepidus is simply an instrument or tool to be used at will. Antony describes him as 'barren-spirited'; 'barren' connotes unfertile land where nothing grows, implying that Lepidus has no original thoughts or initiative. There is the rule of three with 'objects, arts, and imitations' to emphasise Antony's point that there is nothing original about Lepidus, who values what 'out of use and staled by other men'—second-hand and unimaginative. Antony characterises Lepidus as not a leader but a follower, one who has no original thoughts or masculine drive.

By now presenting Antony, the previously loyal friend of Caesar, as critical and manipulative, Shakespeare is hinting that the Second Triumvirate is doomed to failure. The historical Lepidus was manoeuvred into exile by Octavian and in many ways, was lucky to escape with his life. The ironic interaction between Antony and Octavius reveals further political and personal tensions: Antony says 'Octavius, I have seen more days than you', which creates the impression of the older and wiser man sharing his worldly wisdom with the younger, inexperienced man, who is listening carefully. We have seen how Antony criticises Lepidus's lack of independence of spirit; ironically, this independence that Antony appears to admire so much will eventually backfire on him. The historical Octavius defeated Antony (and Cleopatra) at the Battle of Actium in 31 BC and, in several carefully orchestrated stages, declared himself emperor four years later.

ORIGINAL TEXT	MODERN TRANSLATION
Camp near Sardis. Before BRUTUS's tent.	**Camp near Sardis. Before BRUTUS's tent.**
Drum. Enter BRUTUS, LUCILIUS, LUCIUS, and Soldiers; TITINIUS and PINDARUS meeting them	*Drum. Enter BRUTUS, LUCILIUS, LUCIUS, and Soldiers; TITINIUS and PINDARUS meeting them*
BRUTUS Stand, ho!	**BRUTUS** Halt!
LUCILIUS Give the word, ho! and stand!	**LUCILIUS** Pass on the command and halt!
BRUTUS What now, Lucilius, is Cassius near?	**BRUTUS** What is happening, Lucilius? Is Cassius near here?
LUCILIUS He is at hand, and Pindarus is come To do you salutation from his master.	**LUCILIUS** He is nearby, and Pindarus has come To salute you on behalf of his master.
BRUTUS He greets me well. Your master, Pindarus, In his own change, or by ill officers, Hath given me some worthy cause to wish Things done undone; but if he be at hand I shall be satisfied.	**BRUTUS** He sends his greetings with a good man. Your master, Pindarus, Whether from his own change of mind, or because he's been influenced by unworthy subordinates, Has given me considerable cause to wish We hadn't done some of the things we did; but if he is nearby I shall receive a full explanation.
PINDARUS I do not doubt But that my noble master will appear Such as he is, full of regard and honour.	**PINDARUS** I have no doubt That my noble master will be shown to be True to himself, deserving all respect and honour.
BRUTUS He is not doubted. A word, Lucilius; How he received you, let me be resolved.	**BRUTUS** I do not doubt him. Can I have a word with you, Lucilius; How did Cassius treat you? Please tell me everything.
LUCILIUS With courtesy and with respect enough, But not with such familiar instances, Nor with such free and friendly conference, As he hath used of old.	**LUCILIUS** He treated me with courtesy and respect, But not with the same signs of friendship, Nor with the same free and friendly conversation, Which he used in the past.
BRUTUS Thou hast described A hot friend cooling. Ever note, Lucilius, When love begins to sicken and decay, It useth an enforced ceremony. There are no tricks in plain and simple faith;	**BRUTUS** You have described A warm friend who is cooling off. Always observe, Lucilius, When friendship begins to diminish and die, It is evident by the use of strained manners. There is no pretence in plain and simple trust;

But hollow men, like horses hot at hand,
Make gallant show and promise of their mettle;
But when they should endure the bloody spur,
They fall their crests, and like deceitful jades
Sink in the trial. Comes his army on?

LUCILIUS
They mean this night in Sardis to be quarter'd;
The greater part, the horse in general,
Are come with Cassius.

BRUTUS
Hark! he is arrived.
March gently on to meet him.

Enter CASSIUS and his powers

CASSIUS
Stand, ho!

BRUTUS
Stand, ho! Speak the word along.

FIRST SOLDIER
Stand!

SECOND SOLDIER
Stand!

THIRD SOLDIER
Stand!

CASSIUS
Most noble brother, you have done me wrong.

BRUTUS
Judge me, you gods; wrong I mine enemies?
And if not so, how should I wrong a brother?

CASSIUS
Brutus, this sober form of yours hides wrongs;

And when you do them –

BRUTUS
Cassius, be content.
Speak your griefs softly; I do know you well.
Before the eyes of both our armies here,
Which should perceive nothing but love from us,
Let us not wrangle. Bid them move away;
Then in my tent, Cassius, enlarge your griefs,

And I will give you audience.

But insincere men, like horses spirited at the start,
Put on a brave show promising great spirit;
But when they should persevere in adversity,
They lower their necks, and like old worn out horses
Fail when tested. Is his army approaching?

LUCILIUS
They intend to spend the night in Sardis;
The majority of them, all the mounted soldiers,
Have come with Cassius.

BRUTUS
Look! He has arrived.
March slowly on to meet him.

Enter CASSIUS and his powers

CASSIUS
Halt!

BRUTUS
Halt! Pass the order along.

FIRST SOLDIER
Halt!

SECOND SOLDIER
Halt!

THIRD SOLDIER
Halt!

CASSIUS
Most noble brother, you have wronged me.

BRUTUS
May the gods judge me; do I wrong my enemies?
And if I don't wrong my enemies, how could I wrong
a brother?

CASSIUS
Brutus, this restrained manner of yours conceals
your wrongdoings;
And when you do –

BRUTUS
Cassius, keep calm.
Present your grievances quietly; we are old friends.
In the presence of both of our armies,
Who ought to see nothing but love between us,
Let's not argue. Command them to move back;
Then, in my tent, Cassius, you can explain your
grievances,
And I will give you a hearing.

CASSIUS Pindarus, Bid our commanders lead their charges off A little from this ground. **BRUTUS** Lucius, do you the like, and let no man Come to our tent till we have done our conference. Let Lucilius and Titinius guard our door. *Exeunt*	**CASSIUS** Pindarus, Order our commanders to lead their troops away A short distance from this place. **BRUTUS** Lucius, you do the same, and don't allow anyone To come to our tent until we have finished our conference. Lucilius and Titinius can guard our door. *Exeunt*

Part 26: Analysing Act 4 Scene 2

Shakespeare opens this scene by highlighting the differences in personality between Brutus and Cassius. Brutus tells Lucilius that Cassius is a 'hot friend cooling'. This metaphor emphasises the contrast between their relationship when we last saw them together, conspiring to assassinate Caesar, and now, in the aftermath of their actions. There is also the personification of their relationship in imagery of illness and death ('love begins to sicken and decay') which clearly suggests that for a variety of reasons their friendship is breaking down. Moreover, Brutus says that Cassius is like someone presenting himself with 'enforced ceremony' in public. The adjective 'enforced' implies that, in Brutus's opinion, Cassius is making an effort to go through the motions of friendship and politeness but, like a 'ceremony', it is rehearsed and not from the heart. Cassius's behaviour in public is therefore making Brutus increasingly suspicious about their friendship.

The focus on Cassius's behaviour in public is developed through a contrasting use of horse imagery to that of the previous scene (in which Antony compared Lepidus to a horse). In this scene, Brutus criticises Cassius, stating that he is 'like horses hot at hand' who '[m]ake gallant show and promise of their mettle'. In other words, he is like a temperamental horse, unable to control himself. Perhaps Shakespeare is using this imagery to stress the harm that can be caused by an inability to curb passions; alternatively, the earlier criticism of Lepidus reminds the audience that leaders should have initiative, so Shakespeare might be saying that we must create a balance.

When the two men meet in public, Cassius is unable to conceal his private feelings and control his behaviour. His very first words to Brutus include a superlative adjective to create an ironically accusatory tone: 'Most noble brother, you have done me wrong'. The superlative 'most noble' with the noun 'brother' imply great respect and love; however, the monosyllabic 'you have done me wrong' stresses Cassius's feelings of betrayal. Cassius does not even greet Brutus before he says these words, indicating that he has been quietly brooding and is unable to restrain himself. The audience, having seen how ruthlessly even family members can be condemned to death in the previous scene, would be alert to this conversation, well aware that there might be serious consequences to the disagreement.

When Brutus warns Cassius of the public consequences of airing private feelings in front of the armies, his abrupt interruption and use of imperatives illustrate that he has a better understanding of leadership than Cassius:

> *Speak your griefs softly; I do know you well.*
> *Before the eyes of both our armies here,*
> *Which should perceive nothing but love from us,*
> *Let us not wrangle. Bid them move away;*
> *Then in my tent, Cassius, enlarge your griefs,*
> *And I will give you audience.*

The imperatives also suggest that Brutus sees himself as a ruler. This is further developed by his use of the declarative 'I will give you audience', which is a formal and rather grandiose expression, one that we associate with kings granting a hearing to their subjects. This sort of language is certain to lead to friction between the two. However, it confirms Brutus's better understanding of politics and leadership. He is well aware of the importance of behaving appropriately in front of the soldiers: Cassius's inability to control himself is putting everything at risk.

Part 27: Translating Act 4 Scene 3

ORIGINAL TEXT	MODERN TRANSLATION
Brutus's tent.	**Brutus's tent.**
Enter BRUTUS and CASSIUS	*Enter BRUTUS and CASSIUS*
CASSIUS That you have wrong'd me doth appear in this: You have condemn'd and noted Lucius Pella For taking bribes here of the Sardians; Wherein my letters, praying on his side, Because I knew the man, were slighted off.	**CASSIUS** The evidence that you have wronged me is thus: You have condemned and slandered Lucius Pella For taking bribes from the Sardians; And my letters, arguing his innocence, Because I knew the man, were dismissed.
BRUTUS You wronged yourself to write in such a case.	**BRUTUS** You wronged yourself by writing on behalf of such a man.
CASSIUS In such a time as this it is not meet That every nice offence should bear his comment.	**CASSIUS** At a time like this it is not right That every minor offence should be criticised.
BRUTUS Let me tell you, Cassius, you yourself Are much condemn'd to have an itching palm, To sell and mart your offices for gold To undeservers.	**BRUTUS** Let me tell you, Cassius, that you yourself Are accused of having a greedy streak, Selling and dealing, giving your positions in exchange for gold To undeserving men.
CASSIUS I an itching palm! You know that you are Brutus that speak this, Or, by the gods, this speech were else your last.	**CASSIUS** Me, a greedy streak! You know that if it were anyone other than you, Brutus, who said this, I swear by the gods, that this speech would be your last.
BRUTUS The name of Cassius honours this corruption, And chastisement doth therefore hide his head.	**BRUTUS** The name of Cassius lends respect to these corrupt actions, And so punishment is avoided.
CASSIUS Chastisement!	**CASSIUS** Punishment!
BRUTUS Remember March, the ides of March remember. Did not great Julius bleed for justice' sake? What villain touch'd his body, that did stab, And not for justice? What, shall one of us, That struck the foremost man of all this world But for supporting robbers, shall we now Contaminate our fingers with base bribes,	**BRUTUS** Remember March, March 15th remember. Didn't great Julius Caesar bleed for the sake of justice? What villain struck Caesar's body and stabbed him, For any other reason than for justice? What, should one of us, Who struck down the most powerful man in the world Be supporting robbers, and should we now Dirty our hands with sordid bribes,

Original	Modern
And sell the mighty space of our large honours For so much trash as may be grasped thus? I had rather be a dog, and bay the moon, Than such a Roman.	And sell the high and honourable offices in our power For as much money as we can get our hands on? I would rather be a dog and howl at the moon, Than be that kind of a Roman.
CASSIUS Brutus, bait not me; I'll not endure it. You forget yourself, To hedge me in. I am a soldier, I, Older in practice, abler than yourself To make conditions.	**CASSIUS** Brutus, do not harass me; I will not put up with it. You are forgetting yourself, When you limit my authority. I am a soldier, I am, More experienced than you, and more capable than you At managing affairs.
BRUTUS Go to! You are not, Cassius.	**BRUTUS** Get away from me! You are not, Cassius.
CASSIUS I am.	**CASSIUS** I am.
BRUTUS I say you are not.	**BRUTUS** I say that you are not.
CASSIUS Urge me no more, I shall forget myself; Have mind upon your health; tempt me no further.	**CASSIUS** Do not provoke me anymore, or I shall forget to restrain myself; Consider your safety; and don't provoke me anymore.
BRUTUS Away, slight man!	**BRUTUS** Leave, worthless man!
CASSIUS Is't possible?	**CASSIUS** Is this possible?
BRUTUS Hear me, for I will speak. Must I give way and room to your rash choler? Shall I be frighted when a madman stares?	**BRUTUS** Listen to me, because I have something to say. Do I have to indulge and endure your quick temper? Should I be frightened when a madman glares at me?
CASSIUS O ye gods, ye gods! Must I endure all this?	**CASSIUS** Oh ye gods, ye gods! Must I endure all this?
BRUTUS All this? Ay, more: fret till your proud heart break; Go show your slaves how choleric you are, And make your bondmen tremble. Must I budge? Must I observe you? Must I stand and crouch Under your testy humour? By the gods, You shall digest the venom of your spleen, Though it do split you; for, from this day forth, I'll use you for my mirth, yea, for my laughter, When you are waspish.	**BRUTUS** All this? Yes, and more: rage until your proud heart breaks; Go and show your slaves how bad-tempered you are, And make your servants tremble. Do I have to flinch? Do I have to grovel? Do I have to stand and bow To your ill-tempered disposition? By the gods, You shall swallow your own bad-tempered poison, Until it makes you burst; because, from now on, I will use you as an object of fun and ridicule, Whenever you get angry with me.

CASSIUS Is it come to this?	**CASSIUS** Has it come to this?
BRUTUS You say you are a better soldier: Let it appear so; make your vaunting true, And it shall please me well. For mine own part, I shall be glad to learn of noble men.	**BRUTUS** You say you are a better soldier: Show it; make your boasting come true, And I shall be delighted. As for me, I shall be happy to be instructed by brave men.
CASSIUS You wrong me every way; you wrong me, Brutus. I said an elder soldier, not a better; Did I say better?	**CASSIUS** You wrong me in every way; you wrong me, Brutus. I said an older soldier, not a better soldier; Did I say better?
BRUTUS If you did, I care not.	**BRUTUS** If you did, I don't care.
CASSIUS When Caesar lived, he durst not thus have moved me.	**CASSIUS** When Caesar was alive, he wouldn't have dared to exasperate me like this.
BRUTUS Peace, peace! You durst not so have tempted him.	**BRUTUS** Oh, be quiet! You wouldn't have dared to provoke him like this.
CASSIUS I durst not?	**CASSIUS** I wouldn't have dared?
BRUTUS No.	**BRUTUS** No.
CASSIUS What, durst not tempt him?	**CASSIUS** What, not dared to provoke him?
BRUTUS For your life you durst not.	**BRUTUS** For fear of your life, you wouldn't have dared to.
CASSIUS Do not presume too much upon my love; I may do that I shall be sorry for.	**CASSIUS** Do not take my friendship for granted; I may do something I'll regret.
BRUTUS You have done that you should be sorry for. There is no terror, Cassius, in your threats; For I am arm'd so strong in honesty That they pass by me as the idle wind, Which I respect not. I did send to you For certain sums of gold, which you denied me; For I can raise no money by vile means; By heaven, I had rather coin my heart, And drop my blood for drachmas, than to wring From the hard hands of peasants their vile trash	**BRUTUS** You have already done something which you should regret. There is no terror for me, Cassius in your threats; Because I am so secure in my integrity They pass by me like a gentle breeze, Which I ignore. I asked you For a certain amount of gold, which you wouldn't give to me; I cannot raise money by dishonourable means; I swear by heaven, I would rather use my heart as currency, And give my blood for coins than extort From the hard-working hands of peasants, their petty cash

By any indirection. I did send To you for gold to pay my legions. Which you denied me; was that done like Cassius? Should I have answer'd Caius Cassius so? When Marcus Brutus grows so covetous, To lock such rascal counters from his friends, Be ready, gods, with all your thunderbolts, Dash him to pieces!	By devious means. I asked You for gold to pay my soldiers. You refused to give it to me; was that the sort of thing Cassius would do? Would I have responded to Caius Cassius in that way? If I, Marcus Brutus, ever become so greedy, That I hoard such trashy coins from my friends, Be ready, gods, with all your thunderbolts, Dash me to pieces!
CASSIUS I denied you not.	**CASSIUS** I did not refuse you.
BRUTUS You did.	**BRUTUS** You did.
CASSIUS I did not. He was but a fool That brought my answer back. Brutus hath rived my heart; A friend should bear his friend's infirmities; But Brutus makes mine greater than they are.	**CASSIUS** I did not. The man was a fool Who brought my answer to you. Brutus, you have broken my heart; A friend should tolerate his friend's frailties; But you, Brutus, make mine appear worse than they really are.
BRUTUS I do not, till you practise them on me.	**BRUTUS** I do not, until you practise them on me.
CASSIUS You love me not.	**CASSIUS** You do not love me.
BRUTUS I do not like your faults.	**BRUTUS** I do not like your faults.
CASSIUS A friendly eye could never see such faults.	**CASSIUS** A friend would never see such faults.
BRUTUS A flatterer's would not, though they do appear As huge as high Olympus.	**BRUTUS** A flatterer would not see such faults, even if they were As huge as Mount Olympus.
CASSIUS Come, Antony, and young Octavius, come, Revenge yourselves alone on Cassius, For Cassius is aweary of the world; Hated by one he loves; braved by his brother; Checked like a bondman; all his faults observed, Set in a note-book, learn'd, and conn'd by rote, To cast into my teeth. O, I could weep My spirit from mine eyes! There is my dagger, And here my naked breast; within, a heart Dearer than Plutus' mine, richer than gold: If that thou be'st a Roman, take it forth. I, that denied thee gold, will give my heart:	**CASSIUS** Come, Antony, and young Octavius, come, Take your revenge only on Cassius, Because Cassius is weary of this world; Hated by someone he loves; challenged by his brother; Rebuked like a servant; all his faults observed, Recorded in a notebook, studied and committed to memory, To be thrown back in his face. Oh, I could weep My soul out! There's my dagger, And here is my bare chest; inside it there is a heart More precious than Plutus' mine, richer than gold: If you are a Roman, remove my heart. I, who denied you gold, will give you my heart:

Strike, as thou didst at Caesar; for I know,
When thou didst hate him worst, thou lovedst him better
Than ever thou lovedst Cassius.

BRUTUS
Sheathe your dagger.
Be angry when you will, it shall have scope;

Do what you will, dishonour shall be humour.

O Cassius, you are yoked with a lamb
That carries anger as the flint bears fire,
Who, much enforced, shows a hasty spark,
And straight is cold again.

CASSIUS
Hath Cassius lived
To be but mirth and laughter to his Brutus,

When grief and blood ill-temper'd, vexeth him?

BRUTUS
When I spoke that, I was ill-temper'd too.

CASSIUS
Do you confess so much? Give me your hand.

BRUTUS
And my heart too.

CASSIUS
O Brutus!

BRUTUS
What's the matter?

CASSIUS
Have not you love enough to bear with me,
When that rash humour which my mother gave me

Makes me forgetful?

BRUTUS
Yes, Cassius; and from henceforth,
When you are over-earnest with your Brutus,
He'll think your mother chides, and leave you so.

POET
(*Within*) Let me go in to see the Generals.
There is some grudge between 'em; 'tis not meet
They be alone.

LUCILIUS
(*Within*) You shall not come to them.

Strike, as you did at Caesar; because I know,
Even when you hated Caesar the most, you still loved him more
Than you ever loved me.

BRUTUS
Put your dagger away.
Be angry whenever you like, your temper can have free rein;
Do whatever you want, I'll say that your future insults are just the result of a bad mood.
Oh Cassius, you are partners with a lamb
Which carries anger like a flint carries fire,
Which, when struck with force, gives a brief spark,
And then is, at once, cold again.

CASSIUS
Have I lived
Only to be a source of entertainment for you, Brutus,
Whenever grief and frustration make you angry?

BRUTUS
When I said that, I was angry too.

CASSIUS
Do you admit it, then? Give me your hand.

BRUTUS
And my heart too.

CASSIUS
Oh, Brutus!

BRUTUS
What's the matter?

CASSIUS
Don't you have enough love for me to be patient,
When that quick temper which I inherited from my mother
Makes me forget my manners?

BRUTUS
Yes, Cassius; and from now on,
When you are hot-headed with me,
I'll imagine it's your mother speaking, and let it go at that.

POET
(*Off stage*) Let me go in to see the Generals.
There is a grudge between them; it's not right
For them to be alone.

LUCILIUS
(*Off stage*) You can't go in to see them.

POET *(Within)* Nothing but death shall stay me. *Enter Poet, followed by LUCILIUS, TITINIUS, and LUCIUS* **CASSIUS** How now? What's the matter? **POET** For shame, you Generals! What do you mean? Love, and be friends, as two such men should be; For I have seen more years, I'm sure, than ye. **CASSIUS** Ha, ha! How vilely doth this cynic rhyme! **BRUTUS** *(To poet)* Get you hence, sirrah! Saucy fellow, hence! **CASSIUS** Bear with him, Brutus; 'tis his fashion. **BRUTUS** I'll know his humour, when he knows his time. What should the wars do with these jigging fools? Companion, hence! **CASSIUS** Away, away, be gone! *Exit Poet* **BRUTUS** Lucilius and Titinius, bid the commanders Prepare to lodge their companies to-night. **CASSIUS** And come yourselves, and bring Messala with you Immediately to us. *Exeunt LUCILIUS and TITINIUS* **BRUTUS** Lucius, a bowl of wine. *Exit LUCIUS* **CASSIUS** I did not think you could have been so angry.	**POET** *(Off stage)* Only death would stop me from going in. *Enter Poet, followed by LUCILIUS, TITINIUS, and LUCIUS* **CASSIUS** What's this? What's the matter? **POET** Shame on you, Generals! What do you mean by this? Love each other, and be friends, as two men like you should be; For I am sure that I am older than you. **CASSIUS** Ha, ha! How disgusting are this coarse man's rhymes! **BRUTUS** *(To poet)* Get out of here, you! Insolent fellow, get out! **CASSIUS** Be patient with him, Brutus; it's just his way. **BRUTUS** I'll put up with his kind of behaviour, when he keeps it for a proper time and place. What should we do with these rhyming fools? Get out of here, fellow! **CASSIUS** Go, go, get out of here! *Exit Poet* **BRUTUS** Lucilius and Titinius, tell the commanders To prepare their men to camp tonight. **CASSIUS** And you return, bringing Messala with you As soon as possible. *Exeunt LUCILIUS and TITINIUS* **BRUTUS** Lucius, bring a bowl of wine. *Exit LUCIUS* **CASSIUS** I did not think that you could get so angry.

BRUTUS O Cassius, I am sick of many griefs.	**BRUTUS** Oh Cassius, I am troubled by many sorrows.
CASSIUS Of your philosophy you make no use, If you give place to accidental evils.	**CASSIUS** You're not following your philosophy of stoicism, If you allow incidental adversities to upset you.
BRUTUS No man bears sorrow better. Portia is dead.	**BRUTUS** No man endures sorrow better than me. Portia is dead.
CASSIUS Ha? Portia?	**CASSIUS** Portia?
BRUTUS She is dead.	**BRUTUS** She is dead.
CASSIUS How 'scaped I killing, when I cross'd you so? O insupportable and touching loss! Upon what sickness?	**CASSIUS** How did I escape being killed, when I argued with you? Oh, unbearable and grievous loss! As a result of what sickness?
BRUTUS Impatient of my absence, And grief that young Octavius with Mark Antony Have made themselves so strong; for with her death That tidings came. With this she fell distract, And, her attendants absent, swallow'd fire.	**BRUTUS** She was concerned about my absence, And grieved that young Octavius and Mark Antony Have grown so strong; for, at the same time as the news of her death That news came to me. With these concerns, she became overwhelmed with despair, And, when her attendants were away, swallowed burning coals.
CASSIUS And died so?	**CASSIUS** And that is how she died?
BRUTUS Even so.	**BRUTUS** Yes, like that.
CASSIUS O ye immortal gods!	**CASSIUS** Oh, immortal gods!
Re-enter LUCIUS, with wine and taper	*Re-enter LUCIUS, with wine and candle*
BRUTUS Speak no more of her. Give me a bowl of wine. In this I bury all unkindness, Cassius.	**BRUTUS** Don't talk about her any more. Give me a bowl of wine. With this toast I bury all disagreements, Cassius.
CASSIUS My heart is thirsty for that noble pledge. Fill, Lucius, till the wine o'erswell the cup; I cannot drink too much of Brutus' love.	**CASSIUS** My heart is thirsty for that noble promise. Fill my cup, Lucius, until it overflows with wine; I cannot drink too much of Brutus' love.
BRUTUS Come in, Titinius.	**BRUTUS** Come in, Titinius.

Exit LUCIUS. Re-enter TITINIUS, with MESSALA

Exit LUCIUS. Re-enter TITINIUS, with MESSALA

Welcome, good Messala.
Now sit we close about this taper here,
And call in question our necessities.

Welcome, good Messala.
Now let's sit together, here around this candle,
And think carefully about our needs.

CASSIUS
Portia, art thou gone?

CASSIUS
Portia, are you really gone?

BRUTUS
No more, I pray you.
Messala, I have here received letters,
That young Octavius and Mark Antony
Come down upon us with a mighty power,
Bending their expedition toward Philippi.

BRUTUS
Don't talk any more about that, please.
Messala, I have received these letters here,
Saying that young Octavius and Mark Antony
Are bearing down on us with a mighty army,
Directing their expedition towards Philippi.

MESSALA
Myself have letters of the self-same tenor.

MESSALA
I too have letters which say the same thing.

BRUTUS
With what addition?

BRUTUS
And anything else?

MESSALA
That by proscription and bills of outlawry
Octavius, Antony, and Lepidus
Have put to death an hundred senators.

MESSALA
That by condemnation to death and legal writs
Octavius, Antony, and Lepidus
Have executed a hundred senators.

BRUTUS
Therein our letters do not well agree.
Mine speak of seventy senators that died
By their proscriptions, Cicero being one.

BRUTUS
On that point, our letters don't agree.
Mine say that seventy senators lost their lives
By execution, Cicero being one of them.

CASSIUS
Cicero one?

CASSIUS
Cicero was one of them?

MESSALA
Cicero is dead,
And by that order of proscription.
Had you your letters from your wife, my lord?

MESSALA
Cicero is dead,
And that was by their order of execution.
Have you received your letters from your wife, my lord?

BRUTUS
No, Messala.

BRUTUS
No, Messala.

MESSALA
Nor nothing in your letters writ of her?

MESSALA
Nor any news about her in your letters?

BRUTUS
Nothing, Messala.

BRUTUS
Nothing, Messala.

MESSALA
That, methinks, is strange.

MESSALA
I think that is strange.

BRUTUS
Why ask you? Hear you aught of her in yours?

BRUTUS
Why are you asking? Have you heard something about her in your letters?

MESSALA No, my lord.	**MESSALA** No, my lord.
BRUTUS Now, as you are a Roman, tell me true.	**BRUTUS** Now, as you are a Roman, tell me the truth.
MESSALA Then like a Roman bear the truth I tell; For certain she is dead, and by strange manner.	**MESSALA** Then, like a Roman, endure the truth I must tell you; It is certain that she is dead, and she died in a strange way.
BRUTUS Why, farewell, Portia. We must die, Messala. With meditating that she must die once, I have the patience to endure it now.	**BRUTUS** Well, farewell, Portia. We all must die, Messala. By reflecting that she had to die some day, I can endure her death now.
MESSALA Even so great men great losses should endure.	**MESSALA** This is the way great men ought to endure great losses.
CASSIUS I have as much of this in art as you, But yet my nature could not bear it so.	**CASSIUS** I have as much of this stoical fortitude in theory as you have, But my emotions could not bear this news as you do.
BRUTUS Well, to our work alive. What do you think Of marching to Philippi presently?	**BRUTUS** Well, let us move forward in our work with the living. What do you think Of marching to Philippi immediately?
CASSIUS I do not think it good.	**CASSIUS** I do not think it's a good idea.
BRUTUS Your reason?	**BRUTUS** What is your reason?
CASSIUS This it is: 'Tis better that the enemy seek us; So shall he waste his means, weary his soldiers, Doing himself offence, whilst we, lying still, Are full of rest, defence, and nimbleness.	**CASSIUS** This is my reason: It is better that the enemy comes looking for us; That way he will use up his supplies, tire out his soldiers, Doing himself a disservice, whilst we, lying still, Are fully rested, ready to defend, and energetic.
BRUTUS Good reasons must of force give place to better. The people 'twixt Philippi and this ground Do stand but in a forced affection; For they have grudged us contribution. The enemy, marching along by them, By them shall make a fuller number up,	**BRUTUS** Though your reasons are good, they must give way to my plan, which is better. The people who live between Philippi and here Are friendly to us, only because we force them to be; Because they have grudgingly contributed to our cause. If the enemy is marching along past them, They will add them to their numbers,

Come on refresh'd, new-added, and encouraged;

From which advantage shall we cut him off,
If at Philippi we do face him there,
These people at our back.

CASSIUS
Hear me, good brother –

BRUTUS
Under your pardon. You must note beside
That we have tried the utmost of our friends,

Our legions are brim-full, our cause is ripe.
The enemy increaseth every day;
We, at the height, are ready to decline.
There is a tide in the affairs of men,
Which, taken at the flood, leads on to fortune;

Omitted, all the voyage of their life
Is bound in shallows and in miseries.
On such a full sea are we now afloat,
And we must take the current when it serves,

Or lose our ventures.

CASSIUS
Then, with your will, go on;
We'll along ourselves, and meet them at Philippi.

BRUTUS
The deep of night is crept upon our talk,

And nature must obey necessity,
Which we will niggard with a little rest.
There is no more to say?

CASSIUS
No more. Good night.
Early to-morrow will we rise, and hence.

BRUTUS
Lucius!

Enter LUCIUS

My gown.

Exit LUCIUS

Farewell, good Messala.
Good night, Titinius. Noble, noble Cassius,
Good night, and good repose.

CASSIUS
O my dear brother,
This was an ill beginning of the night;

And then come at us refreshed, reinforced, and full
of courage;
We will deprive them of this advantage,
If we meet them at Philippi,
With these people behind us.

CASSIUS:
Listen to me, good brother –

BRUTUS
Begging your pardon. You must acknowledge also
That we have obtained every assistance that we
possibly can from our friends,
Our regiments are full to the brim, and ready to go.
The enemy is increasing in numbers every day;
We, now at maximum numbers, can only decrease.
There is a tide at work in the affairs of men,
Which, when acted upon at high tide, leads to
victory;
If it is missed, the whole journey of their lives
Is confined to the shallows and to misery.
It is on such a high tide that we are now floating,
And we must take advantage of the current while it
is available,
Or lose our campaign.

CASSIUS
Then, as you wish, proceed;
We'll proceed with you, and meet them at Philippi.

BRUTUS
The middle of the night has crept up on us whilst
we've been talking,
And we must give in to tiredness,
Which we will alleviate with a short rest.
Is there anything else you want to say?

CASSIUS
Nothing else. Good night.
Early tomorrow we will rise, and go from here.

BRUTUS
Lucius!

Enter LUCIUS

My nightgown.

Exit LUCIUS

Farewell, good Messala.
Good night, Titinius. Noble, noble Cassius,
Good night, and sleep well.

CASSIUS
Oh, my dear brother,
This was a bad start to the night;

Never come such division 'tween our souls! Let it not, Brutus.	May we never be divided like that again! Let's not, Brutus.
BRUTUS Everything is well.	**BRUTUS** All is well.
CASSIUS Good night, my lord.	**CASSIUS** Good night, my lord.
BRUTUS Good night, good brother.	**BRUTUS** Good night, good brother.
TITINIUS MESSALA Good night, Lord Brutus.	**TITINIUS MESSALA** Good night, Lord Brutus.
BRUTUS Farewell, every one.	**BRUTUS** Farewell, everyone.
Exeunt all but BRUTUS. Re-enter LUCIUS, with the gown.	*Exeunt all but BRUTUS. Re-enter LUCIUS, with the gown.*
Give me the gown. Where is thy instrument?	Give me the gown. Where is your lute?
LUCIUS Here in the tent.	**LUCIUS** Here in the tent.
BRUTUS What, thou speak'st drowsily? Poor knave, I blame thee not; thou art o'er-watch'd. Call Claudius and some other of my men; I'll have them sleep on cushions in my tent.	**BRUTUS** What, do you sound tired? Poor lad, I don't blame you; you've been awake too long. Call Claudius and some of my other men; They can sleep on cushions in my tent.
LUCIUS Varro and Claudius!	**LUCIUS** Varro and Claudius!
Enter VARRO and CLAUDIUS	*Enter VARRO and CLAUDIUS*
VARRO Calls my lord?	**VARRO** Are you calling, my lord?
BRUTUS I pray you, sirs, lie in my tent and sleep; It may be I shall raise you by and by On business to my brother Cassius.	**BRUTUS** I ask you, sirs, to rest in my tent and sleep; I may wake you in a while To send you to my brother Cassius with a message.
VARRO So please you, we will stand and watch your pleasure.	**VARRO** If you like, we shall stay awake to do anything you wish to be done.
BRUTUS I will not have it so; lie down, good sirs. It may be I shall otherwise bethink me. Look, Lucius, here's the book I sought for so; I put it in the pocket of my gown.	**BRUTUS** I don't want you to do that; lie down, good sirs. Otherwise I may change my mind. Look, Lucius, here's the book I was looking for; I put it in the pocket of my night gown.
VARRO and CLAUDIUS lie down	*VARRO and CLAUDIUS lie down*

LUCIUS

I was sure your lordship did not give it me.

BRUTUS

Bear with me, good boy, I am much forgetful.
Canst thou hold up thy heavy eyes awhile,

And touch thy instrument a strain or two?

LUCIUS

Ay, my lord, an't please you.

BRUTUS

It does, my boy.
I trouble thee too much, but thou art willing.

LUCIUS

It is my duty, sir.

BRUTUS

I should not urge thy duty past thy might;
I know young bloods look for a time of rest.

LUCIUS

I have slept, my lord, already.

BRUTUS

It was well done, and thou shalt sleep again;

I will not hold thee long. If I do live,
I will be good to thee.

Music, and a song

This is a sleepy tune; O murderous slumber,
Lay'st thou thy leaden mace upon my boy,
That plays thee music? Gentle knave, good night;

I will not do thee so much wrong to wake thee.
If thou dost nod, thou break'st thy instrument;
I'll take it from thee; and, good boy, good night.
Let me see, let me see; is not the leaf turn'd down
Where I left reading? Here it is, I think.

Enter the Ghost of CAESAR

How ill this taper burns! Ha! Who comes here?

I think it is the weakness of mine eyes
That shapes this monstrous apparition.
It comes upon me. Art thou any thing?
Art thou some god, some angel, or some devil,
That makest my blood cold, and my hair to stare?

Speak to me what thou art.

LUCIUS

I was sure that your lordship had not given it to me.

BRUTUS

Bear with me, good man, I am very forgetful.
Can you keep your tired eyes open for a while longer,
And play a couple of tunes on your lute?

LUCIUS

Yes, my lord, if it pleases you.

BRUTUS

It does, my boy.
I ask too much of you, but you are always willing.

LUCIUS

It is my duty, sir.

BRUTUS

I should not ask too much of you;
I know that young men need a time of rest.

LUCIUS

I have already had a sleep, my lord.

BRUTUS

That's a good thing, and you shall have another sleep;
I will not keep you very long. If I survive this,
I will be good to you.

Music, and a song

This is a sleepy tune; Oh, deathly slumber,
Have you apprehended, my boy,
Who is playing music for you? Gentle servant, good night;
I won't disturb you by waking you.
If you fall forward, you will break your lute;
So I will take it from you; good night, good boy.
Let me see, let me see; did I turn down the page
Where I finished reading? Here it is, I think.

Enter the Ghost of CAESAR

This candle is not giving much light! What! Who is this?
I think it is my poor eyesight
That is causing me to see this dreadful ghost.
It is coming towards me. Are you real?
Are you some god, an angel, or a devil,
That is making my blood run cold, and my hair stand on end?
Tell me what you are.

GHOST Thy evil spirit, Brutus.	**GHOST** I am your evil spirit, Brutus.
BRUTUS Why comest thou?	**BRUTUS** Why have you come here?
GHOST To tell thee thou shalt see me at Philippi.	**GHOST** To tell you that you will see me at Philippi.
BRUTUS Well; then I shall see thee again?	**BRUTUS** Well; then I shall see you again?
GHOST Ay, at Philippi.	**GHOST** Yes, at Philippi.
BRUTUS Why, I will see thee at Philippi then.	**BRUTUS** Alright, I will see you at Philippi then.
Exit Ghost	*Exit Ghost*
Now I have taken heart, thou vanishest. Ill spirit, I would hold more talk with thee. Boy! Lucius! Varro! Claudius! Sirs, awake! Claudius!	Now I have received courage, you have vanished. Evil spirit, I want to talk with you for longer. Boy! Lucius! Varro! Claudius! Sirs, awake! Claudius!
LUCIUS The strings, my lord, are false.	**LUCIUS** The strings, my lord, are out of tune.
BRUTUS He thinks he still is at his instrument. Lucius, awake!	**BRUTUS** He thinks he is still playing his lute. Lucius, wake up!
LUCIUS My lord?	**LUCIUS** My lord?
BRUTUS Didst thou dream, Lucius, that thou so criedst out?	**BRUTUS** Were you dreaming, Lucius, causing you to shout out like that?
LUCIUS My lord, I do not know that I did cry.	**LUCIUS** My lord, I don't think I shouted out.
BRUTUS Yes, that thou didst. Didst thou see any thing?	**BRUTUS** Yes, you did shout out. Did you see anything?
LUCIUS Nothing, my lord.	**LUCIUS** Nothing, my lord.
BRUTUS Sleep again, Lucius. Sirrah Claudius! *(To VARRO)* Fellow thou, awake!	**BRUTUS** Go back to sleep, Lucius. Claudius! *(To VARRO)* You there, wake up!
VARRO My lord?	**VARRO** My lord?
CLAUDIUS My lord?	**CLAUDIUS** My lord?

BRUTUS
Why did you so cry out, sirs, in your sleep?

VARRO, CLAUDIUS:
Did we, my lord?

BRUTUS
Ay; saw you anything?

VARRO
No, my lord, I saw nothing.

CLAUDIUS
Nor I, my lord.

BRUTUS
Go, and commend me to my brother Cassius.
Bid him set on his powers betimes before,

And we will follow.

VARRO, CLAUDIUS:
It shall be done, my lord.

Exeunt

BRUTUS
Why did you shout out like that in your sleep?

VARRO, CLAUDIUS:
Did we, my lord?

BRUTUS
Yes; did you see anything?

VARRO
No, my lord, I didn't see anything.

CLAUDIUS
Nor did I, my lord.

BRUTUS
Go, and deliver my greeting to my brother Cassius.
Order him to advance his forces early in the morning,
And we will follow.

VARRO, CLAUDIUS:
We will do that, my lord.

Exeunt

Part 28: Analysing Act 4 Scene 3

In this scene, the themes of manhood and honour develop, as the frictions and irritations between Brutus and Cassius rub away at each of them. Both men fire rhetorical questions at each other to score points in their argument, but Brutus employs more, indicating that he has more power:

> *Must I budge?*
> *Must I observe you? Must I stand and crouch*
> *Under your testy humour? By the gods,*
> *You shall digest the venom of your spleen,*
> *Though it do split you*

Brutus employs the rule of three with his short rhetorical questions, as he fires them like bullets to criticise Cassius's lack of self-control. He then uses the metaphor of a snake to illustrate that Cassius's inability to control himself is consuming him and could result in his downfall. We see that Brutus has lost control of his emotions, which seems out of character for a Stoic—this is an early signifier to the audience that something is wrong and that he is behaving out of character because he is grieving Portia's death.

In their argument, Shakespeare deliberately uses short sentences and repetition, as the men compete for dominance:

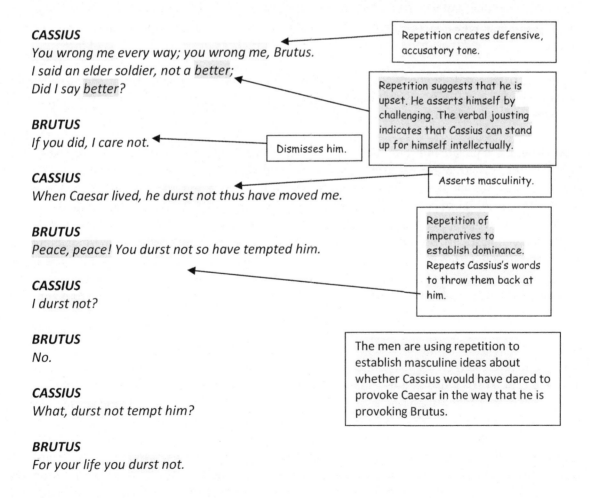

CASSIUS
You wrong me every way; you wrong me, Brutus.
I said an elder soldier, not a better;
Did I say better?

Repetition creates defensive, accusatory tone.

Repetition suggests that he is upset. He asserts himself by challenging. The verbal jousting indicates that Cassius can stand up for himself intellectually.

BRUTUS
If you did, I care not.

Dismisses him.

CASSIUS
When Caesar lived, he durst not thus have moved me.

Asserts masculinity.

BRUTUS
Peace, peace! You durst not so have tempted him.

Repetition of imperatives to establish dominance. Repeats Cassius's words to throw them back at him.

CASSIUS
I durst not?

BRUTUS
No.

The men are using repetition to establish masculine ideas about whether Cassius would have dared to provoke Caesar in the way that he is provoking Brutus.

CASSIUS
What, durst not tempt him?

BRUTUS
For your life you durst not.

This argument reminds us of a playground confrontation, so it does not do either man credit. The rapid exchanges quicken the pace and tension of the quarrel. With his interrogatives, we see that Cassius is the more provocative while Brutus's declaratives in which he accuses Cassius of not daring to provoke Caesar illustrate that he is not backing down. It could be argued that a sensible man would not have embarked on this line of argument; we therefore see again how the impact of the death of Portia has weakened Brutus's self-control.

The differences between the two men's attitudes to the morality of politics also develops in this scene. Brutus regards himself as an honourable man, who will not stoop to raise money in a dishonourable way; however, there is an element of hypocrisy when he comments:

> I did send to you
> For certain sums of gold, which you denied me;
> For I can raise no money by vile means

It seems that Brutus will use any money that Cassius has raised despite knowing that it came to his hands by corrupt means. Brutus's rather smug wish to stand by his principles and Cassius's willingness to adapt his behaviour to the circumstances is therefore beginning to hamper their war effort.

The reconciliation of the two men, which is largely Cassius's doing, is a private moment in the play, which also contains family imagery. Cassius says that he inherited his bad temper from his 'mother', and we once again see how contemporary masculine ideals were at the expense of women. He is also giving a reason for his behaviour so that they can both back down without loss of face.

The Poet is used as a dramatic device to relieve the tension and to create humour. The atrocious rhyming couplet (Cassius laughs 'Ha, ha! How vilely doth this cynic rhyme!') lightens the mood before the focus of the scene changes to Portia.

The theme of the private life continues when we learn that Portia has committed suicide—she 'swallow'd fire', which presumably burnt her throat and lungs. She committed suicide because she was missing Brutus and feared the Triumvirate was getting too strong; these appear to be weak, emotional reasons for suicide, which would fit contemporary ideas about femininity. We are reminded that, when we first met Portia, she insisted that women were the weaker sex, and she later displayed hysterical behaviour in the street. Her manner of dying does contain masculine traits, however: swallowing fire is a brave, painful way to die. This confirms the same masculine strength of character as when she revealed earlier in the play that she had stabbed herself in the thigh. Nevertheless, it is significant that Portia dies offstage—this is not a play about women, but about men.

Shakespeare decides to report Portia's death twice, and this enables the audience first to see Brutus's private and then his public response. In private, he bluntly tells Cassius 'No man bears sorrow better. Portia is dead'. Interestingly, his grief is mentioned before her death, and the two simple sentences emphasise his pain. The verb 'bear' followed by the noun 'sorrow' are significant, as we realise that he is carrying his sorrow around with him like a heavy weight.

We then see the contrast with his public reaction when his subordinate Messala, after sounding Brutus out to see if he has heard anything, states 'she is dead, and by strange manner'. He probably does not want to provide details out of sensitivity to Brutus's feelings—from Shakespeare's point of view, this would also be too repetitious for the audience. Brutus's public response is restrained and philosophical:

> *Why, farewell, Portia. We must die, Messala.*
> *With meditating that she must die once,*
> *I have the patience to endure it now.*

On the surface, this appears to be an uncaring comment to make but, knowing that he has admitted his feelings to Cassius, we realise that Brutus is concealing his true feelings in front of a subordinate. He shows a leader's ability to subordinate the personal to the professional and a Stoic's resolve not to emote self-indulgently. We have not seen Brutus lose his temper before this scene, so Portia's suicide explains his uncharacteristic behaviour and helps the audience to sympathise with him. We have human sympathy for Brutus in his anxiety, but he is not altogether easy to get along with here. In many ways--his vacillation, his occasionally raw emotionality, his constant grappling with the rightness of a course of action—he is a precursor of Hamlet.

Brutus's adherence to the actual Stoical school of philosophy continues through his use of water imagery to illustrate the theme of fate. He tells Cassius:

> *We, at the height, are ready to decline.*
> *There is a tide in the affairs of men,*   Water imagery
> *Which, taken at the flood, leads on to fortune;*
> *Omitted, all the voyage of their life*
> *Is bound in shallows and in miseries.*
> *On such a full sea are we now afloat,*
> *And we must take the current when it serves,*
> *Or lose our ventures.*

Brutus feels that we must 'take the current' that has been offered by the gods and seize the moment. In other words, we should accept what the gods have offered and follow nature's plan. He wins the discussion about marching to Philippi (and their eventual doom), and this provides further evidence of his sometimes counter-productive dominance.

Cassius is the character who most develops during the play's action. He has brought Brutus on board for good reasons but, in this scene and elsewhere in the play, has to watch his own influence diminish as a result. This exchange shows him close to his best: he finally exercises restraint and pledges loyalty to Brutus—even though he knows Brutus has made a military misjudgement.

There are interesting structural features about this scene so far. Firstly, it contains parallel plot elements with Act 1, Scene 2. For example, we saw contemporary ideas about manhood and honour when Caesar offered the crowd 'his throat to cut'. In an equally dramatic gesture, this is mirrored in this scene when Cassius offers Brutus his 'dagger' and invites him to stab him: 'I, that denied thee gold, will give my heart:/Strike, as thou didst at Caesar'. Likewise, before Caesar died, we saw the theme of politics when he refused to grant 'immediate freedom of repeal' to Publius Cimber; in this scene, Brutus refuses to repeal Lucius Pella's punishment for taking bribes. The use of these parallel plot elements encourages the audience to appreciate that both Cassius and Brutus contain aspects of Caesar's personality, but only Caesar contained both. This leads the audience to compare them to Caesar and to judge the characters' individual fitness as politicians. Moreover, the references to Caesar remind the audience of him—after all, he died two acts ago—subconsciously preparing them for his appearance at the end of this scene.

The scene is structured in another way to prepare the audience for Caesar's appearance. We have the tension at the beginning with Cassis's and Brutus's argument, which begins to drop when the argument is resolved and they talk about Portia. The theme of the private self then develops through Brutus's conversation with the servant Lucius and the calm, relaxing bedtime music, as everyone prepares to sleep. This lulls the audience into a false sense of security, heightening the shock at the entrance of Caesar's ghost, after which the tension shoots up.

The plot device of a ghost is a common element of tragedies of the time and it featured very significantly in Shakespeare's own work (for example, 'Richard III' and his later plays 'Hamlet', performed a year or so after 'Julius Caesar' and 'Macbeth'). The ghost states that it is 'Thy evil spirit, Brutus'. This might be interpreted as a manifestation of Brutus's guilt in the form of Brutus's spirit, which is evil. Alternatively, with the possessive pronoun 'thy', coupled with the knowledge that the ghost appears to Brutus only, it could mean that the ghost belongs to Brutus only. The audience suspects that its appearance does not bode well for the future: with the adjective 'evil' linking Brutus to the ghost, we have a sense of inevitability that, when they next meet at Philippi, it will not turn out well for Brutus.

Through the device of the ghost, we learn that although Caesar's body is dead, his spirit is not: it lives in the conscience of Brutus and in the hearts of the people who are avenging his death. We are reminded that, at Caesar's funeral, one of the citizens shouted 'Let him be Caesar' after Brutus's speech in Act 3, Scene 2. The meaning of the proper noun *Caesar* has changed: it has become a synonym for *leader, king, emperor* or *ruler*. The appearance of Caesar's ghost suggests that the spirit of Caesar lives on in people's hearts and minds, and shows that they are receptive to the idea of a monarchy. Thus, it seems, no matter what Brutus does, the Roman Republic is fated to end.

Part 29: Translating Act 5 Scene 1

ORIGINAL TEXT	MODERN TRANSLATION
The plains of Philippi.	**The plains of Philippi.**
Enter OCTAVIUS, ANTONY, and their army	*Enter OCTAVIUS, ANTONY, and their army*
OCTAVIUS Now, Antony, our hopes are answered: You said the enemy would not come down, But keep the hills and upper regions. It proves not so; their battles are at hand; They mean to warn us at Philippi here, Answering before we do demand of them.	**OCTAVIUS** Now, Antony, our prayers have been answered: You said the enemy would not come down, But would keep to the hills and upper regions. It turns out not to be the case; their troops, in battle order, are nearby; They intend to challenge us here at Philippi, Answering a call to battle before we have issued it.
ANTONY Tut, I am in their bosoms, and I know Wherefore they do it. They could be content To visit other places, and come down With fearful bravery, thinking by this face To fasten in our thoughts that they have courage; But 'tis not so.	**ANTONY** I know their secret thoughts, and I know Why they're doing this. They really wish They were somewhere else, and they descend on us With a display of splendour which hides the fear they are feeling, thinking that this outward appearance Will convince us that they are courageous; But they aren't.
Enter a Messenger	*Enter a Messenger*
MESSENGER Prepare you, Generals; The enemy comes on in gallant show. Their bloody sign of battle is hung out, And something to be done immediately.	**MESSENGER** Prepare yourselves, Generals; The enemy is approaching with a splendid display. They're showing us their bloody heralds of battle, And something must be done immediately.
ANTONY Octavius, lead your battle softly on Upon the left hand of the even field.	**ANTONY** Octavius, lead your army slowly out To the left side of the level field.
OCTAVIUS Upon the right hand I. Keep thou the left.	**OCTAVIUS** I will go to the right side. You stay on the left.
ANTONY Why do you cross me in this exigent?	**ANTONY** Why are you opposing me in this emergency?
OCTAVIUS I do not cross you; but I will do so.	**OCTAVIUS** I am not opposing you perversely; but it's what I intend to do.
March. Drum. Enter BRUTUS, CASSIUS, and their Army; LUCILIUS, TITINIUS, MESSALA, and others.	*March. Drum. Enter BRUTUS, CASSIUS, and their Army; LUCILIUS, TITINIUS, MESSALA, and others.*
BRUTUS They stand, and would have parley.	**BRUTUS** They have stopped, and want to talk.
CASSIUS	**CASSIUS**

Stand fast, Titinius; we must out and talk.

OCTAVIUS
Mark Antony, shall we give sign of battle?

ANTONY
No, Caesar, we will answer on their charge.
Make forth; the Generals would have some words.

OCTAVIUS
(To his army) Stir not until the signal.

BRUTUS
Words before blows: is it so, countrymen?

OCTAVIUS
Not that we love words better, as you do.

BRUTUS
Good words are better than bad strokes, Octavius.

ANTONY
In your bad strokes, Brutus, you give good words;

Witness the hole you made in Caesar's heart,
Crying, 'Long live! Hail, Caesar!'

CASSIUS
Antony,
The posture of your blows are yet unknown;

But for your words, they rob the Hybla bees,

And leave them honeyless.

ANTONY
Not stingless too.

BRUTUS
O yes, and soundless too;
For you have stol'n their buzzing, Antony,
And very wisely threat before you sting.

ANTONY
Villains! You did not so, when your vile daggers

Hack'd one another in the sides of Caesar:

You show'd your teeth like apes, and fawn'd like hounds,
And bow'd like bondmen, kissing Caesar's feet;
Whilst damned Casca, like a cur, behind

Struck Caesar on the neck. O you flatterers!

Stay here, Titinius; we must go out and talk to them.

OCTAVIUS
Mark Antony, shall we give the signal to attack?

ANTONY
No, Caesar, we will respond when they attack.
Advance; the Generals want to speak with us.

OCTAVIUS
(To his army) Do not move until we give the signal.

BRUTUS
Words before fighting: is that how it is to be, countrymen?

OCTAVIUS
Not that we love words more than fighting, as you do.

BRUTUS
Good words are better than bad strokes, Octavius.

ANTONY
Accompanying your evil strokes, Brutus, you give a good speech;
Think of the hole you made in Caesar's heart,
Whilst declaring, 'Long live Caesar! Hail, Caesar!'

CASSIUS
Antony,
The nature of the blows you can inflict are as yet unknown;
But as for your words, they are as sweet as honey taken from the Hybla bees,
Leaving them honeyless.

ANTONY
And stingless too?

BRUTUS
Oh yes, and soundless too;
Because you have stolen their buzzing, Antony,
And you very wisely warn us before you sting.

ANTONY
Villains! You didn't warn us before you stung, when your vile daggers
Struck each other as they embedded in Caesar's sides:
You smiled insincerely like apes, and fawned like dogs,
And bowed like servants, kissing Caesar's feet;
Whilst damned Casca, like a mongrel dog, from behind
Struck Caesar on the neck. Oh, you flatterers!

CASSIUS
Flatterers? Now, Brutus, thank yourself:

This tongue had not offended so today,
If Cassius might have ruled.

OCTAVIUS
Come, come, the cause. If arguing make us sweat,

The proof of it will turn to redder drops.
Look,
I draw a sword against conspirators.
When think you that the sword goes up again?

Never till Caesar's three and thirty wounds
Be well avenged; or till another Caesar
Have added slaughter to the sword of traitors.

BRUTUS
Caesar, thou canst not die by traitors' hands,
Unless thou bring'st them with thee.

OCTAVIUS
So I hope.
I was not born to die on Brutus' sword.

BRUTUS
O, if thou wert the noblest of thy strain,
Young man, thou couldst not die more honourable.

CASSIUS
A peevish schoolboy, worthless of such honour,
Join'd with a masker and a reveller.

ANTONY
Old Cassius, still!

OCTAVIUS
Come, Antony; away!
Defiance, traitors, hurl we in your teeth.
If you dare fight to-day, come to the field;
If not, when you have stomachs.

Exeunt OCTAVIUS, ANTONY, and their army.

CASSIUS
Why now, blow wind, swell billow, and swim bark!
The storm is up, and all is on the hazard.

BRUTUS
Ho, Lucilius, hark, a word with you.

LUCILIUS
(Standing forth) My lord?

BRUTUS and LUCILIUS converse apart

CASSIUS
Flatterers? Now, Brutus, you have only yourself to thank:
Antony wouldn't be here to offend us today,
If I had had my way after Caesar's death.

OCTAVIUS
Come, come, let's keep to the matter in hand. If arguing makes us sweat,
The real trial will turn the sweat to drops of blood.
Look,
I draw my sword against conspirators.
When do you think the sword will be sheathed again?
Never, until Caesar's thirty-three wounds
Are well avenged; or until I, Octavius Caesar, too
Have been slaughtered by traitors' swords.

BRUTUS
Caesar, you're not going to be killed by a traitor,
Unless you kill yourself.

OCTAVIUS
I hope you are right.
I was not born to die on your sword, Brutus.

BRUTUS
Oh, if you were the noblest of your family,
Young man, you could not die a more honourable death.

CASSIUS
A silly school boy, unworthy of such an honour,
Joined by a masquerader and a reveller.

ANTONY
You're still the same old Cassius!

OCTAVIUS
Come, Antony; let's go!
Traitors, we fiercely defy you.
If you dare to fight today, come to the field;
If not, then come when you're ready for battle.

Exeunt OCTAVIUS, ANTONY, and their army.

CASSIUS
Now, let the wind blow, waves swell, and ships sink!
The storm is up, and everything is at stake.

BRUTUS
Lucilius, I would like to have a word with you.

LUCILIUS
(Coming forward) My lord?

BRUTUS and LUCILIUS converse to one side

CASSIUS
Messala.

MESSALA
(Standing forth) What says my General?

CASSIUS
Messala,
This is my birthday; as this very day
Was Cassius born. Give me thy hand, Messala:
Be thou my witness that against my will—
As Pompey was—am I compell'd to set
Upon one battle all our liberties.
You know that I held Epicurus strong,

And his opinion; now I change my mind,

And partly credit things that do presage.
Coming from Sardis, on our former ensign

Two mighty eagles fell, and there they perch'd,
Gorging and feeding from our soldiers' hands,
Who to Philippi here consorted us.
This morning are they fled away and gone,
And in their steads do ravens, crows, and kites
Fly o'er our heads and downward look on us,
As we were sickly prey; their shadows seem
A canopy most fatal, under which
Our army lies, ready to give up the ghost.

MESSALA
Believe not so.

CASSIUS
I but believe it partly,
For I am fresh of spirit, and resolved
To meet all perils very constantly.

BRUTUS
Even so, Lucilius.

CASSIUS
Now, most noble Brutus,
The gods to-day stand friendly, that we may,
Lovers in peace, lead on our days to age!
But since the affairs of men rest still incertain,
Let's reason with the worst that may befall.

If we do lose this battle, then is this
The very last time we shall speak together;
What are you then determined to do?

BRUTUS

CASSIUS
Messala.

MESSALA
(Coming forward) What do you want to say, my General?

CASSIUS
Messala,
Today is my birthday; on this very day
Cassius was born. Give me your hand, Messala:
You be my witness that against my will—
Just as Pompey was—I am forced to gamble
All our freedoms on one battle.
You know that I was a convinced follower of Epicurus,
And his disregard for omens; now I have changed my mind,
And partly believe in omens.
When we were traveling from Sardis, upon our foremost flag
Two great eagles landed, and they perched there,
Feasting and feeding from the soldiers' hands,
Who had accompanied us to Philippi.
This morning they have flown away and gone,
And in their place, there are ravens, crows, and kites
Flying over our heads and looking down on us,
As if we were dying prey; their shadows are like
A canopy foreboding death, under which
Our army lies, ready to give up the ghost.

MESSALA
Don't believe this.

CASSIUS
I only partly believe it,
Because I am enthusiastic, and determined
To face all dangers unrelentingly.

BRUTUS
Right, Lucilius.

CASSIUS
Now, most noble Brutus,
May the gods stand friendly today, so that we may,
Dear friends of peace, live on to old age!
But since the affairs of men remain ever uncertain,
Let us consider what is to be done if the worst happens.
If we lose this battle, this will be
The very last time we'll speak to each other;
If we lose, what do you intend to do?

BRUTUS

Even by the rule of that philosophy
By which I did blame Cato for the death
Which he did give himself - I know not how,
But I do find it cowardly and vile,
For fear of what might fall, so to prevent
The time of life - arming myself with patience
To stay the providence of some high powers

That govern us below.

CASSIUS
Then, if we lose this battle,
You are contented to be led in triumph
Thorough the streets of Rome?

BRUTUS
No, Cassius, no; think not, thou noble Roman,
That ever Brutus will go bound to Rome;
He bears too great a mind. But this same day
Must end that work the ides of March begun;

And whether we shall meet again I know not.
Therefore our everlasting farewell take:
For ever, and for ever, farewell, Cassius.
If we do meet again, why, we shall smile;
If not, why then this parting was well made.

CASSIUS
For ever, and for ever, farewell, Brutus.
If we do meet again, we'll smile indeed;
If not, 'tis true this parting was well made.

BRUTUS
Why then, lead on. O, that a man might know
The end of this day's business ere it come!
But it sufficeth that the day will end,
And then the end is known. Come, ho! Away!

Exeunt

By the same guiding principle
Which led me to disapprove of Cato's death
By suicide – I do not know why,
But I consider it cowardly and vile,
That out of fear of what may happen, one ends
One's life early – I intend to be patient
To wait for the fate of whatever the high powers above
Decide for us here below.

CASSIUS
So, if we lose this battle,
You are happy to be led in triumph
Through the streets of Rome?

BRUTUS
No, Cassius, no; do not imagine, noble Roman,
That Brutus will ever go to Rome bound in chains;
His mind is too great for that. But today is the day
When we must finish the work we began on 15th March;
And I don't know whether we shall meet again.
Therefore, let's say our everlasting farewell:
Forever and forever, farewell, Cassius.
If we meet again, then, we shall smile;
If not, then this parting was a good one.

CASSIUS
Forever and forever, farewell, Brutus.
If we meet again, we shall smile indeed;
If not, it is true that this parting was a good one.

BRUTUS
Well, lead on. Oh, I wish that I could know
What will happen today before it happens!
But it's sufficient to know that today will end,
And then the end will be known. Come! Let us go!

Exeunt

Part 30: Analysing Act 5 Scene 1

Octavius and Antony have an army assembled and are preparing to fight Cassius and Brutus. The forthcoming battle is reflected in battles of words.

Brutus's and Cassius's argument in the previous scene is paralleled in this scene when Octavius asserts his authority, refusing to take Antony's battle orders ('I do not cross you; but I will do so'). His assertion, delivered in a calm, collected manner, without explaining his reasons, also mirrors Caesar's decision to stay at home in Act 2, Scene 2 without giving a reason to the Senate. In both cases, the men show authority, which is the quality of a leader. The use of this moment in the play therefore foreshadows Octavius's future role as emperor, as we see his ability to rule. There is another layer of meaning, however. To cross someone is to go against them. The historical Octavius will eventually betray Antony and take the power for himself. We therefore see dramatic irony, as members of the audience are likely to know Antony's eventual fate.

It is also interesting to see that, after this point, Antony begins to call Octavius 'Caesar'. Here we see firstly that the historical Octavius took Caesar's name as he was entitled to do. Secondly, we have also seen in the play that the name *Caesar* has become a synonym for *leader, king, emperor* or *ruler* (although in history, this happened much later). This indicates that Antony is accepting Octavius's authority. Shakespeare demonstrates that Octavius is determined to be his own man and that power between the two is shifting, foreshadowing Octavius's eventual triumph as emperor.

So far in 'Julius Caesar', we have seen the power of rhetoric to plot, plan, persuade, and to incite a rebellion and war. In this scene, the language of the leaders focuses on the power of words and swords:

> **BRUTUS**
> *Words before blows: is it so, countrymen?*
>
> **OCTAVIUS**
> *Not that we love words better, as you do.*
>
> **BRUTUS**
> *Good words are better than bad strokes, Octavius.*

The highlighted phrases illustrate that Octavius believes military might is the ultimate resort; Brutus, on the other hand, is still considering the possibility of negotiation. The use of contrasting attitudes is therefore a metaphor for the pending battle.

More evidence of words no longer having the power to heal the rift between the conspirators and the Triumvirate is seen when Antony cleverly uses words to provoke Brutus into a fight that Antony expects to win. Antony focuses on Brutus's hypocrisy: 'Witness the hole you made in Caesar's heart, /Crying, 'Long live! Hail, Caesar!''. We have the literal meaning of a hole in the heart to explain the stab wound, coupled with the metaphor of Brutus leaving Caesar with a hole in the heart because he betrayed their friendship. Anthony therefore emphasises that Brutus cannot be trusted when he quotes Brutus's exclamations 'Long live! Hail, Caesar!'. Brutus's words, in the opinion of Antony, now mean nothing. By quoting Brutus, we see that words are best met with other words: fire fights fire.

The battle of words continues when Cassius's personifies Antony's words that 'rob the Hybla bees, /And leave them honeyless'. (Honey from the Sicilian village of Hybla was famously sweet.) Brutus extends this metaphor, saying that Antony has 'stol'n their buzzing', implying that Antony's words are as annoying and inconsequential as the buzzing of a bee. This insult challenges Antony's feelings of honour and manhood.

Antony subsequently loses his temper, and he employs exclamatory sentences, violent verbs and similes:

> *Villains! You did not so [threaten before killing], when your vile daggers*
> *Hack'd one another in the sides of Caesar:*
> *You show'd your teeth like apes, and fawn'd like hounds,*
> *And bow'd like bondmen, kissing Caesar's feet;*
> *Whilst damned Casca, like a cur, behind*
> *Struck Caesar on the neck. O you flatterers!*

Exclamatory sentences: 'Villains!', 'O you flatterers!'
Violent verbs: 'Hack'd', 'Struck'
Similes: 'teeth like apes', 'fawn'd like hounds', 'bow'd like bondsmen;, 'like a cur'/

The use of exclamatory sentences ('Villains!' and 'O you flatterers!') reveals his feelings of anger as he attacks and insults Brutus and Cassius. His violently emotive vocabulary with the adjective 'vile' and the verbs 'hack'd' and '[s]truck' recreate the violence of the murder and illustrate the conspirators' bloodlust. This develops into animal imagery with the similes 'show'd your teeth like apes, and fawn'd like hounds' to underline their hypocrisy, smiling like friends and showing slavish devotion like a dog while Casca stabbed Caesar in the back. The animal imagery also dehumanises the pair, adding to the insult. The next simile of servile behaviour 'bow'd like bondmen, kissing Caesar's feet' creates the visual symbolism of the pair publicly revering Caesar, openly acknowledging his higher status. The contrasting imagery of them doing this while Casca—with the simile 'like a cur', an unwanted, stray dog—creeps up 'behind' Caesar to kill him emphasises their duplicity and betrayal.

Caesar's friend Antony has lost his temper when recalling the assassination; we have an interesting contrast when Caesar's adopted son stands quietly to one side, letting Antony rant. Showing his leadership skills, Octavius concludes the conversation with brutally direct imagery, noting that it is useless to negotiate. Only fighting will serve to avenge the death of Caesar:

> *I draw a sword against conspirators.*
> *When think you that the sword goes up again?*
> *Never till Caesar's three and thirty wounds*
> *Be well avenged.*

Every line contains a word to do with a sword, wounds or vengeance, illustrating his determination to fight. His words are simple, direct and they lack Antony's rhetorical flourish. This makes the audience wonder who is the more attractive figure historically and dramatically. Moreover, Octavius's final words before he exits are a challenge: 'If you dare fight to-day, come to the field'. With this taunt, we see him confident now in his leadership, suggesting with the verb 'dare' that the conspirators are cowards. At the end of the exchange of insults, we see that the men's clever rhetoric has been stripped away; it is now all about the naked will to survive.

The theme of fate is picked up again when Cassius tells Messala about the 'ravens, crows, and kites/Flying over our heads and looking down on us, /As if we were dying prey'. These are carrion birds that eat decaying flesh, suggesting that the conspirators are fated to die. Cassius says that he did not, as a 'follower of Epicurus' believe in omens. As we have already seen, the Greek philosopher Epicurus taught that gods did not intervene, so humans had the free will to do what they wanted. Now that Cassius 'partly' believes in omens, we appreciate the impact that the birds have on him.

In contrast, Brutus's decision 'to be patient' if he loses the battle and '[t]o wait for the fate of whatever the high powers above/Decide for us here below' is a Stoic view: he believes that he should just endure life and wait for what it brings.

SCENE II. The same. The field of battle. *Alarum. Enter BRUTUS and MESSALA* **BRUTUS** Ride, ride, Messala, ride, and give these bills Unto the legions on the other side. *Loud alarum* Let them set on at once; for I perceive But cold demeanor in Octavius' wing, And sudden push gives them the overthrow. Ride, ride, Messala; let them all come down. *Exeunt*	**SCENE II. The same. The field of battle.** *Call to arms. Enter BRUTUS and MESSALA* **BRUTUS** Ride, ride, Messala, ride, and give these written orders To our forces on Cassius' wing. *Loud signal calling to arms* Let them attack at once; because I sense A lack of fighting spirit in Octavius' wing, And a sudden assault would overthrow him. Ride, ride, Messala; let the whole army mount an attack. *Exeunt*

Part 32: Analysing Act 5 Scene 2

This scene is short to quicken the pace after the philosophical discussions about death at the end of the previous scene. With the stage direction of the 'alarum' sounding twice, the tension level rises several notches. Actors enter and exit swiftly to mimic the fast pace of unfolding events; the audience hears instant news updates from the individual characters, whose fortunes are the central focus of the play. In Shakespeare's theatre, all battles were offstage because of the practical and financial problems assembling large numbers of expensive actors and their costly equipment. Far better to let the audience imagine a bloody slaughter, which would be more chaotic and brutal than anything a director could organise on the stage.

The theme of fate continues, as the audience wonders if Cassius's evil omens of carrion birds can be believed. Moreover, Octavius's forces are not fighting with enthusiasm (they have a 'cold demeanor'), which leaves them vulnerable to attack. The audience is therefore forced to wonder whether the Stoic philosophy of life (the gods managing our fates) or the Epicurean (humans controlling fate) will win.

Brutus's repetition of '[r]ide, ride' to Messala in the last line of the scene stresses the urgency of the situation and his belief that he is close to winning. He is, however, looking at the short-term benefits and not seeing the long-term consequences. His desire to send Cassius's troops to fight Octavius's forces might possibly win him the battle, but this will put Cassius in a vulnerable position.

Freytag's Pyramid

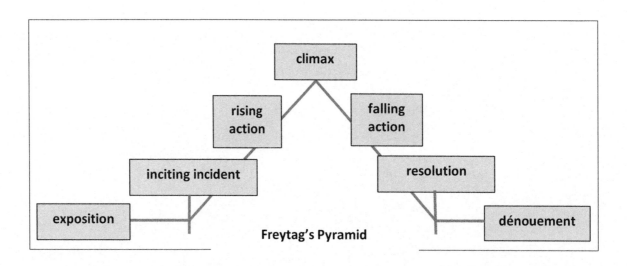

The **falling action**—events that take place because of Caesar's assassination—continue in this scene. After Brutus's disastrous decision to allow Antony to speak at Caesar's funeral, we see the following elements of the falling action:

- Act 3, Scenes 2 – 3. Brutus's oration followed by Antony's oration, which incites anger against the assassins. Brutus and Cassius flee. The mob kills Cinna the Poet.
- Act 4, Scene 1. Antony, Octavius and Lepidus form a Triumvirate to avenge Caesar and to fight Brutus and Cassius. They agree a proscription list.
- Act 4, Scene 2. Brutus and Cassius meet and make plans.
- Act 4, Scene 3. Brutus and Cassius argue and then are reconciled. Brutus reports that Portia has committed suicide. They agree to a battle at Philippi. Brutus sees Caesar's ghost.

- Act 5, Scene 1. Brutus and Cassius meet and exchange words with Antony and Octavius. The armies retire. Brutus and Cassius bid each other goodbye.
- Act 5, Scene 2. The armies meet, and Brutus orders Messala to charge against Octavius.

ORIGINAL TEXT	MODERN TRANSLATION
Another part of the field.	**Another part of the field.**
Alarums. Enter CASSIUS and TITINIUS	*Calling to arms. Enter CASSIUS and TITINIUS*
CASSIUS O, look, Titinius, look, the villains fly. Myself have to mine own turn'd enemy: This Ensign here of mine was turning back; I slew the coward, and did take it from him.	**CASSIUS** Oh, look, Titinius, look, our soldiers are fleeing. I have become an enemy to my own men: This standard bearer here of mine was running away; I killed the coward, and took the standard from him.
TITINIUS O Cassius, Brutus gave the word too early, Who, having some advantage on Octavius, Took it too eagerly; his soldiers fell to spoil, Whilst we by Antony are all enclosed.	**TITINIUS** Oh Cassius, Brutus gave the order too soon, His men, having an advantage over Octavius, Took the order too eagerly; his soldiers began looting, And now we are surrounded by Antony's men.
Enter PINDARUS	*Enter PINDARUS*
PINDARUS Fly further off, my lord, fly further off! Mark Antony is in your tents, my lord. Fly therefore, noble Cassius, fly far off!	**PINDARUS** Retreat further, my lord, retreat further! Mark Antony is in your tents, my lord. Therefore, you must retreat, noble Cassius, retreat further!
CASSIUS This hill is far enough. Look, look, Titinius! Are those my tents where I perceive the fire?	**CASSIUS** This hill is far enough. Look, look, Titinius! Is that my encampment where I see the fire?
TITINIUS They are, my lord.	**TITINIUS** It is, my lord.
CASSIUS Titinius, if thou lovest me, Mount thou my horse, and hide thy spurs in him, Till he have brought thee up to yonder troops And here again, that I may rest assured Whether yond troops are friend or enemy.	**CASSIUS** Titinius, if you love me, Mount my horse, and spur him on, Until he has taken you up to those troops over there And back here again, so that I can be reassured Whether those troops are friends or enemies.
TITINIUS I will be here again, even with a thought.	**TITINIUS** I will be back again, as quick as a thought.
Exit	*Exit*
CASSIUS Go, Pindarus, get higher on that hill; My sight was ever thick. Regard Titinius, And tell me what thou notest about the field.	**CASSIUS** Go, Pindarus, climb that hill; My eyesight has always been poor. Observe Titinius, And tell me what you see in the field.
PINDARUS ascends the hill.	*PINDARUS ascends the hill.*

This day I breathed first. Time is come round,
And where I did begin, there shall I end.
My life is run his compass. Sirrah, what news?

PINDARUS
(Above) O my lord!

CASSIUS
What news?

PINDARUS
(Above) Titinius is enclosed round about
With horsemen, that make to him on the spur,
Yet he spurs on. Now they are almost on him.

Now, Titinius! Now some light. O, he lights too!

He's ta'en!

Shout

And hark! They shout for joy.

CASSIUS
Come down; behold no more.
O, coward that I am, to live so long,
To see my best friend ta'en before my face!

PINDARUS descends

Come hither, sirrah.
In Parthia did I take thee prisoner;
And then I swore thee, saving of thy life,

That whatsoever I did bid thee do,
Thou shouldst attempt it. Come now, keep thine oath;
Now be a freeman; and with this good sword,

That ran through Caesar's bowels, search this bosom.
Stand not to answer. Here, take thou the hilts,

And, when my face is cover'd, as 'tis now,
Guide thou the sword.

PINDARUS stabs him

Caesar, thou art revenged,
Even with the sword that kill'd thee.

Dies

This is the day I breathed my first breath. Time has passed,
And where I began, there I shall end.
My life has gone full circle. What news, boy?

PINDARUS
(Above) Oh, my lord!

CASSIUS
What's happening?

PINDARUS
(Above) Titinius is surrounded completely
By horsemen, who are approaching him at a gallop,
Yet he is galloping forward. Now they're almost on him.
Now, Titinius! Now some are dismounting. Oh, he is dismounting too!
He's been captured!

Shout

And listen! They are shouting for joy.

CASSIUS
Come down; look no more.
Oh, what a coward I am, for living long enough,
To see my best friend captured before my eyes!

PINDARUS descends

Come here, boy.
In Parthia, I took you prisoner;
And at that time, I made you swear, when I spared your life,
That whatever I ordered you to do,
You should perform it. Come here now and keep your oath;
Now you will be a free man; and with this good sword,
Which ran through Caesar's bowels, penetrate this chest.
Do not delay in obeying my order. Here, you take the handle,
And, when my face is covered, as it is now,
You use the sword.

PINDARUS stabs him

Caesar, you are avenged,
With the very sword that killed you.

Dies

PINDARUS So, I am free; yet would not so have been, Durst I have done my will. O Cassius! Far from this country Pindarus shall run, Where never Roman shall take note of him. *Exit. Re-enter TITINIUS with MESSALA* **MESSALA** It is but change, Titinius; for Octavius Is overthrown by noble Brutus' power, As Cassius' legions are by Antony. **TITINIUS** These tidings will well comfort Cassius. **MESSALA** Where did you leave him? **TITINIUS** All disconsolate, With Pindarus his bondman, on this hill. **MESSALA** Is not that he that lies upon the ground? **TITINIUS** He lies not like the living. O my heart! **MESSALA** Is not that he? **TITINIUS** No, this was he, Messala, But Cassius is no more. O setting sun, As in thy red rays thou dost sink to night, So in his red blood Cassius' day is set. The sun of Rome is set. Our day is gone; Clouds, dews, and dangers come; our deeds are done. Mistrust of my success hath done this deed. **MESSALA** Mistrust of good success hath done this deed. O hateful Error, Melancholy's child, Why dost thou show to the apt thoughts of men The things that are not? O Error, soon conceived, Thou never comest unto a happy birth, But kill'st the mother that engender'd thee.	**PINDARUS** In such circumstances as these, I am free; and yet would not have been, If I had my wish rather than Cassius' wish. Oh Cassius! I shall run far from this country, Where no Romans can ever find me. *Exit. Re-enter TITINIUS with MESSALA* **MESSALA** It is merely exchange of fortune, Titinius; because Octavius Has been overthrown by noble Brutus' forces, At the same time as Cassius' legions have been overthrown by Antony. **TITINIUS** This news will greatly comfort Cassius. **MESSALA** Where did you leave him? **TITINIUS** Totally despondent, With Pindarus his slave, on this hill. **MESSALA** Isn't that him lying on the ground? **TITINIUS** He doesn't look as if he is alive. Oh, my heart! **MESSALA** Isn't that him? **TITINIUS** No, this was him, Messala, But Cassius is no more. Oh, setting sun, Just as with red rays you sink at night-time, So, in his red blood Cassius' day has come to an end. The sun of Rome has set. Our day is over; Clouds, dews, and dangers approach; we are done for. Fear of the outcome of my mission has caused his death. **MESSALA** Yes, he thought we'd lost the battle and this led to his death. Oh, dreadful Mistake, which Melancholic thinking gave birth to, Why does Melancholy cause easily impressed men To believe things that are not true? Oh Mistake, the product of Melancholic thinking, You never lead to a happy birth, But instead you kill the one who begot you.

TITINIUS
What, Pindarus! Where art thou, Pindarus?

MESSALA
Seek him, Titinius, whilst I go to meet
The noble Brutus, thrusting this report
Into his ears. I may say 'thrusting' it;
For piercing steel and darts envenomed
Shall be as welcome to the ears of Brutus
As tidings of this sight.

TITINIUS
Hie you, Messala,
And I will seek for Pindarus the while.

Exit MESSALA

Why didst thou send me forth, brave Cassius?
Did I not meet thy friends, and did not they
Put on my brows this wreath of victory,
And bid me give it thee? Didst thou not hear their shouts?
Alas, thou hast misconstrued every thing!
But hold thee, take this garland on thy brow;
Thy Brutus bid me give it thee, and I
Will do his bidding. Brutus, come apace,
And see how I regarded Caius Cassius.
By your leave, gods. This is a Roman's part;
Come, Cassius's sword, and find Titinius's heart.

Kills himself.

Alarum. Re-enter MESSALA, with BRUTUS, CATO, STRATO, VOLUMNIUS, and LUCILIUS

BRUTUS
Where, where, Messala, doth his body lie?

MESSALA
Lo, yonder, and Titinius mourning it.

BRUTUS
Titinius' face is upward.

CATO
He is slain.

BRUTUS
O Julius Caesar, thou art mighty yet!
Thy spirit walks abroad, and turns our swords
In our own proper entrails.

Low alarums

TITINIUS
Pindarus! Where are you, Pindarus?

MESSALA
Look for him, Titinius, whilst I go to meet
The noble Brutus, and inflict this news
On his ears. I say 'inflict' it;
Because sharp blades and poisoned arrows
Would be as welcome to the ears of Brutus
As news of this sight.

TITINIUS
Hurry, Messala,
And I will look for Pindarus in the meantime.

Exit MESSALA

Why did you send me out, noble Cassius?
Didn't I meet your allies, and didn't they
Place on my brow this wreath of victory,
And order me to give it to you? Didn't you hear their shouts?
Alas, you misunderstood everything!
But wait, let me place this wreath on your brow;
Your Brutus ordered me to give it to you, and I
Will carry out his order. Brutus, come quickly,
And see how I esteemed Caius Cassius.
With your permission, gods. This is a Roman's duty;
Come, Cassius's sword, and strike Titinius's heart.

Kills himself.

Alarum. Re-enter MESSALA, with BRUTUS, CATO, STRATO, VOLUMNIUS, and LUCILIUS

BRUTUS
Where is his body, Messala?

MESSALA
Over there, where Titinius is mourning it.

BRUTUS
Titinius is lying face- up.

CATO
He has been killed.

BRUTUS
Oh, Julius Caesar, you are still powerful!
Your ghost walks the earth, and turns our swords
Towards our very own bellies.

Low alarums

CATO Brave Titinius, Look where he have not crown'd dead Cassius.	**CATO** Noble Titinius, Look he has put the crown on dead Cassius.
BRUTUS Are yet two Romans living such as these? The last of all the Romans, fare thee well! It is impossible that ever Rome Should breed thy fellow. Friends, I owe more tears To this dead man than you shall see me pay. I shall find time, Cassius, I shall find time. Come therefore, and to Thasos send his body. His funerals shall not be in our camp, Lest it discomfort us. Lucilius, come; And come, young Cato; let us to the field. Labeo and Flavius, set our battles on. 'Tis three o'clock; and, Romans, yet ere night We shall try fortune in a second fight. *Exeunt*	**BRUTUS** Are there two living Romans who are as good as these two? The last of all the Romans, fare-well to you! It will be impossible for Rome To ever produce your equal. Friends, I owe more tears To this dead man than you will see me shed. I will find the time to weep for you Cassius, I will find the time. Come then, and send his body to Thasos. His funeral will not be in our camp, Because it may dishearten our soldiers. Lucilius, come; And come, young Cato; let us proceed to the field. Labeo and Flavius, push our armies onward. It is three o'clock; and, Romans, before night-fall We shall try our fortune in a second battle. *Exeunt*

Part 34: Analysing Act 5 Scene 3

Once more, the theme of fate dominates as, with Cassius's suicide, Shakespeare presents us with a paradox: we are reminded of the omen of the 'ravens, crows, and kites' and Cassius's feeling that they heralded his death. If he had held fast to his Epicurean philosophy, he would have told Pindarus to stay at the top of the hill, and he would have learnt that they had not lost the battle. We have irony that the Epicurean Cassius succumbs to fate; depression is part and parcel of his emotional approach to life, and his errors of judgement have precipitated his death.

Personification is used when Messala says, 'O hateful Error, Melancholy's child' to emphasise that the primary cause of Cassius's suicide is his loss of heart at the supposed capture of his loyal friend Titinius. The personifications 'Error' and 'Melancholy' emphasise the consequences of miscommunication. The exclamatory sentence is lengthened with the interjection 'O' to create a feeling of anguish, emphasising the role of fate or destiny in the death of Cassius.

Contemporary ideas of manhood and honour encourage the audience to regard Cassius as a coward. First, his death is devalued by his misreading of the circumstances that triggered it. This lack of judgement combines with his manner of dying to make his death less noble. He is not brave enough to kill himself or look death in the face when he instructs Pindarus 'when my face is cover'd, as 'tis now, /Guide thou the sword'. He attempts to elevate his death with a reference to justice from beyond the grave with his final words: 'Caesar, thou art revenged, /Even with the sword that kill'd thee'. However, a slave uses the sword to kill Cassius, so this cheapens his words, which he intends to be eloquent.

Another interpretation of his character is that, instead of trying to elevate his death, Cassius is employing the instincts of a dramatist: he dies on his birthday, creating a sense of completion, and he gets Pindarus to kill him with Caesar's assassination weapon, thereby coming around in a full circle. Moreover, Cassius persuades Pindarus to hold the sword by promising him his freedom, which is a generous gesture—Pindarus is thus under extreme pressure to obey the order. Cassius might also be covering his face to help Pindarus; victims of contemporary firing squads have covered faces for this very reason. Immediately after Cassius dies, the slave expresses huge regret: 'So, I am free; yet would not so have been, /Durst I have done my will. O Cassius!'. Moreover, Titinius kills himself almost immediately afterwards out of loyalty to Cassius. Thus, Cassius cannot have been altogether such a bad man to have inspired such loyalty.

The theme of fate continues when Brutus suggests a supernatural hand in Cassius's death: 'O Julius Caesar, thou art mighty yet! /Thy spirit walks abroad, and turns our swords/In our own proper entrails'. He is interpreting the event from the experience of seeing Caesar's ghost the previous night, and this suggests that, with a supernatural hand controlling events, Brutus is more vulnerable than ever.

The contrast between the Brutus and Cassius is heightened by the former's response to the latter's death. There are no long speeches to eulogise Cassius as there were with Caesar; instead, Brutus stoically says that he will 'find time' to mourn later. Then, like any man of action, he exits to fight.

In the final line of this scene, Brutus announces his intention to 'try' his 'fortune' in a second battle. Such a gamble is a huge un-Brutus-like risk when Caesar appears to be demonstrating his power from beyond the grave.

ORIGINAL TEXT	MODERN TRANSLATION
Another part of the field.	**Another part of the field.**
Alarum. Enter fighting, Soldiers of both armies; then BRUTUS, CATO, LUCILIUS, and others	*Sounds of battle. Enter fighting, Soldiers of both armies; then BRUTUS, CATO, LUCILIUS, and others*
BRUTUS Yet countrymen, O, yet hold up your heads!	**BRUTUS** Keep on countrymen, oh, keep holding your heads high!
CATO What bastard doth not? Who will go with me? I will proclaim my name about the field. I am the son of Marcus Cato, ho! A foe to tyrants, and my country's friend. I am the son of Marcus Cato, ho!	**CATO** Who is so lowbred that he wouldn't do so? Who will advance with me? I will proclaim my name around the field. I am the son of Marcus Cato! An enemy to tyrants, and a friend to my country. I am the son of Marcus Cato!
LUCILIUS: And I am Brutus, Marcus Brutus, I! Brutus, my country's friend; know me for Brutus!	**LUCILIUS** And I am Brutus, Marcus Brutus! Brutus, my country's friend; know that I am Brutus!
Soldiers kill young Cato.	*Soldiers kill young Cato.*
LUCILIUS O young and noble Cato, art thou down? Why, now thou diest as bravely as Titinius, And mayst be honour'd, being Cato's son.	**LUCILIUS** Oh, young and noble Cato, have you been killed? Why, you are as brave in death as Titinius was, And will be honoured, because you are Cato's son.
FIRST SOLDIER *(To Lucilius)* Yield, or thou diest.	**FIRST SOLDIER** *(To Lucilius)* Surrender, or you will die.
LUCILIUS Only I yield to die. There is so much that thou wilt kill me straight: Kill Brutus, and be honour'd in his death.	**LUCILIUS** I surrender simply to die. There is so much inducement that you will surely kill me immediately: Kill Brutus, and in doing so win great honour.
FIRST SOLDIER We must not. A noble prisoner!	**FIRST SOLDIER** We must not. He is a noble prisoner!
SECOND SOLDIER Room, ho! Tell Antony, Brutus is ta'en.	**SECOND SOLDIER** Make room! Tell Antony that Brutus has been captured.
FIRST SOLDIER I'll tell the news. Here comes the General.	**FIRST SOLDIER** I will tell him the news. Here comes the General.
Enter ANTONY	*Enter ANTONY*
Brutus is ta'en, Brutus is ta'en, my lord.	Brutus has been captured, Brutus has been captured, my lord.

ANTONY

Where is he?

LUCILIUS

Safe, Antony; Brutus is safe enough.
I dare assure thee that no enemy
Shall ever take alive the noble Brutus;
The gods defend him from so great a shame!
When you do find him, or alive or dead,
He will be found like Brutus, like himself.

ANTONY

(To soldiers) This is not Brutus, friend; but, I assure you,
A prize no less in worth. Keep this man safe;

Give him all kindness. I had rather have
Such men my friends than enemies. Go on,
And see whether Brutus be alive or dead;
And bring us word unto Octavius' tent
How every thing is chanced.

Exeunt

ANTONY

Where is he?

LUCILIUS

He is safe, Antony; Brutus is safe and sound.
I can safely assure you that no enemy
Will ever take the noble Brutus alive;
The gods protect him from so great a shame!
When you do find him, alive or dead,
He will be found like Brutus, true to his own noble nature.

ANTONY

(To soldiers) This is not Brutus, friend; but, I assure you,
He is a prize equally as valuable as Brutus. Keep this man safe;
Treat him kindly. I would rather have
Such men as my friends than my enemies. Proceed,
And find out whether Brutus is alive or dead;
And bring us news to Octavius' tent
About everything that has happened.

Exeunt

Part 36: Analysing Act 5 Scene 4

Following Cassius's suicide in the previous scene, Shakespeare presents the audience with a contrasting example of manhood with Cato the soldier. (If you're interested in family relationships, Cato is Portia's brother.) Knowing that everything is over, Cato's final words are:

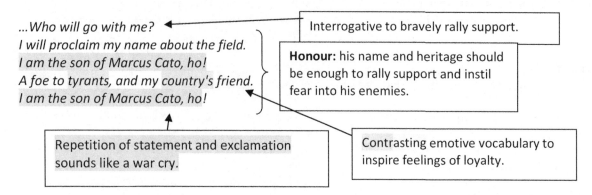

...Who will go with me?
I will proclaim my name about the field.
I am the son of Marcus Cato, ho!
A foe to tyrants, and my country's friend.
I am the son of Marcus Cato, ho!

Interrogative to bravely rally support.

Honour: his name and heritage should be enough to rally support and instil fear into his enemies.

Repetition of statement and exclamation sounds like a war cry.

Contrasting emotive vocabulary to inspire feelings of loyalty.

The soldier's words illustrate his bravery in the face of adversity: he intends to die fighting. Plutarch reports that the historical Cato, refusing to retreat, charged enemy ranks in a final act of bravery, wearing neither helmet nor armour. This sacrifice for his country was seen as a noble death. Shakespeare probably included Cato's honourable death to encourage the audience to draw comparisons with Cassius's suicide.

The second honourable deed is when the captured Lucilius pretends to be Brutus and invites the soldiers to kill him, saying 'Kill Brutus, and be honour'd in his death'. He knows that should the soldiers kill him, the real Brutus will be safe. This would indeed be an honourable death for Lucilius.

The fate of Lucilius provides the audience with the opportunity to reflect on the politics of war. Just as Brutus once spared Antony, Antony offers to spare Lucilius. Brutus naively trusted Antony's sense of honour, but Antony's reasons for sparing Lucilius are more political: 'I had rather have/Such men my friends than enemies'. He knows that, should he win him to his side, Lucilius will be a good ally. Antony's comment reveals a belief that out of self-interest people will switch sides, regardless of their principles. Perhaps this reflects his own opportunism as a politician. The audience wonders whether the loyal Lucilius will bend his principles and switch sides.

Part 37: Translating Act 5 Scene 5

ORIGINAL TEXT	MODERN TRANSLATION
Another part of the field.	**Another part of the field.**
Enter BRUTUS, DARDANIUS, CLITUS, STRATO, and VOLUMNIUS	*Enter BRUTUS, DARDANIUS, CLITUS, STRATO, and VOLUMNIUS*
BRUTUS Come, poor remains of friends, rest on this rock.	**BRUTUS** Come, pitiful surviving friends, rest on this rock.
CLITUS Statilius show'd the torch-light; but, my lord, He came not back; he is or ta'en or slain.	**CLITUS** Statilius waved the torch-light for us to see; but, my lord He has not come back; he has been captured or killed.
BRUTUS Sit thee down, Clitus. Slaying is the word; It is a deed in fashion. Hark thee, Clitus.	**BRUTUS** Sit down, Clitus. Killed, most probably; It's the current fashion. Listen, Clitus.
Whispers	*He whispers*
CLITUS What, I, my lord? No, not for all the world.	**CLITUS** What, me, my lord? No, not for all the world.
BRUTUS Peace then. No words.	**BRUTUS** Silence then. Don't breathe a word.
CLITUS I'll rather kill myself.	**CLITUS** I would rather kill myself.
BRUTUS Hark thee, Dardanius.	**BRUTUS** Listen, Dardanius.
Whispers	*He whispers*
DARDANIUS Shall I do such a deed?	**DARDANIUS** How could I do something like that?
CLITUS O Dardanius!	**CLITUS** Oh Dardanius!
DARDANIUS O Clitus!	**DARDANIUS** Oh Clitus!
CLITUS What ill request did Brutus make to thee?	**CLITUS** What dreadful thing did Brutus ask you to do?
DARDANIUS To kill him, Clitus. Look, he meditates.	**DARDANIUS** To kill him, Clitus. Look, he is lost in thought.
CLITUS Now is that noble vessel full of grief, That it runs over even at his eyes.	**CLITUS** Now that noble man is so full of grief, That it is overflowing from his eyes.

BRUTUS
Come hither, good Volumnius; list a word.

VOLUMNIUS
What says my lord?

BRUTUS
Why, this, Volumnius:
The ghost of Caesar hath appear'd to me
Two several times by night: at Sardis once,
And this last night, here in Philippi fields.
I know my hour is come.

VOLUMNIUS
Not so, my lord.

BRUTUS
Nay, I am sure it is, Volumnius.
Thou seest the world, Volumnius, how it goes:
Our enemies have beat us to the pit.

Low alarums

It is more worthy to leap in ourselves
Than tarry till they push us. Good Volumnius,
Thou know'st that we two went to school together;
Even for that our love of old, I prithee

Hold thou my sword-hilts whilst I run on it.

VOLUMNIUS
That's not an office for a friend, my lord.

Alarum still

CLITUS
Fly, fly, my lord, there is no tarrying here.

BRUTUS
Farewell to you; and you; and you, Volumnius.
Strato, thou hast been all this while asleep;
Farewell to thee too, Strato. Countrymen,
My heart doth joy that yet in all my life
I found no man but he was true to me.
I shall have glory by this losing day
More than Octavius and Mark Antony
By this vile conquest shall attain unto.
So fare you well at once; for Brutus' tongue
Hath almost ended his life's history.
Night hangs upon mine eyes; my bones would rest,

That have but labour'd to attain this hour.

Alarum. Cry within, 'Fly, fly, fly!'

BRUTUS
Come here, good Volumnius; listen to what I say.

VOLUMNIUS
What do you want to say, my lord?

BRUTUS
Just this, Volumnius:
The ghost of Caesar has appeared to me
Twice in the night-time: once at Sardis,
And last night, here in the Philippi fields.
I know that my hour has come.

VOLUMNIUS
No, it has not, my lord.

BRUTUS
No, I am sure it has, Volumnius.
You see how things are, Volumnius:
Our enemies have driven us to the edge of the grave.

Faint sounds of battle

It is nobler to leap in ourselves
Than wait until they push us. Good Volumnius,
You know that we two went to school together;
For the sake of our long-standing friendship, I ask you to please
Hold my sword handle whilst I run onto it.

VOLUMNIUS
That is not a job for a friend to do, my lord.

Continuing sounds of battle

CLITUS
Run away, run away, my lord, we can't stay here.

BRUTUS
Farewell to you; and you; and you, Volumnius.
Strato, you have been asleep all this time;
Farewell to you too, Strato. Countrymen,
My heart rejoices that throughout all my life
I knew no men who were disloyal to me.
I shall have glory in this losing day
More than Octavius and Mark Antony
Will gain by this vile conquest.
So, farewell without further ado; for my tongue
Has almost said everything it has to say.
Night time is closing in on my eyes; my bones want to rest,
After working hard right up to this hour of my death.

Sounds of battle. Someone cries, 'Run! Run! Run!'

CLITUS
Fly, my lord, fly.

BRUTUS
Hence! I will follow.

Exeunt CLITUS, DARDANIUS, and VOLUMNIUS

I prithee, Strato, stay thou by thy lord.
Thou art a fellow of a good respect;
Thy life hath had some smatch of honour in it.
Hold then my sword, and turn away thy face,
While I do run upon it. Wilt thou, Strato?

STRATO
Give me your hand first. Fare you well, my lord.

BRUTUS
Farewell, good Strato.

Runs on his sword

Caesar, now be still;
I kill'd not thee with half so good a will. *(Dies)*

Alarum. Retreat. Enter OCTAVIUS, ANTONY, MESSALA, LUCILIUS, and the army.

OCTAVIUS
What man is that?

MESSALA
My master's man. Strato, where is thy master?

STRATO
Free from the bondage you are in, Messala.
The conquerors can but make a fire of him;

For Brutus only overcame himself,
And no man else hath honour by his death.

LUCILIUS
So Brutus should be found. I thank thee, Brutus,

That thou hast proved Lucilius' saying true.

OCTAVIUS
All that served Brutus, I will entertain them.

Fellow, wilt thou bestow thy time with me?

STRATO
Ay, if Messala will prefer me to you.

CLITUS
Run, my lord, run.

BRUTUS
Go on! I will follow.

Exeunt CLITUS, DARDANIUS, and VOLUMNIUS

I beg you, Strato, stay with me.
You are a man of good reputation;
Your life has been flavoured with honour.
Then hold my sword, and turn your face away,
While I run onto it. Will you, Strato?

STRATO
Give me your hand first. Farewell, my lord.

BRUTUS
Farewell, good Strato.

Runs on his sword

Caesar, now you can rest peacefully;
I didn't kill you half as willingly. *(He dies)*

Sounds of battle. Trumpets sound a retreat. Enter OCTAVIUS, ANTONY, MESSALA, LUCILIUS, and the army.

OCTAVIUS
What man is that?

MESSALA
My master's man. Strato, where is your master?

STRATO
Free from the bondage you are in, Messala.
The conquerors can only put his corpse on a funeral pyre;
Because only Brutus triumphed over himself,
And no other man gains honour through Brutus' death.

LUCILIUS
It is right that Brutus should be found like this. I thank you, Brutus,
That you have proved my prediction was true.

OCTAVIUS
I will take everyone who served Brutus into my service.
Young man, will you join with me?

STRATO
Yes, if Messala recommends me to you.

OCTAVIUS
Do so, good Messala.

MESSALA
How died my master, Strato?

STRATO
I held the sword, and he did run on it.

MESSALA
Octavius, then take him to follow thee,
That did the latest service to my master.

ANTONY
This was the noblest Roman of them all.
All the conspirators save only he
Did that they did in envy of great Caesar;
He only, in a general honest thought
And common good to all, made one of them.
His life was gentle, and the elements

So mix'd in him, that Nature might stand up
And say to all the world, 'This was a man!'

OCTAVIUS
According to his virtue let us use him,
With all respect and rites of burial.
Within my tent his bones to-night shall lie,
Most like a soldier, order'd honourably.
So call the field to rest, and let's away,
To part the glories of this happy day.

Exeunt omnes

OCTAVIUS
Do so, good Messala.

MESSALA
How did my master die, Strato?

STRATO
I held the sword, and he ran onto it.

MESSALA
Octavius, then take him to serve you,
He that did the final service to my master.

ANTONY
This was the noblest Roman of them all.
All the conspirators except Brutus
Acted out of envy of great Caesar;
He was the only one moved by a sincerer belief
That what he was doing was for the public good.
His life was noble and magnanimous, and the four elements
So well balanced in him, that Nature could stand up
And announce to the whole world, 'This was a man!'

OCTAVIUS
Let us treat him according to his goodness,
With all respect and rituals of burial.
His body shall lie in my tent tonight,
Treated with all honour, appropriate for a soldier.
So, order the armies to rest, and let us go home,
To share the glories of this happy day.

Everyone exits

Part 38: Analysing Act 5 Scene 5

When Brutus decides that suicide is an honourable death, we see contemporary ideas of manhood and honour through his decision to commit suicide. The scene is structured so that the audience does not hear the words that Brutus whispers to Clitus and Dardanius when he tries to persuade them to assist him. This dramatic device excites the interest of the audience, who must guess the topic of conversation from the soldiers' replies.

Brutus attempts to persuade Volumnius in a rational manner; the theme of manhood combines with fate when he explains his belief that Caesar's ghost is an omen of his death: 'I <u>know</u> my <u>hour</u> is <u>come</u>'. The monosyllabic words and regular rhythm (underlined) indicate that he accepts the inevitability of his death with calmness, thereby underlining his bravery.

When Volumnius refuses to assist Brutus, the latter varies his persuasive strategies:

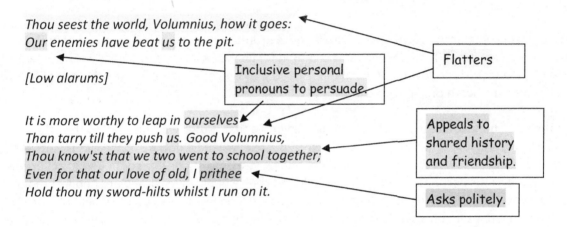

Thou seest the world, Volumnius, how it goes:
Our enemies have beat us to the pit.

[Low alarums]

Inclusive personal pronouns to persuade.

Flatters

It is more worthy to leap in ourselves
Than tarry till they push us. Good Volumnius,
Thou know'st that we two went to school together;
Even for that our love of old, I prithee
Hold thou my sword-hilts whilst I run on it.

Appeals to shared history and friendship.

Asks politely.

Because he knows Volumnius personally, Brutus can also employ the strategy of appealing to their shared school days. However, his rhetoric backfires when Volumnius politely and respectfully refuses to help: 'That's not an office for a friend, my lord'. By including refusals from three people, Shakespeare is showing that Brutus is so loved by his friends that not one of them can face killing him.

Brutus changes tactics by pulling rank over his servant Strato ('I prithee, Strato, stay thou by thy lord'), and he appeals to contemporary ideas of manhood and integrity with the nouns 'respect' and 'honour':

> *Thou art a fellow of a good respect;*
> *Thy life hath had some smatch of honour in it.*

Even at this perilous hour, Brutus talks to him as a fellow human being, according him the respect he says Strato deserves. The above quotation is deeply ironic because Brutus is talking to a man many levels below him in rank. Furthermore, Brutus inspires such loyalty and respect that Strato is moved to behave above and beyond what would reasonably have been required of a servant by agreeing to assist the suicide.

Shakespeare stresses that this is an honourable death through Strato's desire to shake hands with Brutus and bid him a formal farewell before assisting him. This sign of sincere respect between the two, despite the chasm of social rank that separates them, is designed to have maximum impact on the Elizabethan audience—an audience similarly afflicted with a tendency to dehumanise servants.

Brutus then employs two short imperatives 'Hold then my sword, and turn away thy face, /While I do run upon it', as he understands that Strato will feel anguish at the outcome of his action. With this embedded stage direction, Shakespeare stresses that Brutus actively impales himself, to focus the audience on his determination and bravery. This is a direct contrast to Cassius, who asked his slave to kill him. Afterwards, we see more evidence of the loyalty that Brutus inspired when Strato stays with the body, a morally correct gesture that Brutus's enemies praise.

Like Cassius, Brutus addresses the dead Caesar before he dies to acknowledge his revenge. Unlike Cassius, Brutus's final words are a rhyming couplet:

> *Caesar, now be still;*
> *I kill'd not thee with half so good a will.*

The couplet illustrates his acceptance of death: he is utterly convinced of the rightness of both the assassination and his self-impalement. It is common for Shakespeare to end scenes with rhyming couplets; the scene is not over, but Brutus's life is, so the couplet appears to mark the end of his life and honours the death of a tragic hero.

The theme of honour continues when Antony recognises that Brutus was different to the other conspirators, employing the superlative adjective 'noblest' when he declares 'This was the noblest Roman of them all'. With the proper noun 'Roman', he stresses that Brutus continued to act in what he regarded as the best interests of the Republic. His choice of positive vocabulary ('honest thought' and 'common good') focuses the attention of the audience on Brutus's sincerity of belief. This heightens the impact of his death, extending the tragedy. By the end of the play, Caesar is not quite forgotten—his name is mentioned at the death of each conspirator. But the protagonist now appears to be Brutus, the tragic hero who mistakenly ignored his private feelings of friendship for Caesar in favour of the 'common good'.

Shakespeare chooses to give Octavius the closing lines of the play, and this symbolises continuing politics after the play ends. It might also signify that Shakespeare perceives Octavius, the future emperor, to be the highest-ranking character. Caesar's heir outlived the members of the Second Triumvirate: the historical Antony died in 30 BC, and Lepidus died in 13 BC. Octavius ruled as the Roman Empire's first emperor from 27 BC until his death in AD 14.

Freytag's Pyramid
The **resolution and dénouement** in the final scenes bring the play to a close.

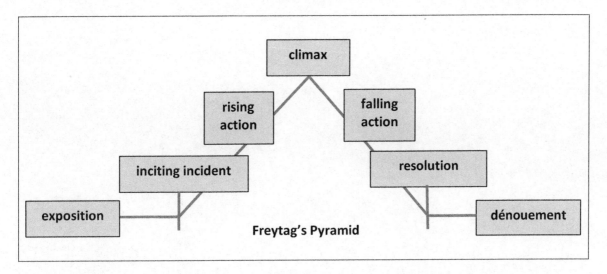

Freytag's Pyramid

In the **resolution**, the main problem or conflict is solved. We see this with the deaths of the conspirators:

- Act 5, Scene 3. Cassius orders his slave Pindarus to stab him.
- Act 5, Scene 5. Brutus commits suicide.

With the **dénouement**, the audience is presented with the outcome of the play. In this, the final scene, Antony praises Brutus; Octavius announces his intention to give him an honourable funeral. Brutus's death signifies the end of the Republican government. Their historic victory led to Octavius eventually becoming the first Roman emperor.

Printed in Great Britain
by Amazon

21352404R00093